Architectural Study of
the Temple of Messene at Ancient Messene

Japanese Architectural Mission to Greece, Kumamoto University, Japan
J. Ito, Director / Editor

Architectural Study of the Temple of Messene at Ancient Messene

N. Yasui and J. Ito

English translation by J. Yoneoka

Kyushu University Press

All rights reserved. No part of this publication may be reproduced or transmitted in any form or by any means, electronic or mechanical, including photocopying and recording, or by any information storage and retrieval system, without written permission from the publisher.

©Copyright 2016 by Kyushu University Press
3-8-34 Momochihama, Sawara-ku, Fukuoka 814-0001, Japan
Tel. 092-833-9150, Fax. 092-833-9160
Email: info@kup.or.jp

Translation by Prof. J. Yoneoka, Kumamoto Gakuen University

ISBN978-4-7985-0177-2

Printed by Shinano Co., Ltd

This book was published with the assistance of Grant-in-aid for Scientific Research, provided by Japan Society for the Promotion of Science (JSPS).

Preface

This book is the result of our survey and research on the Temple of deified Messene, which was found in the center of the agora at ancient Messene and excavated by Prof. P. Themelis, Professor Emeritus at University of Crete and the president of the Society of Messenian Archaeological Studies. It was the third target of our architectural studies following the grave monuments in the gymnasion area and the Stoas of the Asklepieion. And, this became the second publication of our Japanese Architectural Mission to Greece on the architecture of ancient Messene, following the Stoas at the Asklepieion.

It has been one of my biggest dreams as an architect to work on a Doric temple at an archaeological site in Greece, ever since I started my architectural fieldwork in Greece in 1994. This is certainly because temples exhibit the highest quality of Greek architecture. The chance came suddenly in 2003, when we were surveying the Stoas of the Asklepieion. On the way to the site, we passed the agora site, where excavation was going on. Some large orthostate blocks started to appear one after another from under the earth, and I guessed that they were temple blocks from their size and technical quality. Finally, the next year, we saw the temple which exposed its outline and many architectural blocks to the eyes of public view. The blocks were found scattered around on the site, but only a few blocks were excavated in situ except poros foundation blocks and a staircase at the west end of the temple, but there seemed to be enough blocks to reconstruct its original form. I asked Prof. Themelis to get permission for me to study the temple, and he accepted my request with pleasure, probably because we had already worked together almost ten years at the site until then. The survey work started in 2005 and ended the next year.

It was the greatest honor that our Japanese team, all the members of which were architects, was able to engage in the survey and research work on the Doric Temple of Messene. This was one of the earliest and most important temples in the agora, judging from the fact that it was dedicated to the goddess Messene from which the name of the city derived. In addition, the temple was located almost in the center of the agora and must have played an important architectural role in the agora. The view of the temple must have been grandiose against the acropolis on the back to the north and also against the North Stoa at its foot, which was the largest stoa in ancient Greece.

It is mentioned in Pausanias' "Description of Greece" that there were some other temples in the agora. These are going to be excavated one after another together with other buildings. It will be my great pleasure if our brief report on this temple is useful in the future study of ancient Messene and its architecture.

This report was completed together with Dr. N. Yasui, the co-author. We advanced our study together discussing closely every detail of the temple. We shared ideas, writing and description together, but basically, detailed analysis was done by him and I directed and edited the total work of the research all through from the fieldwork to the lab work.

Acknowledgments

Field research projects at archaeological sites always requires the cooperation of many people and organizations. I would like to express my deepest thank to each of them.

In terms of financial support, I have received much scientific research assistance and subsidies from the Japan Society for the Promotion of Science (JSPS), an auxiliary organization of Japan Ministry of Education. Most of the monetary source for our work was the Grant-in-Aid for Scientific Research of JSPS. Without its support, our work would not have been not possible.

I wish to express my acknowledgements to my friends in Greece. First and foremost of these is Prof. P. Themelis, Professor Emeritus at the University of Crete and president of the Society of Messenian Archaeological Studies. He has conducted systematic and extensive excavations in Messene since 1986, and graciously granted our survey team permission to measure and study the architectural remains that he himself originally excavated. Our joint research owes its existence to our excellent working relationship with Prof. Themelis.

I also wish to express sincere gratitude to our colleagues in Japan: first, to my long-term research partners Prof. Yoshinobu Hayashida of Miyakonojo Technical College and Assist. Prof. Ryuichi Yoshitake of Kumamoto University for their cooperative work and proper advice to the students at the sites.

Also, many thanks should go to J. J. Coulton, former Reader at Oxford University and our old friend who always gave us academic suggestions for our research.

I also would like to express my appreciation to all the students in my lab as well as participating students from other faculties and other universities. Without their hard work drawing and measuring blocks at the site, the survey would not have been possible, and without their organized efforts in the lab after returning home, this report could not have been completed. Especially, Dr. N. Yasui, the co-author of this report, worked on the temple enthusiastically, and his dissertation became the base of this report. I was his supervisor and we discussed together about every detail of this temple to complete this final report. We could share the happiest time as researcher of the ancient Greek architecture,

Finally, I thank Prof. J. Yoneoka of Kumamoto Gakuen University who always translates our Japanese into proper English.

Juko Ito
Professor and leader
Kumamoto University Architectural Mission to Greece

February 2016

Authors

Preface	Juko Ito
Chapter 1	Juko Ito
Chapter 2	Nobuaki Yasui, Juko Ito
Chapter 3	Nobuaki Yasui, Juko Ito
Chapter 4	Nobuaki Yasui, Juko Ito
Chapter 5	Juko Ito, Nobuaki Yasui
Catalogue	Juko Ito, Nobuaki Yasui
Tables	Nobuaki Yasui
Photographs	Juko Ito

Juko Ito — Professor, D.Eng, Graduate School of Science and Technology, Kumamoto University, Japan

Nobuaki Yasui — D.Eng, Research staff, Keisoku Research Consultant CO. Former doctor candidate, Graduate School of Science and Technology, Kumamoto University, Japan, presently,

Survey Outline

Duration
2006-2007, August-September

Research subsidies and grant
Grant-in-aid for Scientific Promotion 2005, 2006, no.16254005, Japan Society for the Promotion of Science (JSPS)

Participants
　　*Titles and affiliations are at the time of participation.
2005
Juko Ito (leader, Professor, Graduate School of Science and Technology, Kumamoto University)
Yoshinobu Hayashida (Professor, Miyakonojo National College of Technology)
Keiko Ogawa, Yoshihiro Kasho, Keisuke Kimoto, Satoko Sueyasu (Students, Graduate School of Science and Technology, Kumamoto University)
Nobuaki Yasui (Student, Department of Architecture, Kumamoto University)

2006
Juko Ito (leader)
Yoshinobu Hayashida (as above)
Mayumi Kunitake, Satoko Sueyasu, Yosuke Kameyama, Isamu Koyanagi, Nobuaki Yasui
(Students, Graduate School of Science and Technology, Kumamoto University)
Asahi Kato (Doctor candidate, Maebashi Institute of Technology)

2007
Juko Ito (leader, as above)
Ryuichi Yoshitake (Doctor candidate, Aristotelian University of Thessaloniki)
Nobuaki Yasui (as above)

Contents

Preface	i
Acknowledgments	ii

Chapter 1   Introduction

1-1 Background of the research	1
1-2 Purpose of the research	2

Chapter 2   Present State of the Temple of Messene

2-1 Overview of ancient Messene	5
2-1-1 History of Messene	5
2-1-2 Ruins of ancient Messene	5
2-1-3 The Agora	7
2-2 Ruins of the Temple of Messene	8
2-2-1 Ancient literary sources	8
2-2-2 Present state of the site	9
2-2-3 Temple perimeter	10
2-2-4 West stairs	11
2-2-5 Temple interior	11
2-3 Overview of the excavated blocks	11
2-3-1 Crepis blocks	11
2-3-2 Stylobate blocks	12
2-3-3 Flooring blocks	13
2-3-4 Toichobate blocks	13
1) For the antae, 2) L-shaped blocks for intersections, 3) For the side walls of the naos, 4) For the dividing wall of the opisthodomos, 5) For the side walls of the pronaos and opisthodomos, 6) For the dividing wall of the pronaos	
2-3-5 Threshold	16
2-3-6 Orthostate blocks	17
1) For the antae, 2) For the intersections, 3) For the side walls of the pronaos and the opisthodomos, 4) For the dividing wall of the pronaos, 5) For the dividing wall of the opisthodomos, 6) For the side walls of the naos, 7) Unidentified block	
2-3-7 Wall blocks	19
2-3-8 Column drums	19
2-3-9 Column capitals	19
2-3-10 Architrave blocks	20
2-3-11 Frieze blocks	21

2-3-12 Cornice blocks	21
2-3-13 Sima blocks	21

Chapter 3   Reconstruction of the Temple

3-1 Reconstruction of plan of the peripteral columns	23
3-1-1 Intercolumniation	23
3-1-2 Angle contraction of corner intercolumniation	24
3-1-3 Crepis	25
3-1-4 Number of front columns	26
3-1-5 Number of side columns	27
3-1-6 West staircase	28
3-2 Reconstruction of the cella	29
3-2-1 Threshold and adjacent blocks	30
3-2-2 Anta blocks	31
3-2-3 Side walls of the pronaos and the opisthodomos	33
1) Length of the side walls of the pronaos, 2) Length of the side walls of the opisthodomos	
3-2-4 Side walls of the naos	35
3-2-5 Dividing wall of the opisthodomos	38
3-2-6 Wall blocks	39
3-2-7 Order of placement of the blocks	40
1) Toichobate blocks, 2) Orthostate blocks, 3) Wall blocks above the orthostate	
3-2-8 Entrance to the pronaos	41
3-2-9 Relative height of the floor	44
3-2-10 Location of the cella walls	44
3-3 Reconstruction of the elevation	45
3-3-1 Reconstruction of the entablature	45
1) Architrave, 2) Frieze, 3) Cornice and sima, 4) Organization of the entablature,	
3-3-2 Peripteral columns	50

Chapter 4   Parallels and Comparative Study

4-1 Temple size	52
4-2 Doric order proportions	52
4-2-1 Column proportions	52
1) Abacus width to upper diameter (AbW/d), 2) Abacus width to column capital height (AbW/CH), 3) Abacus height to capital height (AbH/CH), 4) Echinus height to abacus height (EH/AbH), 5) Abacus width to lower column diameter (AbW/D), 6) Upper diameter to lower diameter (d/D), 7) Column height to upper column diameter (H/D), 8) Proportion of capital height to column height (H/CH), 9) Summary of column proportions	
4-2-2 Entablature proportions	56
1) Frieze height to triglyph front width (FH/TW), 2) Frieze	

height to metope front width (FH/MW), 3) Metope front width to triglyph front width (MW/TW), 4) Frieze height to architrave height (FH/AH), 5) Column height to entablature height (H/FH+AH+CorH), 6) Summary of entablature proportions

    4-2-3 Column height of the Temple of Messene   58
  4-3 Comparison with the Temple of Asklepios at Messene   59
    4-3-1 Size and plan   60
    4-3-2 Comparison of the orders   60
      1) Column proportions, 2) Entablature proportions
    4-3-3 Ornament   60
      1) Crepis, stylobate and orthostate, 2) Toichobate moulding, 3) Triglyph at the cella walls
    4-3-4 Materials   61
      1) Stone blocks, 2) Condition and setting of the blocks
    4-3-5 Summary of the comparison with the Temple of Asklepios   62
  4-4 Details and date   62
    4-4-1 Riser of crepis and stylobate   62
    4-4-2 Orthostate   63
    4-4-3 Doric capital   63
    4-4-4 Triglyph   64
  4-5 Mouldings   65
    4-5-1 Cyma reversa of cornice soffit   65
    4-5-2 Sima   65
    4-5-3 Cyma reversa on toichobate   65
    4-5-4 Combination of cyma reversa and scotia of the threshold   66
  4-6 Summary   67

Chapter 5   Summary and Conclusion

  5-1 Suummary   69
  5-2 Hellenistic Doric temple in the agora   70

Appendix: Block Catalog   73

Bibliography   91
List of Plates   99
    Photographs   99
      Drawings   102
Plates   105
Tables   224

Chapter 1

Introduction

1-1 Background of the research

The site of ancient Messene is located on the eastern edge of Messenian mountains, looking down the Messenian plain to the east. The city was outlined with the hills which connect Mt. Ithome or acropolis to the north and Mt. Eva to the east. The city area opens to the southward on the gentle slope of these hills. (PL. 108). A several hundred meters of the city wall with round and square towers has been still preserved in very good condition on its west and on the north around the Laconian Gate, showing its marvelous masonry skills. The city was built in 369 BC after the Battle of Leuktra in 371 BC by Epaminondas, the Theban hero, as the capital of Messenia[1].

Up to the present date, excavations of the Agora has proceeded in the center of the city; the Asklepieion, the Gymnasion with Stadion, the Agora, the Theater and the Fountain of Arsinoe, etc. The size of the city limits reveals us that there seems to have been an ancient population of at least tens of thousands, which seems to have disappeared gradually with the downfall of the city of Messene together with the fall of the Roman Empire. Concerning the remains of the Middle Ages, only a small basilica and some houses have been uncovered. Presently, most of the city limit is covered by the agricultural fields of fig and olive, and some 50 local houses forms a small village called Mavromati on the south slope of the Mt. Ithome.

There is a record of ancient Messene in the *Description of Greece* by Roman traveler Pausanias, who visited the city in the 2nd century AD[2]. He described some monuments and sculptures but nothing was recorded unfortunately about the Temple of Messene.

The first survey of Messene in the modern age was conducted by a French team in the first half of the 19th century. They surveyed and investigated the Peloponnese region, and the team discovered part of the stadion in Messene and other architectural remains and left plans and drawings of the city wall, stadion, Klepsydra fountain and other ruins[3]. However, they did not find the Temple of Messene or even the agora itself in the center of the city.

After the Second World War, Prof. A. K. Orlandos, the Greek archaeologist at Athens University, started and continued the excavation from 1957 to 1975, and found the ruins of the Asklepieion; the Temple of Asklepios and its surrounding square stoa[4]. After the intermission

---

[1] Pausanias 4, 27, 9. About the detailed history of independence and fortifications of Messene, see Luragi 2008 with its references. It describes and discusses the history Messenians before the independence.

[2] Pausanias 4, 31, 9-14.

[3] Blouet 1831, pp. 19-46. Pls. 18-47. The book includes 27 plates, including the general plan of the city, city walls, city gates, stadion, theater, and restored drawings of the remains, although some of them are imaginative and cannot be identified.

[4] Orlandos published his excavation results as annual reports in *Prakt*, *Ergon*, *BCH*, etc., and they were also summarized in A. K. Orlandos, "Νεώτεραι Έρευναι εν Μεσσήνη (1957-1973)," in Jantzen 1976, pp. 9-38. The annual reports in each site are as follows: A. K. Orlandos, "Ανασκαφή Μεσσήνης," *Prakt* 1957, pp. 121-125, pls. 53-58; *id.*, 1958, pp. 177-183, pls. 137-142; *id.*, 1959, pp. 162-173, pls. 136-145; *id.*, 1960, pp. 210-227, pls. 162-169; *id.*, 1962, pp. 99-112, pls. 103-

of some ten years, Prof. P. G. Themelis at the University of Crete started the systematic excavation work as a president of the Society of Messenian Archaeological Studies entrusted by Archaeological Society of Greece. He extended the excavation to the Gymnasion with Stadion to the south of the Asklepieion, to the Theater and the Fountain of Arsinoe to the north, to the Agora also to the north, and Roman houses, etc. Through the series of excavation works, he found numerous findings at ancient Messene, which revealed its history and life in the city, adding new pages to the history of Peloponnesos. The excavation has progressed extensively with his vigorous work, and the site was conserved and restored to show the monuments to the visitors.

Presently in 2010s, the excavation is proceeding in the agora, and it started to show its outline which was surrounded by stoas. The excavation of the North Stoa was completed recently and its whole view was exposed. In addition, some buildings as the Temple of Messene, the Bouleuterion, the stoa of meat market, etc. were also unearthed, and the buildings and the life in the agora are going to be made clear[5].

1-2 Purpose of the research

In the process of the excavation at the Agora, a small Doric temple was unearthed by Greek team in 2003. The trace of the temple was found in its central area, being completely destroyed to the foundation, and only steps of the west front and some poros blocks of foundations of the pteron were exposed. More than 200 architectural blocks, including fragments, were also found scattered around the site. P. Themelis, the excavator, identified it as the Temple of Messene which was dedicated to the deified city goddess of Messene. The objective of this study is to make a document of the architectural remains of the Temple of Messene and to reconstruct its original form, and to date the building from the view point of architecture.

No previous reports exist on its architecture. The authors of the present volume are architects' group of the Japanese Architectural Mission to Greece, Kumamoto University, Japan (Leader: Juko Ito), which spent every summer from 2005-2007 on site, surveying the architectural remains of the temple to make a document, including drawings and photographs.

It has been said that the Doric style temples were popular from the archaic to classical period in antiquity, and that they were replaced by Ionic and Corinthian style temples in the Hellenistic period, mainly because the taste to the architectural style changed from simple and tough style of Doric order to elegant and decorative style of Ionic and Corinthian styles. In fact, the tendency was observed in the stylistic mixture of Doric and Ionic orders, as we see already in 5th century BC acropolis at Athens. Ionic style was introduced to the two main monuments: four columns in the opisthodomos of the Parthenon and six columns of the central corridor of the Propylaia. It is also said that the Doric style was evaded due to its difficulty and

---

120; *id.*, 1963, pp. 122-129, pls. 94-105; *id.*, 1964, pp. 96-101, pls. 99-109; *id.*, 1969, pp. 98-120, pls. 121-136; *id.*, 1970, pp. 125-141, pls. 172-184; *id.*, 1971, pp. 157-171, pls. 191-203; *id.*, 1972, pp. 127-138, pls.103-116; *id.*, 1973, pp. 106-111; *id.*, 1974, pp. 102-109, pls. 83-87; *id.*, 1975, pp.176-161, pls. 154-161; A. K. Orlandos, "Μεσσήνη," *Ergon* 1957, pp. 75-80; *id.*, 1958, pp. 142-148; *id.*, 1959, pp. 110-117; *id.*, 1960, pp. 159-167; *id.*, 1962, pp. 119-132; *id.*, 1963, pp. 88-102; 1964, pp. 90-101; *id.*, 1969, pp. 97-132; *id.*, 1970, pp. 100-131; *id.*, 1971, pp. 144-173; *id.*, 1972, pp. 67-83; *id.*, 1973, pp. 79-82; *id.*, 1974, pp. 62-73; *id.*, 1975, pp. 107-116; A. K. Orlandos, "Messene," *BCH* 82, 1958, pp. 714-717; *id.*, 83, 1959, pp. 636-639; *id.*, 84, 1960, pp. 695-700; *id.*, 85, 1961, pp. 697-703; *id.*, 87, 1963, pp. 768-777; *id.*, 88, 1964, pp. 734-742; *id.*, 89, 1965, pp. 729-732; *id.*, 94, 1970, pp. 984-989; *id.*, 95, 1971, pp. 892-895; *id.*, 96, 1972, pp. 60-66; A. K. Orlandos, "Messene," *AJA* 67, 1963, pp. 281-282; 75, 1971, pp. 308-310. It was pity that Orlandos never published his final report of the excavation, although he reported partially in these periodicals. Finally, the architecture of the Temple of Asklepios and its surroundings as the Ekkllesiasterion and stoas was studied by Birtacha, Sioumpara, and our Japanese team. See Birtacha 2008, Sioumpara 2011 and Hayashida/Yoshitake/Ito 2013.

5   The preliminary reports for the excavation are in *Praktika* 2002, pp.42-46; 2003, pp.34-38; 2004, p.38, pl. 8.

Chapter 1   Introduction

troublesomeness of angle contraction of corner columns[6], corresponding to the arrangement of triglyphs and metopes on frieze above.

However, in Messene, as far as we see the result of the excavations, the Doric style buildings had been built continuously in the heart of its city as main monuments even in the Hellenistic period. It is quite important that the Temple of Asklepios, dated to the end of the 3rd century BC[7], with its surrounding Corinthian stoas was built in Doric order as a main temple of the city. In addition, the Temple of Messene, which was dedicated to the city goddess and might be dated to the 2nd half of the 4th century, was built also in Doric order right in the center of the agora, the heart of the citizens' lives. Some other buildings as the stoa of the meat market from 3rd century BC in the agora, the stoa for the court of the Palaestra from the 3rd century, the U-shaped stoa which surrounded the Stadion, the Mausoleum of the Saithidae Family from the Roman imperial era, were built also in Doric. It seems that Doric style, which was the main traditional style of temples in Peloponnesos, had continued to be the main architectural order in Messene[8].

The purpose of this research is to reconstruct the Temple of Messene based on the actual measurements in order to clarify the architectural characteristics of the Temple and to place it in the history of Doric architecture. Especially, as the Hellenistic era is known as the declining phase of the Doric style, we aim to explain the transformation of Doric temples in this era based on new information obtained from our on-site investigations.

In ancient Greece, temples were usually placed in the acropolis. Also in Messene, the temple of Zeus Ithomata was placed on the acropolis, although it has not been identified architecturally yet, but some architectural blocks are observed in the Monastary of Voulkano on the acropolis. However, temples which were placed in the agora were not popular in ancient Greece especially in Peloponnesos except a few examples.

There is no previous study on the Temple of Messene because it was unearthed for the first time. The most important Doric temple in Messene, the Temple of Asklepios, with surrounding stoas[9] was thoroughly studied by E. Sioumpara[10] recently. No other Doric peripteral temple has been found yet in Messene. So, the newly excavated Temple of Messene can also be considered one of the most important examples.

---

6   The problems of Doric design were pointed out by many authors. For example, see Coulton 1977, pp.60-62.
7   Siumpara 2011. pp. 211-216.
8   Coulton 2002, The choice of Doric order in Hellenistic era was discussed by Coulton.
9   Concerning the surrounding stoas of the Asklepieion, see Hayashida 2012. It is the final report for the architecture of the stoa.
10 Sioumpara 2011.

Chapter 2

Present State of the Temple of Messene

2-1 Overview of ancient Messene
2-1-1 History of Messene

The ancient city of Messene is located on the southwestern part in Peloponnesos about 20 km northwest of the present day town of Kalamata. (Fig. 2-1) Descriptions of the city can be read in traveler and geographer Pausanias' *Description of Greece* written in the 2nd century AD.

Messene was built by the Messenians in 369 BC after the surrender of Sparta at the battle of Leuctra, over a period of about 85 days under the leadership and direction of Epaminondas. In the 3rd century BC, it was repeatedly attacked by Sparta and Macedonia, but persevered and maintained its independence until it became a Roman state in 146 BC[11]. The city is built on a slope surrounded by mountains, and borders on Mt. Ithome to the north and Mt. Eva to the east. According to its modern excavator P. Themelis, the wall that joins the ridges of these mountains has an overall length of almost 9.5 km[12]. With the demise of the Roman Empire, the city was abandoned and started to be buried by sediment during the Middle Ages.

The present-day small village of Mavromati is currently located on the south slope of Mt. Ithomi around the ancient Klepsidra Fountain, which is still being used, an elevated area overlooking the ancient city. A few hundred meters of the north wall of the city is in relatively good condition, but most of the city itself was completely ruined and is now covered with agricultural land of olive and fig.

2-1-2 Ruins of ancient Messene

Ancient Messene was surrounded by a solid wall around 9.5 km long, inside of which many public buildings and residential quarters must have filled the area in its prosperous period. There were turrets along the city wall, and two gates remain: the Arcadian Gate on the north facing Arcadia, and Laconian Gate on the east facing Laconia. There was an Acropolis built on the summit of Mt. Ithome to the north of the city, but at present only a small building remains on the side of the mountain, and remains of the Voulkano Monastery from the Byzantine period are located on top of the mountain. (PL. 108)

---

11 Pausanias 4. 27. 5-7. The general history of Messenia and the Messenians was written by N. Luraghi recently, and it should be referred for the detailed history and discussions. See Luraghi 2008. The building of the city wall is suggested to date soon after the liberation of Messene through the study of architectural technique of the city walls. Müth-Herda 2005, pp. 214-218.

12 Themelis 2003, pp. 42-43.

In the center of Ancient Messene have been excavated main public buildings: the Agora, the Theater, the Fountain of Arsinoe, the Asklepieion, and the Stadion. The agora was still under excavation and the huge North Stoa has been exposed recently[13].

The Asklepieion[14] is located next to the south of the agora, and it consists of a Doric temple built in the central court, surrounded by rectangular stoas with 2 rows of columns (Fig. 2-4). Asclepius is known as the god of medicine, and Asklepions generally served as hospitals during the Hellenistic period. However, according to Pausanias, the Asklepieion at Messene was closer to a museum than a hospital, and housed art exhibits[15]. In addition, there was a series of rooms behind the stoas called Sebastion, Ekklesiasterion, Bouleuterion and Artemision, which indicate that this was also the political center of the city.

To the south of the Asklepieion is the Stadion area (PL. 109), whose south end is bordered by the city wall. The Stadion features horseshoe-shaped seating opening towards the south, where the Mausoleum of the Saithidae Family was built at the castle wall. Doric stoas were built in the other three directions surrounding the Stadion. A propylaea on the north side and a group of funerary monuments on the west side can be seen. In addition, a palaestra was built at the southern end of West Stoa.

The Agora area spread out to the north of the Asklepieion, and was surrounded by stoas in all four directions. Currently the North stoa has been excavated, and the excavation has revealed it was a huge Doric stoa and had two rows of inner colonnades with projecting wings on both ends. The Arsinoe Fountain is located on the northwest corner of the agora next to the west end of the North Stoa. The terrain to the north of the Agora is high, and currently slopes gently within the Agora. The Temple of Messene was excavated almost in the center but a little southwest part of the Agora. The Agora will be described in more detail in a later section.

There was also a theater that used the natural inclination of the area located about 20 m to the west of the northwest corner of the Agora (Fig. 2-2). The date of construction is uncertain, but the excavator Themelis surmised that a Greek style theater was first built in the

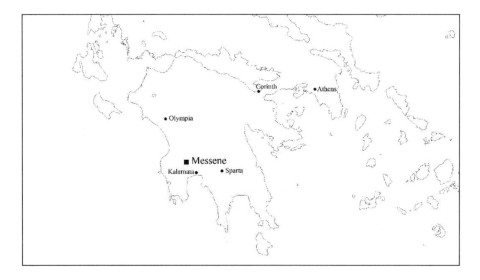

Fig. 2-1　Location of Messene.

13　The result of the excavations has been reported annually in *Praktika*. Themelis 2008, 41-42; 2009, 75-78; 2011, 35-39.

14　The stoas of the Asklepieion were surveyed by our Kumamoto University Architectural Mission to Greece directed by J. Ito from 2001-2004. See Hayashida 2013. Concerning the temple itself, Siumpara studied almost thoroughly. See Siumpara 2011.

15　Pausanias 4. 30. 10.

Chapter 2   Present State of the Temple of Messene

3rd century BC, and that the skene was later reconstructed in the 2nd century AD. The theater is about 100 m east-west in length, and its overall size is on the magnitude of the Asklepion and the Stadion, making it one of the largest structures of the city. The orchestra, scene building, parodos walls, and part of the façade remain today. The orchestra has a diameter of approximately 21.6 m, and a stage approximately 46.6 m in length is built into approximately one-fourth of this. The stage building has three niches, making it a "western type".

2-1-3   The Agora

The Agora excavations were still in progress at the writing of this publication, and the overall organization of its buildings is still unclear. According to Pausanias, the Agora included a statue of Zeus the savior, Fountain of Arsinoe, Temple of Poseidon, and Temple of Aphrodite[16]. As of 2010, only the Fountain of Arsinoe has been confirmed (PL. 15-2). During 2010s, the Doric Stoa of meat market and the Bouteuteion were newly excavated[17].

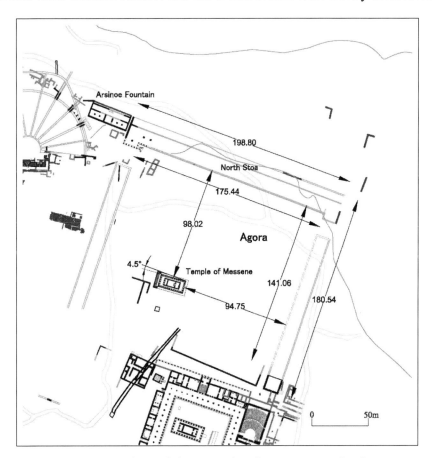

Fig. 2-2   Location of the Temple of Messene at the Agora.

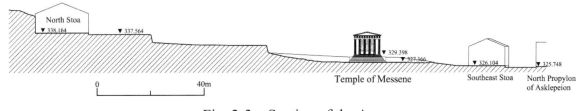

Fig. 2-3   Section of the Agora.

---

16   Pausanias 4. 31. 6, Themelis 2012b, p.42.
17   Themelis 2010, p.59; 2012a, p.57, 60.

The stoas surrounding the Agora on four sides were partially excavated. According to our measurement, it can be determined that the inside of the Agora was 175.4 long from east to west and 141.1 m from south to west. The stoas were approximately 13 to 19 m deep. The North Stoa is winged and has two rows of columns. The north side of the Agora is approximately 13 m higher than the south side; that is, the ground surface is slanted (Fig. 2-3). Therefore, it is possible that the East and West Stoas were divided into 2 or 3 buildings, and according to the ground height and judging from the terrain and buildings, the Agora must have been complex plane surfaces with supporting wall[18].

The Temple of Messene was excavated almost in the center of the Agora but a little southwest part of its center. According to our measurement, it is located approximately 94.8m from the East Stoa, and about 98 m from the North Stoa (Fig. 2-2). The temple is not parallel to the North Stoa, but is tilted 4.5 degrees anti-clockwise[19] and it is neither parallel to the south stoa. The reason is unknown. It's floor level is also approximately 9 m lower than that of the North Stoa, which is almost the height of a two-storied building.

Some traces of buildings have been found around the Temple of Messene. On the west side, a Doric stoa, dated 3rd century BC by Prof. Themelis, was excavated approximately 3.2 m from the west steps. The stoa is connected to another building which is called meat market with peristyle court. To the north of the Temple of Messene, the Bouleuterion of 17.5 × 25.8 m from the 4th century was excavated (PL. 14-1, 2)[20]. Also, a small treasury was excavated about 16.3 m south of the temple. It is roughly 2 m square and 1.4 m in depth underground room, with perimeter of approximately 3.7 × 3.4 m. It was built of rectangular blocks which are clamped together and joined by dowels. The construction date is unclear, but one record says that it was used as a prison in 183 BC[21], so it must have been constructed before that time (PL. 15-1).

2-2 Ruins of the Temple of Messene
2-2-1 Ancient literary sources

Besides the travel log of Pausanias, no other written descriptions of the ancient Temple of Messene have been found. Pausanias writes "There is also a temple of Messene, the daughter of Triopas, with a statue of gold and Parian marble. At the back of the temple are paintings of the kings of Messene"[22].

Triopas was a member of the royal family of Argos, and his daughter Messene became the wife of Polykaon, the first ruler of the region. It is said that the entire region was named after Messene when Polykaon came to rule[23]. However, there is something unnatural about this conclusion in the light of the description of Pausanias, who did not mention this temple in his discussion on the Agora, but instead wrote about it after the sanctuary of Asklepius[24]. In addition, no traces of the statue or paintings mentioned in the description of Pausanias, or other evidence linking the temple with this description, were found during the

---

18 As a matter of fact, a supporting wall was unearthed 50 m north from the Temple of Messene. The height of the remaining wall is approximately 1.5-2 m.
19 Measurements were taken using a total station. As a result, it was found that the Temple of Messene is slanted 4.5 degrees counterclockwise with respect to the North Stoa.
20 These two buildings were excavated in 2010s and still being studied. Themelis 2010, p.59.
21 Themelis 2006, 49-52; Themelis 2010b, 122-123.
22 Pausanias discusses the Temple of Messene, and mentions the artists and names of the kings portrayed in paintings at the at the back of the temple. (Pausanias 4. 30. 11)
23 Pausanias 5. 1. 1.
24 Pausanias 4. 30. 11.

Chapter 2   Present State of the Temple of Messene

excavations; therefore the survey team had come to believe that it was actually the temple of Zeus described by Pausanias in connection with the Agora.

However, temple artifacts obtained by excavation have confirmed that it was indeed the temple of Messene. The excavator Themelis points out that, based on his discovery of gold and marble fragments in the vicinity of the temple (similar to those described by Pausanias), inscriptions along the north side of the temple which are dated to 4th-early 3rd century, and also a long inscription on a large statue base found in the area and dated to the first half of the 2nd century, the temple is indeed dedicated to the goddess Messene[25]. This means that Pausanias completed his description of the Agora, then went on to describe the Asklepieion, and afterwards returned to the Agora to write about the Temple of Messene[26]. Themelis also concludes that based on his analysis of the artifacts, the Temple of Messene was part of a larger municipal public works project on structures within the Agora, similar to that of the Asklepieion. Themelis states that the construction of the Agora and sanctuary was a great undertaking by the city, the purpose of which was to promote the unique ethnic tradition of Messene on the Peloponnesian peninsula[27].

2-2-2   Present state of the site

The Temple of Messene was built to the northwest of the Asklepieion, slightly southwest of the center of the Agora. The site of the temple measures approx. 15 × 30 m. At the site many architectural blocks of the stylobate, crepis, wall, columns, architrave, etc. were observed scattered around from place to place, when the site was exposed. Almost all the blocks of the temple itself found removed and only small parts of the poros foundation are in situ on the west and east ends. Thus, the site was almost hollow space when the site was cleared by excavation. The horizontal level of the site was as shallow as some of the blocks were scratched by plows. On the west front, a staircase of 5 steps still exists in situ, which is unusual for normal Doric temples[28], to adjust the level difference of the temple floor level and the ground level on the west. The foundation of the temple still has six rows of foundation blocks on the west side and three on the east side, and these are made of poros (soft, coarse, dark brown limestone) and are believed to have supported the floor. There is only a small portion of carved bedrock excavated, with almost no traces of it otherwise (Fig. 2-4).

The blocks unearthed from the temple are currently grouped together in one location, and our survey team has catalogued their actual measurements and drew each block. Based on the excavated column capitals, the temple is known to have been in the Doric style. The Agora is still under excavation, and existence of stoas and a treasure room were found near the temple, but no new blocks have been discovered. Based on the excavated evidence, the

---

25   Themelis 2006, p.43. Themelis notes that a fragment of a statue dedicated to the gods made of marble and gold was discovered in the temple. The fragment was part of the lower portion of a woman's face, and reflects the style of the late 4th century BC. Themelis 2007, 509-528, Themelis 2010, p.117, Themelis 2012b, 44. Themelis also suggests the date of the temple to around the 4th century BC from the inscription found along the north side of the temple. Themelis 2004, p. 41; Themelis 2006, p.30; Themelis 2012, p.44, Themelis 2012b, 118p.

26   Themelis 2005, pp.48-49. Here, Themelis compares various kinds of excavation data to clarify that the Temple of Messene was located to the southwest of the Agora; that is, northwest of the Temple of Asklepios. Also, based on this, he concludes that Pausanias, after completing his description of the Temple of Asklepios, returned to the Agora and then went on to describe the Temple of Messene.

27   Themelis 2006, p.44. Themelis states that the construction of the Agora and sanctuary was a great undertaking by the city, the purpose of which was to promote the unique ethnic tradition of Messene on the Peloponnesian peninsula.

28   Doric temples usually do not have extra steps except stylobate, crepis and euthynteria. The west staircase of the temple here looks like high stepped stereobate of Ionic temples in Ionia. Probably there is no other parallels like this staircase in Doric temples.

temple is believed to have been constructed at around the end of the 4th century BC[29]. Actual measurement of 86 blocks was completed by 2007 for our measurement survey, of which 73 were illustrated by hand. Detailed descriptions of the remains of each part of the temple follow below.

At the present site, the Temple of Messene was reconstructed by Themelis based on our reconstruction plan for visitors to have better understanding of the site. The peristylar column drums were set on concrete stylobate and the orthostate blocks were placed on the preserved toichobate blocks which were put on concrete foundation. (PLs. 8~13)

2-2-3 Temple perimeter

The temple was located on ground sloping slightly from east to west, and the rockbed is exposed in places. Therefore, stairs were built on the west side to raise the ground level artificially, while the temple foundation was partly dug into the bedrock on the east side. Today, there is still evidence of indentations carved in the ground level on the north, south and east sides, and of stairs on the west side and north and south corners. The distance between the north and south indentations is approximately 11.5 m, and that between the indentation on the eastside and the lowest stair on the west side is approximately 26.9 m. A rough stone foundation for narrow terrace around the temple approximately 1.2 m in width and 10 m in length was built on the west half of the north side. There is the same rubble foundation of approximately 1.1 m in width and 6 m in length on the west half of the south side as well, but to the east of it the bedrock itself is carved out to form the foundation (Fig. 2-4).

This east foundation of the temple was carved approximately 50 cm deep into the ground, and there are 9 thin rectangular limestone slabs lined up along the east side. In the middle of the east side, a sloping poros foundation (width 1.6 m, length 1.6 m) that supported slab ramps to walk up to the temple is seen. Four stelae bases in roughly the same height were unearthed along the north side of the temple (Fig. 2-4).

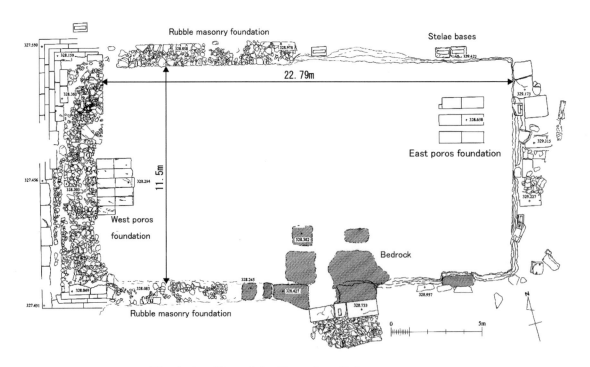

Fig. 2-4　Site of the Temple of Messene.

29　Themelis 2004, p. 41; Themelis 2006, p.30; Themelis 2012, p.44, Themelis 2012b, 118p.

Chapter 2 Present State of the Temple of Messene

2-2-4 West stairs

A set of five stairs remains on the west side of the temple, and the bottom stair is 14.195 m in length[30]. The stairs are crumbling and have shifted in parts, so they are impossible to measure for certain, but the tread is 0.280-0.310 m on the east side, and 0.205-0.250 m north-south, and the rise is 0.185-0.260 m. There are no clamps or dowels on the west stairs, nor are there any recessed joint for the rise as seen on the crepis (to be discussed later). Rough stone foundation for the top part of the west stairs remains along the preserved west stairs (Fig. 2-4, PLs. 2-1, 3-1~2).

2-2-5 Temple interior

There is almost nothing left in the area where the temple itself was built. There should have been a stylobate base to support columns on the cut bedrock foundation as well as foundation blocks for the inner walls, but these blocks have all been removed. However, there are poros foundation blocks in the northeast part of the Temple, 1.68 m inside of the cut bedrock on the east side. It is believed that they supported the pteron inside the flank columns. The long narrow poros blocks each measure 0.580 × 1.20 m, and 2 blocks are placed lengthwise in 3 rows (PL. 6-1). The axial distance between each row is about 96 cm, which is about equal to the length of the stylobate blocks to be discussed later. Therefore, it is believed that the blocks placed atop these were of the same size as well. On the east side of the west stairs, there is also a 2 × 3 m section of 11 poros blocks (approx. 0.5 × 1.0 m) which are arranged in rows of 2 × 6 with no space between them (PL. 4-1). These are also believed have been foundation for the stylobate[31]. However, these blocks are lower than the cut bedrock on the east side, so it is also possible that more layers of foundation blocks were added on top of them (Fig. 2-4).

2-3 Overview of the excavated blocks

2-3-1 Crepis blocks

(PLs. 16, 39~43; Table 2-1)

The crepis is located under the stylobate, and forms the stereobate or platform of the temple. In Doric order temples, it is generally formed of two steps. Several blocks believed to be part of the crepis were excavated, but most were badly damaged and only 7 of them were in relatively good condition. All 7 of these blocks were measured, and 5 of them were illustrated.

Most of the blocks were in sufficient condition to determine the original length, but 2 different block sizes (approx. 0.96 m and approx. 0.80 m) were determined. Their depths ranged from 0.397 m to 0.410 m, and heights from 0.206 m to 0.215 m (Table 2-1).

The front faces of the blocks are double-recessed at the bottom. Additionally, the other faces were joined and anathyrosis can be seen. From the clamp holes seen at the tops of the blocks, it can be determined that they were joined at one place each on the right and left sides and in two places at the back. There are also marks indicating that other crepis or stylobate blocks were placed on top of them. From the location of these marks, the width of the crepis tread was estimated to be 0.240-0.260m. All the blocks were made of limestone.

---

30 According to the Messenian Archaeological Society, the portion that is missing today was present at the earlier excavation, and on the plane drawing of the Agora by, the length of the bottom step was 14.319 m. Chapter 3 makes use of this measurement for the temple reconstruction.

31 Hodge 1966, Plates V, XI. For example, the research report on the Temple of Zeus at Nemea, a Doric style temple built in Peloponnesos in the seemingly same era as the Temple of Messene, describes it as having a similar type of foundation.

2-3-2 Stylobate blocks

(PLs. 17~20, 44~49, Table 2-2~3)

There have been excavated 17 blocks: the larger 15 of them are for exterior colonnade and smaller 2 of them (Δ117+Δ118, Δ130) for the entrance colonnade of the pronaos. All blocks are of limestone.

The exterior blocks were all measured, and 4 of them were illustrated. They are categorized in two types: one has a square dowel hole at the top center on which the columns were placed, and the other does not. The blocks measure 0.956 - 0.962 m in front length, 0.880 m-0.888 m in depth, and 0.211 - 0.240 m in height. Every block has raised panel on its front and the recessed joint can be seen along the bottom and the right edge (as far as observed in the remaining blocks) but not along the top. There is another recessed joint or relieving margin at the bottom, and thus the bottom of the blocks is double recessed. The

Table 2-1 Dimensions of crepis blocks (m)

Block No.	Front length	Depth	Height	Tread	Depth of relieving margin	Note	
Δ50			0.208	0.250	0.017	Corner	
				0.250			
Δ52	0.958	0.409	0.212	0.260			undrawn
Δ59			0.215	0.240	0.020	Corner	
Δ157	0.958	0.397	0.213	0.263			undrawn
Δ181	0.802	0.410	0.209	0.261			
Δ555		0.400	0.214	0.250	0.022		
Δ556	0.804	0.400	0.206				
Ave.		0.403	0.211	0.253	0.020		

Table 2-2 Dimensions of stylobate blocks (m)

Block No.	Front length	Depth	Height	Depth of relieving margin	Note	
Δ43		0.885	0.221	0.021	with column	undrawn
Δ56	0.962		0.223		with column	
Δ64+Δ161+Δ383	0.960	0.880	0.218	0.020		undrawn
Δ75			0.223			
Δ147	0.961	0.884	0.222	0.022	with column	undrawn
Δ267			0.220		with column	
Δ353		0.884	0.221		with column	
Δ454			0.220		with column	
Δ590			0.225		with column	
Δ670			0.222		with column	
ΔX4			0.223		with column	
ΔX5		0.880	0.240			
ΔX9	0.956	0.881	0.211			
ΔX10			0.224			
Δ96a+b		0.888		0.020	Corner	undrawn
		0.880		0.025		
Ave.	0.960	0.883	0.222			

Table 2-3 Dimensions of inner stylobate blocks (m)

Block No.	Front length	Depth	Height	Depth of relieving margin	Note	
Δ117+Δ118			0.215			
Δ130	0.964		0.217			

detail drawing is shown with dimensions in the block Δ147 (PL. 49). This surface finishing of the front of the stylobate can be seen in the Temple of Asklepios at Mesene as well[32]. On the bottom of the corner stylobate blocks, there are square dowel hole probably to make the corner of the temple fixed.

Two interior stylobate blocks were found. They were badly damaged and their original sizes cannot be determined. It is obvious that the sides are joint faces, and recessed joint at the bottom cannot be seen. The blocks are divided into two parts: a higher square part on which the columns were placed and the lower peripheral edges which is larger than the higher part.

2-3-3 Flooring blocks
(PLs. 20, 50~51, Table 2-4)

The temple floor was covered with square flooring blocks of limestone. Due to their simple square shape and easy handing size, these blocks were easily processed, and may have been taken and reused for other buildings in later times. Several fragmentary blocks were excavated, but none of them were completely intact. Two of the blocks are in relatively good condition, and these were measured and illustrated. They are basically the same size as the stylobate blocks: approx. 0.96 m in length and 0.22 m in height. However, the Δ55 is larger in depth, and ΔX2 seems to have projected in L-shape. The sizes for blocks for pteron and cella could have been different in size, but there is no evidence to show it.

Table 2-4 Dimensions of floor paving blocks (m)

Block No.	Front length	Depth	Height	Note
Δ55	0.962		0.217	
ΔX2	0.96	0.96	0.225	L-shaped

2-3-4 Toichobate blocks
(PLs. 21~25, 52~79)

The toichobate is located just below the orthostate, and forms the base for the walls. More than 80 % of the all the toichobate blocks of limestone have been preserved, 28 of these were measured and illustrated. Thus, this made it possible to decide the place of original position of the blocks.

The top of the blocks are finished well to set the orthostate blocks. Two clamp holes were seen on the top edges where the toichobate blocks connected with each other, and a dowel hole in the center. The exterior side of the blocks, which faces to the pteron are divided into two: the lower part is the vertical joint face (height: 0.024-0.050 m) with flooring blocks and the upper is a part is vertical face (height: 0.123 m) with raised panel (height 0.091). The exterior edge of the top is a moulding of cyma reversa or Lesbian cyma (height: 0.035 m, PL. 21-5, 54) These mouldings are noteworthy as architectural ornament for toichobate. The top of the interior face of the block is cut away to set flooring blocks.

Blocks were classified into the following six types based on their geometry.

---

32 Relieving margin was popular finishing of stylobate not only in Messene but also in Peloponnesos. In Messene, it can be seen in the Temple of Messene, the grave monuments K2, K3. Also see Sioumpara 2011, Abb. 121, 122, Tafel 22, 24 for the Temple of Asklepios. Also seen in the temples at Nemea and Tegea.

1) For the antae
(PLs. 21, 52~55, Table 2-5)

The anta is the end of the cella wall, and the blocks form anta pillars which project outward from the wall itself. They are easily recognized by their shape and 3-sided molding. All the 4 anta blocks remain intact. However, their front bottom joint faces were all damaged, so the original size could not be determined. Presently, the biggest size is 0.705 m in width and 1.023 m in length, and the heights range from 0.392 m-0.406 m (Table 2-5). The molding of cyma reversa and raised panel are common with the other toichobate blocks on their exterior faces. The inner wall sides have only raised panel but no molding. On the top of the anta pillar part, there are square dowel holes of 0.10 m square with lead groove to fix the block. This type of dowel can be found on the corner crepis of west staircases, although they are a little smaller.

2) L-shaped blocks for intersections
(PLs. 22, 56~60, Table 2-6)

All the four L-shaped processed blocks, which were used at the intersection of the outer cella wall and dividing walls of the pronaos and opisthosomos, were excavated, measured and illustrated. One tip of the L is a joint face for dividing wall, another tip is the joint face for cella wall. Each of them has a shallow 45° cut for the joint for the toichobate blocks of cella wall at the outer faces. Thus, the blocks form intersection in three directions.

These intersection blocks average 1.009 × 0.967 m with a height of 0.403 m. At the

Table 2-5 Dimensions of toichobate blocks for antae (m)

Block No.	Width of finished top face (wall)	Width of finished top face (anta)	Top length	Width	Length	Height	Height of raised panel (outer)	Height of raised panel (inner)	Projection of raised panel
Δ47	0.522	0.572		(0.701)	(0.986)	0.405	0.155		0.013
Δ223				(0.695)	(0.983)	0.392		0.154	
Δ349	0.514	0.571	0.899	0.705	(0.972)	0.406	0.158		0.014
Δ577+Δ580				0.669	(1.023)	0.403	0.160		
Ave.	0.518	0.572	0.899	0.703	0.980	0.401			0.0135

Table 2-6 Dimensions of toichobate L-shaped blocks for intersection (m)

Block No.	Width of finished top face (A)	Width of finished top face (B)	Width of finished top face (C)	Width	Length	Height	Projection of raised panel	Projection of raised panel
Δ3	0.498	0.490	0.529	0.969	1.007	0.406		
Δ9	0.503	0.483		0.964	1.005	0.400	0.012	
Δ140						0.404		
Δ145	0.506	0.486	0.515	0.967	1.014	0.403		0.013
Ave.	0.502	0.486	0.522	0.967	1.009	0.403	0.012	0.013

Table 2-7 Dimensions of toichobate blocks for the naos side wall (m)

Block No.	Width of finished top face (wall)	Width	Length	Height	Moulding height	Moulding width	Dowel holes
Δ1	0.488	0.663	0.960	0.403	0.160	0.012	–
Δ8		0.713	0.958	0.402	0.154	0.016	✔
Δ15	0.482	0.675	0.961	0.408	0.160	0.013	–
Δ16	0.484	0.660	0.942	0.404	0.158	0.013	✔
Δ18	0.484	0.655	0.957	0.405	0.155	0.015	–
Δ48	0.476	0.635	0.973	0.405	0.150	0.013	✔
Δ143			0.955	0.401			✔
Δ465	0.485	0.632	0.968	0.403	0.162	0.013	–
Δ575+Δ576+Δ579	0.481	0.631	0.963		0.150		–
Ave.	0.483	0.658	0.960	0.404	0.156	0.014	

Chapter 2 Present State of the Temple of Messene

inside part of the L-shape, there is a cut for the flooring material, measuring 0.114 - 0.185 m in width (Table 2-6). On one side, there is molding of cyma reversa and a raised panel above the joint face, as can be seen on outer sides of the other toichobate blocks. Another side which has a raised panel is s the inside of the temple. The width of the top finishing differs in each of the 3 directions, corresponding to the difference of wall widths of each direction. On the top, there are two clamp holes at the edge of joint face. Two sets of one pry hole and two dowel holes used to set the orthostate blocks were also seen.

3) For the side walls of the naos
(PLs. 23~24, 60~68, Table 2-7)

These are blocks which are cut away on the inside to set flooring and have the cyma reversa moulding and raised panel with joint face underneath on the outside. Nine blocks of this type were excavated, measured and illustrated. The blocks averaged 0.960 m in length and ranged from 0.957-0.968 m, which is equal to the front width of the stylobate blocks[33]. Including the cut away parts, the widths ranged from 0.660 - 0.713 m, indicating that the area hidden below the flooring was not always the same size. The heights ranged 0.401-0.408 m. The top finishing was 0.476 - 0.488 m wide, and some of the blocks had dowel holes and lever holes at the center of the top while others did not (Table 2-7).

4) For the dividing wall of the opisthodomos
(PLs. 24-2~6, 69~71, Table 2-8)

Three blocks with cut-away portions for the flooring on the inside and raised panels on the outside were unearthed, measured and illustrated. They are believed to have been used for the dividing wall of the opisthodomos based on the fact that one side of the L-shaped piece for the intersection was made in the same way as the side extending along the inside of the temple. The length of the block is 0.858-0.860 m, making it shorter than the blocks for the cella wall of the naos. The widths of finishing at the top were 0.527 m and 0.512 m (Table 2-8). Some of the blocks had dowel holes and lever holes at the top center, but others did not.

5) For the side walls of the pronaos and opisthodomos
(PLs. 25, 72~77, Table 2-9)

Six blocks with exterior moulding and raised panel were discovered. Their conditions are the same as those on the blocks for the anta, so they are believed to have been used for the cella walls of the opisthodomos or pronaos.

The blocks range in length from 0.949 m to 0.976 m, and average 0.959 m, which is approximately the same size as the blocks for the cella wall of the naos. The width of the finished part on which the orthostate were set ranged from 0.510 m to 0.519 m, which is larger than that of the cella wall of the naos (Table 2-9). Some of the blocks have dowel and pry holes in the center of the top. Block 131 had a large square-shaped dowel hole on the top, which is also seen on the bottom of the orthostate blocks for the anta, therefore it is believed to have connected to a toichobate block for the anta. The inside corners of Blocks 21 and 220 have a small 45° angle cut on its corner, from which it was determined that they connected to intersecting toichobate blocks.

---

33 The perimeter stylobate block front length averaged 0.960 m, which is similar to that for the toichobate blocks of the pronaos and opisthodomos side walls. Therefore, we know that the toichobate blocks were made to correspond to the stylobate blocks.

Table 2-8 Dimensions of toichobate blocks for opisthodomos dividing wall (m)

Block No.	Width of finished top face (wall)	Width	Width of cut-away part	Length	Height	Moulding height	Moulding width	Dowel holes
Δ2			0.206	0.858	0.410			-
Δ14	0.527	0.690	0.160	0.858	0.404	0.158	0.011	-
Δ169	0.512	0.692	0.180	0.860	0.400	0.153		✔
Ave.	0.520	0.691	0.182	0.859	0.405		0.011	

Table 2-9 Dimensions of toichobate blocks for pronaos and opisthodomos side walls (m)

Block No.	Width of finished top face (wall)	Width	Length	Height	Height of raised panel (outer)	Height of raised panel (inner)	Height of raised panel (outer)	Height of raised panel (inner)	Dowel holes	Diagonal cut
Δ21	0.519	0.585	0.955	0.405	0.157	0.152	0.015	0.013	✔	✔
Δ49		0.585		0.405	0.155	0.155	0.015	0.013	-	-
Δ131			0.954	0.408	0.157		0.013	0.013	✔	-
Δ220	0.510	0.579	0.949	0.401	0.156	0.150	0.013	0.013	-	✔
Δ243	0.512	0.582	0.976	0.403	0.158	0.152	0.016	0.01	-	-
ΔX8			0.963	0.400	0.158		0.015		-	-
Ave.	0.514	0.583	0.959	0.404	0.156	0.154	0.015	0.012		

Table 2-10 Dimensions of toichobate blocks for pronaos dividing wall (m)

Block No.	Width of finished top face (wall)	Top length A	Top length B	Top length C	Top length D	Height	Length	Width	Projection of raised panel
Δ11	0.526	0.699	0.831	0.611	0.220	0.404	1.073	0.872	0.012
Δ17	0.515	0.706	0.862	0.632	0.230	0.402		0.870	
Ave.	0.521	0.703	0.847	0.622	0.225	0.403	1.073	0.871	0.012

6) For the dividing wall of the pronaos
(PLs. 25-5~6, 78~79; Table 2-10)

Two of the unearthed blocks have a cut-away part on the edge of the top, and are therefore believed to have adjoined the threshold. Connecting to the threshold, the tops are finished so that the orthostate can be set on top of them, so they were determined to be toichobate blocks for the dividing wall of the pronaos. The top is L-shaped, and one side of the short end of the L has a cut-away part on which the flooring was set, while the other has a cut-away part on which the threshold rested. The vertical front face without moulding has raised panel, with a joint face underneath. The two blocks have the opposite shape and were set to join the either end of the threshold.

2-3-5 Threshold
(PLs. 26~27, 80~81)

The blocks that make up the threshold can be divided into two main groups: those for the entrance to the naos, and those for the entrance to the pronaos. The naos threshold is composed of one large limestone block which was unearthed broken in several pieces. It is damaged and has not been preserved in good condition, but still has complicated markings at the top for installment of the door and doorframe. The inside edge on the top is cut away part, 0.065 m in depth and 0.300 m in width, to stop the door. The front vertical face has double moulding of cyma reversa and cavett on its upper part and a raised panel on the lower part. On either end of the block, there are several square holes to set the doorframe and pivot, and in the middle of the block, two square holes for vertical bolts are observed.

The pronaos threshold blocks are almost all missing, so it is difficult to estimate their original shape. However, it is possible to tell they are pronaos threshold blocks judging from their corresponding shape of the anta toichobate blocks. The fragmental blocks tell us that there were doors for pronaos and the threshold has cut-away part on its inside edge to close the door.

Chapter 2   Present State of the Temple of Messene

2-3-6   Orthostate blocks
(PLs. 28~29, 82~91)

The orthostate makes up the lower part of the cella wall, and the blocks are set on top of the toichobate. They are the largest blocks among unearthed architectural of the temple. Here, the nine blocks that were in the best condition were measured and illustrated. From their shapes, the orthostate blocks were grouped into six categories.

1)   For the antae
(PLs. 28-1~4, 82~85; Table 2-11)

All the four blocks for the anta were excavated. They could clearly be determined as orthostate blocks for the anta due to the fact that one end of the block was a parastade or an anta pillar and another one was a joint face that continued to the wall. Their heights ranged from 0.962 m to 0.965 m and the lengths were between 1.384 m and 1.390 m. The front widths of anta pillar were between 0.572 m and 0.573 m and the wall widths which continued from the pillar ranged from 0.488 m to 0.493 m. The interior widths of anta pillars range between 0.625 m and 0.637 m and their exterior widths between 0.316 m and 0.325 m. In addition, the anta pillars taper upward, corresponding to the taper of the orthostate block itself. All of the blocks had recessed joint at the bottom on both the inside and outside surfaces. On both the top and bottom of the anta pillars, one square dowel hole of some 0.08 m square and some 0.004 m in depth could be seen on each block. The same type of dowel hole was observed also on the bottom at another end of each block.

2)   For the intersections
(PLs. 28-5, -6, 86~87, Table 2-12)

Two blocks with clear traces of anathyrosis on the inside are thought to have been used as intersecting blocks. Recessed joints were seen on the outside at the bottom. Also, one of the blocks has a recessed joint at the bottom of the inside, bordering the anathyrosis, but the other block has no such recessed joint. From analysis of previous blocks, it was determined that the sides with recessed joints were located at the inside of the pronaos or opisthodomos but not at the naos.

3)   For the side walls of the pronaos and the opisthodomos
(PLs. 29-1, 88, Table 2-13)

One block (Δ27) was excavated which, like the orthostate blocks for the anta, had a recessed joint at the bottom on both the inside and outside faces. Therefore it was believed to have been used for the inside wall of the pronaos or the opisthodomos.

4)   For the dividing wall of the pronaos
(PLs. 29-2, 89, Table 2-14)

One of the excavated blocks had a cut-away part at the bottom of an end, which corresponds and connects to the threshold block. Therefore this block (Δ20) was determined to be for the dividing wall of the pronaos.

5)   For the dividing wall of the opisthodomos
(PLs. 29-3, 90, Table 2-15)

One (Δ7) of the excavated blocks was shorter in length than the other orthostate blocks, but was approximately twice the length of the toichobate blocks for the opisthodomos dividing wall. It was too long to be for the dividing wall of the pronaos, therefore it was determined to be for the opisthodomos dividing wall.

6) For the side walls of the naos

No orthostate blocks for the side wall of the naos were found during the present excavation. However, from the shapes of the other orthostate blocks, the height of such blocks was estimated to be 0.96 m, and the length would have been approximately 1.92 m, or twice the length of the toichobate blocks for the side wall of the naos. The width would have been approximately 0.48 m. Also, considering the shape of the intersecting blocks, there would have been a recessed joint on the outside face only, but not on the inside face[34].

Table 2-11 Dimensions of orthostate blocks for antae (m)

Block No.	Bottom width	Bottom width (anta)	Top width	Top width (anta)	Length	Height
Δ4+Δ568+ΔX	0.493	0.573	0.483	0.563		0.964
Δ6	0.488		0.485	0.552	1.384	0.959
Δ22	0.490	0.572	0.483	0.558	1.390	0.962
Δ40+Δ45				0.557	1.390	0.965
Ave.	0.490	0.573	0.484	0.558	1.388	0.963

Table 2-12 Dimensions of orthostate blocks for intersection (m)

Block No.	Bottom width	Top width	Length	Height
Δ19	0.484	0.483	1.920	0.962
Δ144	0.477	0.477	1.904	0.955
Ave.	0.481	0.480	1.912	0.959

Table 2-13 Dimensions of orthostate blocks for pronaos side walls (m)

Block No.	Bottom width	Top width	Length	Height
Δ27	0.485	0.477	1.924	0.966

Table 2-14 Dimensions of orthostate blocks for pronaos dividing wall (m)

Block No.	Bottom width	Top width	Length	Height
Δ20				0.965

Table 2-15 Dimensions of orthostate blocks for opisthodomos dividing wall (m)

Block No.	Bottom width	Top width	Length	Height
Δ7	0.487	0.480	1.708	0.953

Table 2-16 Dimensions of unidentified orthostate block (m)

Block No.	Bottom width	Top width	Length	Height
Δ98+98a	0.490	0.484		0.969

Table 2-17 Dimensions of orthostate block (m)

	Bottom width	Top width	Length	Height
Average (total)	0.487	0.482	※	0.962

Table 2-18 Average block length (m)

for antae	1.388
for side walls	1.916
for opisthodomos dividing wall	1.708

---

[34] The orthostate block height and width was the same for all block types, so the thickness of the inner court walls must have all been the same. Also, the orthostate blocks were staggered with respect to the toichobate blocks and fixed in place using the dowel holes in the center of the toichobate blocks, and the orthostate blocks were twice as long as the toichobate blocks below them. No deep seam was found on the inside of the bottom of blocks for the dividing wall of the opisthodomos, meaning that the inside of the naos did not have such a seam.

Chapter 2   Present State of the Temple of Messene

8) Unidentified block
(PLs. 29-4, 91, Table 2-16)

From the shape and dimension, this block (Δ98+98a) is believed to have been for the inside wall of the naos or for the dividing wall of the opisthodomos. However it cannot be determined for sure, as the original length of the block is unknown.

2-3-7 Wall blocks
(PLs. 29-5, -6, 92~93)

These blocks were simple cuboid blocks of poros and set on top of the orthostate to form the main body of the cella wall. There must have been a plenty of this type, but only a few blocks were excavated. Most likely, few of these blocks were excavated as they were conveniently sized and probably reused as building materials for houses or other buildings in later eras. Two blocks were measured and illustrated, but both were badly damaged and their original length is unknown. Their widths were approximately 0.47 m and their heights 0.33 m.

2-3-8 Column drums
(PLs. 30~34, 94, Table 2-19)

24 column drum blocks were excavated in all. They are made of soft poros and are badly damaged due to weathering. Evidence of stucco can be found on their surfaces (plate 34-3)[35], and it shows the column drums must have been all covered with stucco. One of the blocks in good condition was illustrated, but the other blocks where measured only. The Table 2-19 shows the dimensions of the column drums. They were measured as precisely as possible but includes some errors due to weathering and damages. On the remaining blocks, the largest diameter was 0.747 m and the smallest diameter was 0.655 m. Their heights varied from 0.650 to 0.906 m. The bottom diameters of the capitals, which will be discussed later, ranged from 0.648 m to 0.655 m, and it was determined that blocks Δ122, Δ124 and Δ193, which had smaller diameters than the capitals, were for the inner columns of pronaos and opisthodomos.

The blocks taper slightly and have 20 flutes. There are dowel holes in the center of both on the top and bottom. The dowel holes are usually worked double-bottomed; that is, there is a smaller deeper hole in the larger surface hole. Some of them have rectangular markings on the sides that looked like dowel holes, the purpose of which is unknown but could be traces of later restoration for breakage (PL. 34-2).

2-3-9 Column capitals
(PLs. 35, 95~97)

Two Doric column capitals were excavated and these were measured and illustrated. They were made of poros. Both were badly damaged due to weathering and plowing, and only a part of the fluting, annulets and other decorations remained. The octagonal bedding with the height of 0.004 m for architrave can be seen on the top of the blocks. A set of a square dowel hole in the center and two long narrow dowel holes also can be seen on the top. The dimensions of the two blocks are as follows. Δ32: the abacus is 0.882 m square and 0.128 m in height, echinus 0.088 m, annulet 0.030, shaft 0.082 m and the total 0.332 m in height. The upper column diameter is estimated at 0.689 m between arrises. ΔX1: the abacus is 0.885 m square and 0.136 m in height, echinus 0.084 m, annulet 0.031 m, 0.084 m and the total 0.342 m in height. The upper column diameter is estimated at 0.676 m between arrises. From

---

35 Remnants of stucco were also found on the architrave blocks, so it is believed that the surfaces of blocks made of poros were generally finished with stucco. On the architrave of the stoas of the Asklepieion at Messene, the stucco remnant is also seen. Hayashida/Yoshitake/Ito 2013, Pl. 83a.

their sizes, both blocks were believed to have been used in outer columns[36]. The section of echinus is almost straight but only slightly curved outward and shows Hellenistic feature. No capitals were found for inner columns.

2-3-10 Architrave blocks
(PLs. 36, 98~100)

The architrave located above the column serves as the beam block. The blocks were all made of poros. Three such blocks were excavated, measured and illustrated. They were badly damaged, and none of their original shapes are completely intact. Their heights range

Table 2-19 Dimensions of column drums (m)

Block No.	Height	Lower diameter	Upper diameter	Flute width
Outer column				
Δ61	-	0.747	-	0.121
Δ62	0.779	-	0.743	0.125
Δ63	0.760	-	0.749	0.125
Δ84	0.748	-	0.654	0.110
Δ87	0.774	0.704	0.680	0.110
Δ88	0.704	-	-	0.110
Δ102	-	-	0.654	0.105
Δ111	0.809	-	0.651	0.109
Δ121	0.840	-	-	0.110
Δ126	0.811	-	-	0.116
Δ127	0.781	0.734	0.714	0.122
Δ128	0.736	-	-	0.113
Δ148	0.746	-	-	0.110
Δ149	0.650	0.722	-	0.120
Δ150	0.745	-	0.657	0.110
Δ165	-	-	-	0.123
Δ167	-	0.703	-	0.115
Δ168	-	-	0.658	0.110
Δ190	0.731	-	-	0.110
Δ191	-	-	0.664	0.117
Δ202	0.758	-	-	0.090
Inner column				
Δ122	0.700	0.681	-	0.117
Δ124	0.768	0.681	-	0.114
Δ193	0.760	0.602	-	0.101

---

36 Judging from the architrave width, the column capitals have appropriate dimensions. Column drums with smaller lower column diameters than the column capital lower column diameters were also found. Therefore, these capitals are believed to have been used in the outer colonnade.

from 0.511 to 0.514 m and widths from 0.385 m to 0.389 m. The largest of the damaged blocks was 1.783 m in length. Both an exterior block with reglae and guttae and an interior backer block without reglae or guttae were excavated, so we know that these two types of blocks were set together back to back. On the top, clamp holes are observed at the back edge and at the center.

2-3-11 Frieze blocks
(PLs. 37, 38-1, -2, 101~104)

Several frieze blocks on top of the architrave were found, but they were badly damaged and none of them were completely intact. Seven blocks were measured and four of these were illustrated. Each block is made of poros and has triglyphs and metopes. Three blocks show that the left edges of their triglyph are joint faces. The restored width of the triglyph is 0.378 m and the height 0.589 m. From the block (Δ293), the total width of the frieze would be a little wider than 0.777 m. On the back at the bottom, there is a section to set the ceiling block of the pteron.

2-3-12 Cornice blocks
(PL. 38-3, -4, 105~106)

Only a few of these blocks were excavated, and they were heavily damaged and fragmental. None were completely intact. Two blocks were measured and illustrated. The moulding of cyma reversa can be seen at the transitional part to the eave. The angle of the cornice show that the slope of the roof was 1: 4.48 or 13°.

2-3-13 Sima blocks
(PLs. 38-5, 107)

Only one block which was found is 0.653 m long and 0.214 m high, but the width is unknown due to breakage. The outer face is processed in cavet which rises up straightly and gradually curves outward.

Chapter 3

Reconstruction of the Temple

3-1 Reconstruction of plan of the peripteral columns
3-1-1 Intercolumniation

In order to reconstruct the temple, the intercolumniation, or the axial distance between columns, was decided by analyzing the stylobate blocks. Fifteen outer column stylobate blocks were actually measured, but the front lengths could be measured only on four of these blocks (Δ56, Δ64+Δ161+Δ383, Δ147, ΔX9) and were 0.962 m, 0.961 m, 0.960 m, and 0.956 m respectively. The length of the flooring blocks also corresponds to that of the stylobate blocks due to the correspondence of joint lines and thus is almost the same dimension. Two flooring blocks were measured, and their front lengths were 0.962 m and 0.960 m, and the measurement error was 2 mm. Similarly, there were 14 corresponding toichobate blocks whose block length averaged 0.960 m (0.009 m standard error)[37].

As stylobate blocks are used as bases for the visually important columns, they could have been made with better accuracy than other blocks. When considering the average size of these blocks and the estimated error, even though the front length could be measured directly on only four blocks, the original front length could safely be estimated as the average of these blocks, or 0.960 m.

The intercolumniation was determined to be two times the length of the front stylobate blocks, in other words[38],

0.960 × 2 = 1.920 m.

Next, the one excavated corner stylobate block (Δ96a+b) measured 0.880 × 0.888 m, and the depth of the regular stylobate blocks (Δ43, Δ64+Δ161+Δ383, Δ147, Δ353, ΔX5, ΔX9) were 0.885m, 0.880m, 0.884m, 0.884m, 0.880m and 0.881 respectively. The two sides of the corner stylobate block should have the same depth as the regular stylobate blocks, and these 6 blocks should theoretically all have the same dimensions. Although the maximum error was

---

37 The stylobate blocks, flooring blocks, and toichobate blocks, which had corresponding dimensions, were analyzed and compared (Fig. 3-1, 3-2, 3-3). The front width for regular stylobate blocks, flooring blocks, and the 14 remaining toichobate blocks averaged 0.960 m, 0.961 m and 0.960 m respectively, so the latter two measurements were found to correspond with the former. However, the standard deviation for the toichobate block length was found to be 0.009 m, showing some variation. This variation might be due to the difference of location of the blocks; that is, the naos, pronaos, opisthodomos, cella wall and dividing walls. For reconstruction purposes, this variation is attributed to simple construction error at the corner stylobate blocks.

38 There were dowel holes located at almost the exact center of the top of the stylobate blocks supporting columns. Therefore, the columns are judged to have been located at the center of the stylobate blocks. These blocks were set to alternate with stylobate blocks that did not support columns, so the intercolumniation would be the half of the front length of the column-supporting stylobate blocks doubled, plus the front length of the stylobate blocks without columns. Based on note 37 above, the stylobate blocks with and without supported columns both measured 0.960 m, so the intercolumniation works out to be twice the stylobate block front length, or 1.920 m.

found to be 8 mm, some blocks had the average dimension of 0.884 m or 0.885 m. In some cases, temple stylobate blocks differ in size at the front and at the sides of the temple[39], but it is impossible to tell whether the stylobate blocks at the Temple of Messene were used at the front that their difference in dimensions was not on purpose, but rather due to construction error. The average depth of the six blocks and the corner block was taken as 0.883 m[40].

Thus, it was assumed that the front and side corner stylobate blocks all have the same dimensions, and the reconstructed or original dimensions of the corner stylobate block were determined to be 0.883 × 0.883 m.

Table 3-1 Dimensions of normal stylobate blocks (m)

Block No.	Front Width	Depth
Δ43		0.885
Δ56	0.962	
Δ64+Δ161+Δ383	0.960	0.880
Δ147	0.961	0.884
Δ353		0.884
ΔX5		0.880
ΔX9	0.956	0.881
Δ96		0.888
		0.880
Average	0.960	0.883

Table 3-2 Length of toichobate blocks (m)

Block No.	Length
Δ1	0.960
Δ8	0.958
Δ15	0.961
Δ16	0.942
Δ18	0.957
Δ21	0.955
Δ48	0.973
Δ131	0.954
Δ143	0.955
Δ220	0.949
Δ243	0.976
Δ465	0.968
Δ575+Δ576+Δ579	0.963
ΔX8	0.963
Average	0.960

Table 3-3 Dimensions of flooring blocks (m)

Block No.	Front width
Δ55	0.962
ΔX2	0.960
Average	0.961

3-1-2 Angle contraction of the corner intercolumniation

On Doric temple orders, as a rule triglyphs are arranged at equal intervals on the frieze, and the corner column intercolumniation was generally shortened at the corners (angle contraction). This was also the case at the Temple of Asklepius as well, which was the Doric temple more than a century later at Messene[41]. Theoretically the length of contraction would be half the width of the architrave minus half the triglyph width. According to actual survey data, Doric temples do not necessarily follow this principle[42]. At this temple, there must have been some contraction at any rate, but there is no positive evidence to determine how it was

---

39 In many temples, the axial spacings of the exterior columns differ at their fronts and flanks. It means that the stylobate front length also differ as well respectively. In the Doric temples from the 4th to 3rd century, the axial spacings are as follows; Temple of Athena Alea at Tegeta, 3.613 m (front), 3.585 m (flank); Temple of Zeus at Nemea, 3.750 m, 3.746 m; Temple of Zeus at Stratos, 3.17 m, 3.17 m; Metroon at Olympia, 2.01m, 2.01 m; Temple of Apollo at Delos, 2.905 m, 2.905 m; Temple of Athena Polias, 2.367 m, 2.371 m. This suggests that the axial spacings at front and flanks become the same or almost the same with only a few millimeters in the Hellenistic period, and the stylobate front lengths are also the same as well at their fronts and flanks. The data are from the tables of Dinsmoor. See Dinsmoor p.339.

40 See note 37 above.

41 Sioumpara 2011, Tafel 6, 7, 15. Orlandos, *Prakt* 1971. Pl. B´, Γ´, Δ´. The corner intercolumniation is 2.20 m by Orlandos and Sioumpara, but the normal one is a little different: 2.43 m by Orlandos and 2.398 m by Sioumpara.

42 The angle contraction is an essential problem for Doric design and many authors mention about the problem. Its solution is not uniform with theoretical formula but some variation can be observed. Coulton 1977, pp. 79-80.

determined. Thus, in our reconstruction here, we follow the theoretical angle contraction.

The architrave was made up of two front and back block and each of these blocks averaged 0.387 m in width. Therefore the overall architrave width would have been twice this, or 0.774 m. This width would be reasonable considering that the total width of the frieze block Δ293 which was set on the architrave is presumed to have been 0.777 m in width. (PL. 103).

Block Δ279, on which the triglyph front length was well preserved, was used to determine the reconstructed measurement of 0.383 m (PL. 102). The triglyph front length theoretically should be the same as the regulae on the architrave block, and this dimension is almost equal to the length of the regulae on other architrave blocks, so it was considered appropriate[43].

Using these values, the angle contraction at the column corner was theoretically calculated as the following:

$(0.774 - 0.383)/2 = 0.1955$ (m)

Therefore the column contraction would have been

$1.920 - 0.1955 = 1.7245$ (m)

The stylobate block front width was 0.960 m, and the corner stylobate block front width was 0.883 m. Therefore the front length of the second stylobate block from the corner would have been

$1.7245 - (0.960/2 + 0.883/2) = 0.803$ (m)

3-1-3 Crepis

The crepis blocks were analyzed first in order to determine the front width of the temple. The crepis blocks make up stereobate or platform located underneath the stylobate, and are generally arranged in two tiers in the Doric style. Several crepis blocks were excavated, but they were in extremely poor condition and the original size could be determined for only a few of them. Seven of the blocks were in relatively good condition, and these were measured. They were found to be of two types, with front lengths of about 0.8 m and 0.96 m respectively. These dimensions are essentially equal to the front length of the stylobate blocks, so the 0.8 m block length was determined to be that of the second block from the corner[44], and the 0.96 m blocks were the regular crepis blocks.

We were also able to determine the tread width based on markings left on the top of the blocks. Corner crepis blocks Δ50 and Δ59 had the same dimensions for the tread at the front and the side, therefore we know that the width and length of the tread at the temple are equal. We determined the average value of the six blocks on which markings remain on the surface in order to reconstruct this dimension, and the result was 0.253 m.

The front face of each crepis block has raised panel as well as stylobate blocks. At the bottom there is a recess or margin to articulate the horizontal bottom line of the crepis. The height is 0.046 m and the depth 0.019 m. The vertical front face has a shallow raised panel with the recessed edges along the bottom and either left or right side. The width is 0.028 m and the depth 0.003 m. The detail was measured in block Δ555 (PL. 42).

With these recess at the bottom with 0.022 m, the depth at the bottom is 0.020 m smaller than that at the top, considering the slight inclination of the crepis front. Therefore the visible tread width in floor plan would have been 0.020 m smaller than 0.253 m, or actual tread

---

43 The front length of the regulae was reconstructed as 0.384 m based on architrave block Δ166. The triglyph front length was reconstructed based on the reconstructed value of the frieze. Cf. p.46.

44 The front length of the second stylobate block from the corner, based on reconstruction so far, was determined to be 0.803 m. The vertical joints of blocks were staggered during placement, so this shorter value is assumed to have been used for the second crepis block from the corner as well.

width. That is 0.233m. As the crepis is usually made up of two tiers[45], the overall length of 0.233 × 4 = 0.932 m would be added to the front width of the temple at the stylobate to obtain the front width of the temple at the lower tier of the crepis.

3-1-4 Number of front columns

The number of front columns for Doric temples is generally six. Especially, the size of this temple is very small compared with other Doric temples and the number of the front columns must have been six as well[46]. As mentioned above, the western half of north and south sides of the temple site had foundations of rubble masonry, inside of which the area was dug out approximately 50 cm deep, and almost nothing remained. Generally, the temple foundations are built of ashlar poros blocks on rubble bedding or directly on bedrock which is trimmed for foundations. The levels of these rubble foundations are too high to build foundations of ashlar blocks on them. Moreover, along the extended lines of the north foundation, some stelae bases were excavated, and under the west staircase of the temple, which is the only light structure, had this same rubble foundation. For this reason, it is unlikely that the temple, which must have been of a great weight, would have been set on the foundations of rubble masonry. Therefore it seems reasonable to assume that the temple was located inside these rubble foundations, to the north and the south. Actual survey measurements show that the inside distance between the north and south foundations of rubble masonry was 11.5 m, and the front width of the temple including the crepis would have been smaller than this. The foundations of rubble masonry would have been for paved floor around the temple. With this in mind, a front colonnade of six, seven and eight columns was considered in turn.

In the case of six front columns. If there were six front columns, there would have been

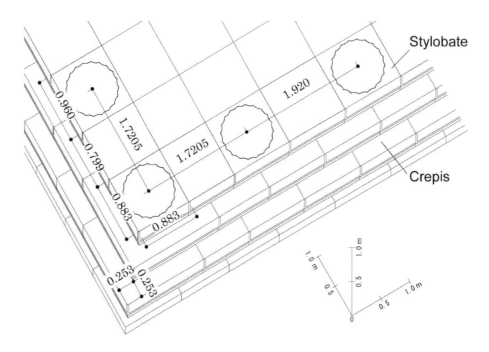

Fig. 3-1 Reconstruction of the corner of the stylobate.

---

[45] Temples built on 3-tiered foundations also exist, but they are exceptional. For example, we see this very rare construction style, for example, at the Temple of Apollo at Syracusa.

[46] The size of the Messene Temple shows the similarity with the Temple of Athena Polias at Pergamon (12.27 × 21.77 m), and the Metroon at Olympia (10.62 × 20.67 m).

Chapter 3   Reconstruction of the Temple

11 stylobate blocks. Of these, seven would have been regular stylobate blocks (with a front width of 0.960 m), two would have been corner stylobate blocks (with two front widths of 0.883 m), and the remaining two would have been contracted angle stylobate blocks second from the corner (with a front width of 0.803 m). Therefore, the total stylobate length would have been
$$0.960 \times 7 + 0.883 \times 2 + 0.803 \times 2 = 10.092 \text{ m} \quad < \quad 11.5 \text{ m}$$
Adding to this the value of two crepis blocks widths on either side
$$10.092 + 0.233 \times 2 \times 2 = 11.024 \text{ m} \quad < \quad 11.5 \text{ m}$$
Here, it is clear that a colonnade of six front columns would fulfill the necessary conditions.

In the cases of seven front columns. In some larger temples, there are also examples of seven or eight columns[47], and it would be necessary to make sure of that. If there were seven front columns, there would have had to have been 13 stylobate blocks. Using the same calculations as with six front columns, we obtain
$$0.960 \times 9 + 0.883 \times 2 + 0.803 \times 2 = 12.012 \text{ m} \quad > \quad 11.5 \text{ m}$$
From this we see that seven front columns do not fulfill the necessary conditions. Therefore, neither seven nor eight front columns is possible, and six columns is the best answer.

3-1-5   Number of side columns

It was confirmed that the number of front columns at the temple was determined to be six as above. Next, the number of side columns and the side length of the temple should be determined and conditions of the surrounding area should be analyzed to do that.

On the west and east ends of the temple, rectangular poros blocks were unearthed in situ, which are believed to have been for the foundation. The ashlar poros blocks (0.580 × 1.20 m) on the east end are placed with an axial distance of ca 0.96 m that is roughly equal to the front length of the stylobate and flooring blocks. Therefore, these poros blocks are believed to have been the foundation for the flooring blocks of the east pteron, where the flooring block were usually spanned between two foundation blocks. There are preserved no other foundation and the bedrock is partially cut away to set the stylobate foundation on the east end.

On the west end, in contrast to the poros blocks on the east end, the ashlar poros blocks are laid out solid with their edges connecting, and therefore are believed to have supported surrounding stylobate and columns on it[48]. Abutting this poros foundation, there are foundation of rubble masonry which turn toward east on its north and south sides. The distance between the east edge of this rubble foundation to the cut-away bedrock on the east end is believed to equal the approximate length of the temple itself. This actual measured length was 22.79 m.

Additionally, there were joint faces on the outside surfaces of the toichobate blocks, which are believed to have adjoined the flooring of the pteron. If this temple had been prostyle, there would be no pteron and thus no need to adjoin the flooring. Thus it is assumed that this temple was peristyle and had a surrounding colonnade.

Taking 22.79 m as an approximate value for the number of side columns, a stylobate length with 12 side columns would be
$$0.960 \times 19 + 0.883 \times 2 + 0.803 \times 2 = 21.612 \text{ m}$$
To this we add the lengths of the two crepis tiers on either side to obtain
$$21.612 + 0.233 \times 2 \times 2 = 22.544 \text{ m} \quad < \quad 22.79 \text{ m}$$
which is a reasonable value. If there were 13 side columns, the length would exceed that of the dug-out foundation, and 11 columns would be too short. Therefore the number of side columns

---

47   Doric style temples with 6 columns at the front are very common and are assumed to have been the more generalized style. See Dinsmoor 1975, figs. 33, 35, 36, 42, 43, 55, 56, 67. As examples of more exceptional styles, the 7-column Temple of Zeus at Acragas (ibid., Fig. 57) and the 8-column Parthenon at Athens can be mentioned.

48   Usually, the foundation blocks are laid connectedly without gap for stylobate and cella walls, although they were laid with a gap for pavement of the pteron floor. Cf. Hodge 1966, Plate V, XI.

was determined as 12. Based on the above, the Temple of Messene was determined to have six columns in the front and 12 columns on the side. With this arrangement, the poros foundation on the west side was determined to be for the stylobate and the poros blocks on the east side would have been for the flooring.

3-1-6 West staircase

The steps on the west end are best preserved part in the temple, but the upper part of the southern half is lost. The steps turn around toward east ca. 3.5 m on its south and north ends. The blocks are weathered and tread widths differ at different locations. There also seems to be some deformation and dislocation of the blocks. Also, the level of the steps was found to be approximately 10 cm lower on the south side than on the north side. From this, it seems that the original positions of the blocks have shifted due to topographical changes during the long history of the sloped site. Therefore the west steps were reconstructed with an error of some centimeters in mind.

The lowest step of the west staircase has a length of 14.319 m. The tread surfaces vary greatly, from 0.160 m to 0.270 m on the north side, 0.220 m to 0.270 m on the south side, and 0.240 m to 0.310 m on the west side. There do not seem to be any tread surfaces for climbing the stairs on the north and south sides, and the tread surfaces become smaller at the higher steps. Also, the rubble foundation of the west steps shows that the steps were not joined together to the previously mentioned ashlar foundation, which is believed to have been located on the edge of the west side of the temple. It is assumed that the staircase was not connected to the temple itself, but rather added to the west end as an extension probably in order to adjust the level

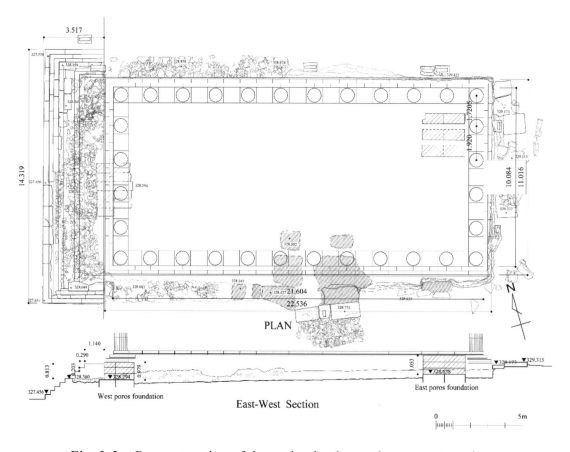

Fig. 3-2 Reconstruction of the peristyle plan and east-west section.

Chapter 3   Reconstruction of the Temple

difference between the temple floor and the west ground.

In our measurement, the lowest step was set as a standard value 0 m (the absolute height was 327.550 m). Using this, the highest existing step (the fifth) was at a height of +0.810 m (absolute height 328.360 m). The height of the poros foundation at the west end of the temple was +0.744 m (absolute height 328.294 m) and the poros foundation at the east end was +1.088 m (absolute value 328.638 m). The height of two blocks, which seems to have been pavement in front of the temple, at the north end of east end cut-away edge was +1.623 m (absolute value 329.173 m). The blocks were higher by 0.8-1 m than the rubble masonry foundation on the west end, so the blocks at the east end was considered to have been the original ground level for the temple. This is considered a reasonable conclusion judging from the height of the foundation of entrance slope to the temple, which can be seen in the center of the east end[49].

Based on these observations, we know that the original ground level for the temple was 1.623 m higher than the first step of the west stairs, and it would be possible that this ground level might have been at the same level all around the temple. Thus, supposing that the top step of the west stair was at the same level as the ground level of the east end (+1.623 m, absolute level 329.173 m), the difference in level between the remaining top step (+0.810 m, absolute level 328.360 m) and the original top step or the ground level on the west end was 0.813 m. Judging from the present value of the rise, it is reasonable to assume that there were four more steps in the staircase (the rise of one step would have been 0.203 m). Similarly, the front tread of the west stairs averages 0.290 m, if we add another four steps, the original top of the west stairs would have reached closer the west edge of the rubble foundation which would have been the line of euthynteria; that is, the distance would have been 1.140 m in width up to the location of the euthynteria[50]. (See PL. 113, East-west section.)

As above, the plan of the surrounding colonnade plane design of the surrounding columns of the temple was decided. Positioning the temple in cross-section, the difference between the top of the poros blocks on the east end and the bottom level of the stylobate is 1.057 m[51]. It is believed that foundation blocks were also set in this space. The height of the poros blocks is unknown, but it is believed that three tiers of poros blocks with a height of approximately 35 cm were arranged here. Similarly, it is thought that three tiers of poros blocks were also set on the west side.

Usually euthynteria foundation blocks are set underneath the crepis blocks, and only one portion of the top part of the euthynteria is above the ground. In this case, however, there were no euthynteria blocks unearthed, and the crepis and stylobate blocks here are somewhat higher than the blocks used at other Doric style temples. At this temple, the euthynteria blocks are hypothesized to have been approximately 1.5 times thicker than the crepis or stylobate blocks, or approximately 0.300 m. Therefore, it is believed that two tiers of blocks approximately 0.350 m in thickness were set on the poros blocks both on the west side and on the east side.

3-2   Reconstruction of the cella

To reconstruct the cella wall, it is necessary to analyze the abovementioned toichobate blocks and orthostate blocks. First of all, from the fact that four toichobate blocks and four orthostate blocks for the antae were found, there the cella had pronaos and opisthodomos which

---

49   The absolute height of the foundation on the east slope was measured using a total station, and the result was 329.193 m.

50   Absolute height of the 5th step - the height of the first step) /4 = (328.360−327.55) /4 = 0.203 m.

51   The absolute ground level is 329.173m. The total height of two crepis is 0.422 m (0.211 × 2). The difference between the bottom of the lower crepis and ground level is unknown and we supposed it 10 cm hypothetically, a half of the crepis height. Thus, the absolute height of the top of the upper crepis or bottom of the stylobate is 329.173 + 0.10 + (0.211x2) 329.695. The absolute level of the top of the east poros foundation is 328.638. Therefore, the difference between the bottom of the stylobate and the top of the east poros foundation is 1.057 m. (329.695 − 328.638 = 1.057 m)

have two antae respectively on both sides, and naos between them.

In addition, foundation blocks excavated on the northeast side of the temple are believed to have supported flooring for the east end pteron. We also know that the poros foundation blocks on the west end of the temple were for the stylobate, based on their shape[52]. From these facts, it was determined that the extent of the cella wall was, at most, the area from the west edge of the poros foundation blocks on the east end to the poros foundation blocks for the stylobate on the west end. This distance was actually measured as 17.137 m. That is, the length of the inner court should reconstructed with a dimension less than 17.137m.

In the previous chapter, the toichobate and orthostate blocks in good condition were categorized into six different categories:
    1. for the anta
    2. for the intersection
    3. for the side wall of the naos
    4. for the dividing wall of the opisthodomos
    5. for the side wall of the opisthodomos and the pronaos
    6. for the dividing wall of the pronaos

With these categories, the dimensions of the toichobate and orthostate and evidence from clamp holes and dowel holes were analyzed in order to reconstruct the combination of the blocks and order in which the blocks were set.

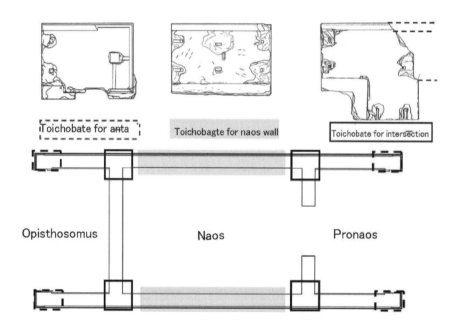

Fig. 3-3　Plan of the cella wall and toichobate block types.

3-2-1　Threshold and adjacent blocks

The threshold block (Δ133+Δ13+Δ477) is an almost half of the threshold and has a door pivot hole and a pair of bolt holes for the doors. With these traces, we would determine that the width of one door leaf was 1.015m, the opening for the door was twice as wide or 2.030 m, and the overall length of the threshold blocks was estimated to be 2.955 m. From the

---

52   See note 48 above.

condition of protruding edges of the threshold blocks and the fact that the location and shape of the cut-away parts of toichobate blocks Δ11 and Δ17 for the dividing wall of the pronaos corresponded to each other, the either end of the threshold block is believed to have rested on these two blocks respectively.

In addition, the shape of the large cut-away portion seen on the bottom of orthostate block Δ20 has the same shape as toichobate block Δ17. No other orthostate blocks have a similar shape; therefore it is believed that the orthostate block Δ20 was located on top of block Δ17.

Next the toichobate block that would have been next to block Δ17 is considered. From our assumptions this far, we know that the Temple of Messene was peristylar with six columns on the ends. In general Doric temples, the axial width of cella corresponds to three central intercolumniations, which is here $0.960 \times 5 = 4.800$ m, and its width from inside-inside width is approximately $0.960 \times 4 = 3.84$ m. Considering these conditions and the width of the threshold block, or 2.955m, it is impossible to lay another toichobate block between Δ17 and the cella wall. Therefore the toichobate block next to block Δ17 must have been a block for the intersection. It is reasonable to think that block Δ144 for the intersection would have adjoined block number Δ17, judging from the location of the clamp holes and the surface finishing. This was also judged to be a reasonable conclusion because the length of the cut-away part of block Δ20 was 1.110 m, which is approximately equal to the sum of the length of one edge of block Δ140 and the length of the part of block Δ17 that fell on the orthostate, or 1.109 m. If a similar block for the intersection was on the opposite side, block Δ3 was judged to be a reasonable candidate to correspond to block Δ11, based on the location of the clamp holes and the surface finishing. (Fig. 3-4, 3-5)

Based on the above, the interior length of the pronaos was estimated as 5.175 m. The orthostate block Δ20, whose inner face to the naos and joint face to the doorway jamb are missing, would have been L-shaped in plan, considering the fact that toichobate block Δ17 is L-shaped in plan, corresponding to the wider width of the threshold block. In addition, the remains of dowel holes on top of the threshold block indicate that orthostate block Δ20 was fixed by three dowels to the end of the threshold.

The general size of block Δ20 was reconstructed based on surface markings. The front length of the block is 1.460 m, the depth on the threshold side is 0.793 m, and the width of the wall supporting the doorway jamb is 0.425 m. Similarly, the width of the dividing wall of the pronaos is 0.486 m. The detailed shape of the doorway jamb, which covered the ends of the pronaos dividing wall, is unknown, but from the surface markings on the threshold it seems that it was constructed of three blocks: one block covering the front corner of the orthostate, one block in the middle, and one block covering the back corner.

We have now reconstructed the threshold and surrounding blocks. The location of two of the toichobate blocks for intersection and two other blocks was also decided, and we know that they were set to intersect with the dividing wall of the opisthodomos. From their shapes, block Δ9 was located at the northwest and block Δ45 at the southwest.

3-2-2 Anta blocks

Two of the four excavated toichobate blocks for the anta have notches on the inside surface which are believed to have been used for a door. From this, we know that there was a door located either at the pronaos or the opisthodomos. We could not clearly determine which room had the door, but the notch on toichobate block Δ47 for the anta was similar to that on stylobate block Δ117+Δ118 for the pronaos and the opisthodomos, excavated at the southeast side of the temple. From this, it is highly likely that the door was not set at the opisthodomos but at the pronaos. Therefore we have reconstructed the present temple with door at the entrance to the pronaos. Based on this, the toichobate blocks for the anta would have been set as follows:

Fig. 3-4 Threshold and dividing wall of the pronaos.

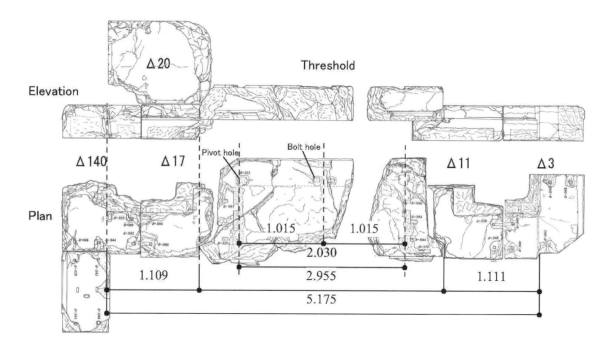

Fig. 3-5 Position of the blocks for threshold and dividing wall of the pronaos.

block Δ349 in the northeast, block Δ47 in the southeast, block Δ577+Δ580 in the northwest, and block Δ223 in the southwest.

The orthostate blocks for the anta have anta pillar or parastade at the end. One side of the anta pillar is approximately 30 cm in width and the other side is approximately 60 cm in width, so we know that the anta pillar width differed with the side. From the finishing on the toichobate blocks for the anta, we know that the wider side of the anta pillar (the 60 cm side) was on the inside, because it should correspond with the diameter of the inner columns of the pronaos. Therefore, of the anta orthostate blocks, block Δ4+Δ568+Δ574+ΔX4 and block Δ22 were set at the southeast or northwest corner, and block Δ6 and block Δ40+Δ45 were set at the northeast or southwest corner[53]. With this in mind, the locations of the dowel holes on each block were analyzed, and it was found that the toichobate block Δ47 for the southeast anta had a dowel hole of ca 0.09 m square on the top which could only correspond to orthostate block

---

53 Based on the location of the square dowel holes on the bottom, none of the other anta orthostate blocks are possible without corresponding dowel holes. Block Δ22 was only choice as the bottom part is missing. It is also an additional reason to indicate that blocks Δ22, Δ45 and Δ47 were found at the east half of the excavated site. See PL.110.

Chapter 3   Reconstruction of the Temple

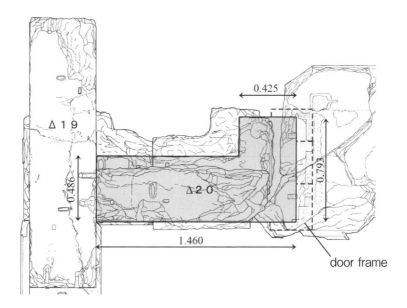

Fig. 3-6   Position of block Δ20 for dividing wall of the pronaos.

Δ22. Therefore, the orthostate blocks for anta were located in the following corners: block Δ40+Δ45 in the northeast, block Δ22 in the southeast, and block Δ4+Δ568+Δ574+ΔX4 in the northwest.

3-2-3   Side walls of the pronaos and opisthodomos

The side walls of the pronaos and the opisthodomos were reconstructed by setting the three related toichobate blocks Δ21, Δ220 and Δ131. The toichobate blocks Δ21 and Δ220 for the side walls of the pronaos and the opisthodomos have corners cut at a 45° angle, therefore they clearly connected to the toichobate blocks for intersection. From the shape and location of the dowel holes, we found that block Δ21 connected to block Δ140, and block Δ220 connected to block Δ145.

Additionally, toichobate block Δ13 had the same square dowel hole on its surface as those on the toichobate and orthostate blocks for the anta, so it was probably connected to an anta block. The square dowel hole on block Δ131 was set somewhat inside the center of the block, and so the corresponding dowel hole must have been only on orthostate block 22[14]. Therefore block Δ131 would have connected to toichobate block Δ47 for the anta, which was located underneath block Δ22.

Next we considered the location of orthostate blocks Δ19 and Δ144 for the intersection. Orthostate block Δ19 is long and has anathyrosis on one side in the center, so it would have been set overlapping two toichobate blocks for the intersection. It could not have been above intersection blocks Δ9 or Δ145 because these have dowel holes on their top surfaces. In addition, there was a recessed joint at the bottom only toward left from the anathyrosis part. This recessed joint is also seen on anta orthostate blocks, so we know that the side on which the recessed joint is visible should have been the pronaos or opisthodomos side. From the above, it was concluded that block Δ19 was set above three toichobate blocks; toichobate block Δ140 for the intersection and orthostate blocks Δ48 and Δ21.

Orthostate block Δ144 also has anathyrosis on the intersecting part of the side edge and a recessed joint on the bottom. There is a dowel hole underneath the anathyrosis part, and the only toichobate block with a corresponding dowel hole is block Δ145. Therefore, block Δ144 was clearly set on toichobate block Δ145 for the intersection.

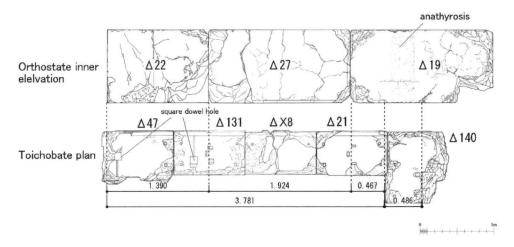

Fig. 3-7 Reconstruction of the south side wall of the pronaos.

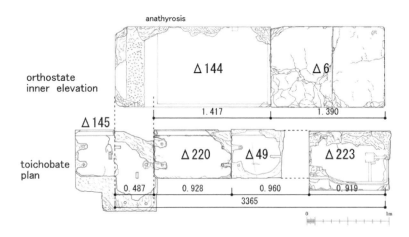

Fig. 3-8 Reconstruction of the opisthodomos side wall of the southwest cella.

Based on the locations of the blocks discussed so far, the locations of other blocks and the dimensions of each part will be decided.

1) Length of the side walls of the pronaos

The length of the side wall of the pronaos was decided based on the southeast side of the temple, for which many of the blocks making up the pronaos side wall remain. In the analysis thus far, toichobate blocks Δ47, Δ131, Δ21 and Δ140 and orthostate blocks Δ22 and Δ19 were used in pronaos side wall in the southeast. Next, the number of connecting blocks between blocks Δ21 and Δ131 is considered. From the abovementioned locations relative to the orthostate, the toichobate must have been arranged with alternating blocks with and without dowel holes on their surfaces[54]. If there had been two blocks between orthostate blocks Δ22 and Δ19, which were set above toichobate blocks Δ21 and Δ131, three toichobate blocks underneath these would have been necessary. This is difficult to imagine considering the length

---

54 This is approximately twice the length of toichobate blocks set underneath the orthostate. Moreover, as some of the toichobate blocks have dowel holes on the top, we know that the bottom edge of the orthostate blocks were positioned with dowels at the center of the toichobate block tops so that they spanned and covered the toichobate blocks without dowel holes.

Chapter 3   Reconstruction of the Temple

of the naos and opisthodomos which will be discussed later[55]. Therefore, it is more natural to assume that only one block was set between these two orthostate blocks, and correspondingly one toichobate block between toichobate blocks Δ21 and Δ131. Because they did not have dowel holes, blocks Δ243 and ΔX8 were considered for the center position, but ΔX8 was determined to be correct because of the position of the clamp hole. Therefore, block Δ243 was determined to have been set at the opposite location (the northeast side). As a result, the southeast toichobate blocks were completely reconstructed, and the length of the side wall of the pronaos was determined as 3.781 m.

Orthostate block Δ27 for the side wall of the pronaos or opisthodomos was found from its length and clamp hole position to have been set between blocks Δ19 and Δ22 and on top of toichobate blocks Δ21 and Δ131 and block ΔX8.

2) Length of the side walls of the opisthodomos

The southwest side of the temple, where most of the blocks making up the side wall of the opisthodomos are remaining, was used to determine the length. The placement of othostate blocks Δ6 and Δ144 was clarified as in the previous discussion, and from their lengths it was determined that neither block Δ220 nor Δ223 would directly fit between them. Therefore there must have been more than one block used. As with the pronaos reconstruction, we considered the possibility of a second block here, but in such a case, there would have to have been 3 toichobate blocks below them, which would not have been possible in light of the temple length to be discussed later[56]. Therefore there should be only one block in the center. Based on this, we found that orthostate blocks Δ6 and Δ144 were directly connected, and that the block between blocks Δ220 and Δ223 would probably have been toichobate block 49. Like toichobate block 131 which connects to the anta at the southeast pronaos, block Δ49 also has part of a groove for pouring lead into a square dowel on its top surface, although the part of the block for the dowel is lost by breakage. Therefore it was clearly next to an anta block. Also, although block Δ49 does not have a set of dowel and lever holes as seen on block Δ131, it would not have needed a dowel hole in the considered location as orthostate block Δ144 and toichobate block Δ145 would both have been held in place by dowels. Thus the location of block Δ49 was set here. From the length of orthostate blocks Δ144 and Δ6, the distance between blocks Δ220 and 223 would have been 0.960 m, which is an appropriate length for one toichobate block. From the above, the length of the side wall of the opisthodomos was determined as 2.807 m based on the length of the present orthostate blocks Δ6 and Δ144 (Fig. 3-9).

3-2-4   Side walls of the naos

There were 9 excavated toichobate blocks for the side wall of the naos, but few hints remained on each block as to how they would have been arranged, thus their locations are difficult to determine. For this reason, dowel and lever holes were used to decide the block order, from which the location of the toichobate blocks was determined. From the construction markings on the blocks that have already been set in place, it is evident that the orthostate blocks for the side walls of the opisthodomos and the pronaos were set from west to east[57]. Therefore,

---

55   Based on the discussion so far, the length of the cella must have been smaller than 17.137 m. If one orthostate block is added to the pronaos, the pronaos length would be 5.695 m. As the length of the naos side wall is 7.708 m and the length of the opisthodomos side wall is 2.807 m (explanations follow later), the sum of these three measurements is 16.210 m, which is only 0.927 m smaller than the maximum possible cella length.

56   See note 55 above.

57   Thus far, the pronaos and opisthodomos side wall toichobate blocks, for which the placement has been identified, all have lever holes on top to the east of the corresponding dowel holes. These indicated that the blocks were moved westward with levers to the dowels to set them to their final position, therefore we know that the orthostate blocks were set from west to east.

it is natural to assume that the toichobate blocks for the naos side wall were also set from west to east. This means that, like the toichobate blocks for other side walls, the tops of toichobate blocks for the naos side wall should have lever holes on the east side corresponding to dowel holes. From this, blocks Δ8 and Δ16 can be positioned on the north side, and blocks 48 and 143 on the south side. With the knowledge that each two toichobate blocks with dowel holes on top were set on each wall (north and south), and with 5 other excavated blocks, the naos side walls had to have at least 3 orthostate blocks each minus the intersecting orthostate blocks. Our analysis begins with the south side of the temple.

If 4 orthostate blocks had been located between blocks Δ144 and Δ19, the distance from the anta to the outer colonnade on the west pteron would have been only 1 m. This would have been too small a distance for the approach from the west, so 4 blocks is impossible. Therefore, the reconstruction with 3 orthostate blocks between blocks Δ144 and Δ19 would be reasonable. The location of the toichobate blocks was determined based on the above considerations.

Considering that the dowel holes on the bottom of the toichobate blocks were located at the joint face edges, the sides with dowel holes would not have been connected with each

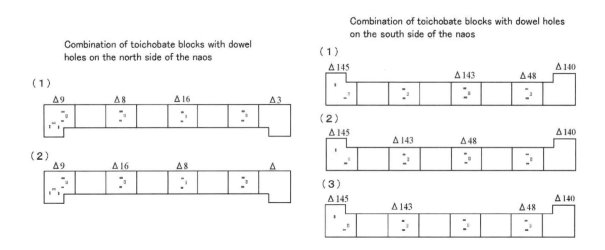

Fig. 3-9　Combination patterns of toichobate blocks of naos side wall.

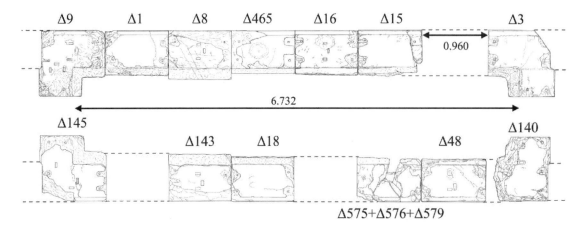

Fig. 3-10　Position of the toichobate blocks on the naos side wall.

Chapter 3   Reconstruction of the Temple

other. Also, as the dowel holes on the bottom of the 4 toichobate blocks for intersection are all facing the center of the naos side walls, we know that the toichobate blocks for the north and south naos side walls were set from the east and west sides, with one block being dropped in from above to complete it. With this, the toichobate blocks with dowel holes on top were distributed between the north and south walls. As the toichobate blocks would have alternated between those with and without dowel holes, there would have been 3 blocks on each side with dowel holes, or 6 blocks altogether. This means that one block on each side is missing.

For explanation purposes, the positions of each block are referred to as north left (northwest block), north center (north center block), north right (northeast block), south left (southwest block), south center (south center block) and south right (southeast block). As blocks

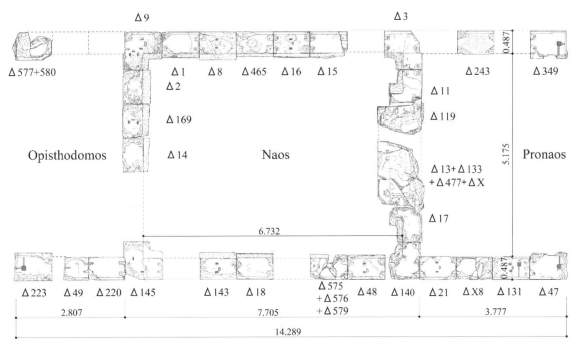

Fig. 3-11   Position of the toichobate blocks of the cella wall.

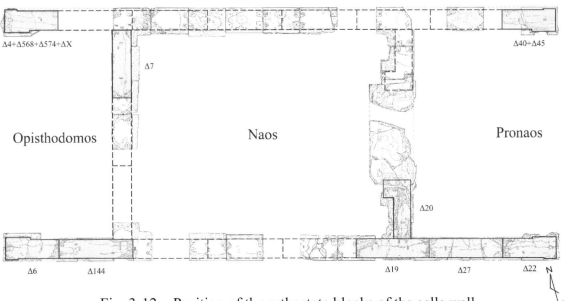

Fig. 3-12   Position of the orthostate blocks of the cella wall.

Δ8 and Δ16 on the north side had dowel holes facing the east side, they cannot have connected with intersecting block Δ3, thus we know that the north right toichobate block is missing. Similarly, judging from the dowel holes on the bottom of the blocks on the south side, block Δ143 has a dowel hole on the east side and block Δ48 has a dowel hole on the west side. Therefore, we know that block Δ48 had to have been set further east than block Δ143.

Based on the above, there are two different possible patterns for setting the toichobate blocks with dowel holes on the north side: block Δ8 as north left block and block Δ16 as north center block, and block Δ16 as north left block and block Δ8 as north center block. Similarly, the south side could have three patterns: block Δ143 as south center block and blockΔ48 as south right block; block Δ148 as south left block and block Δ48 as south center block; and block Δ143 as south left block and block 48 as south right block. 6 patterns in all were hypothesized for the north and south sides, and the most appropriate locations of the other toichobate blocks were considered based on the position of their bottom dowel and clamp holes, breakage, etc. As a result, the north toichobate from the west was determined to be composed of blocks Δ1, Δ8, Δ465, Δ16, Δ15, missing block, and the south toichobate was, from the west, missing block, blocks Δ143, Δ18, missing block, blocks Δ575+Δ576+Δ579, Δ48.

With the above, the arrangement of the toichobate blocks at the side wall of the naos was completed. However, some of the blocks have not been excavated, so we cannot reconstruct the overall length of the naos side wall from the block arrangement alone. Therefore, the overall length was reconstructed using the length of the north wall toichobate, from which one block was missing, plus the average length of one toichobate block; that is, 0.960 m. The result was 6.732 m[58].

3-2-5 Dividing wall of the opisthodomos

The length of the opisthodomos dividing wall was assumed to equal the length of the dividing wall of the pronaos, or 5.175 m. Three toichobate blocks have been excavated for the dividing wall of the opisthodomos. They are somewhat shorter compared with other toichobate blocks, and their average length is 0.859 m. From this, it was surmised that the dividing wall had 5 toichobate blocks and 3 orthostate blocks[59]. As with the naos dividing wall, none of the blocks had much indication of their relative positions, but judging from the location of dowel and clamp holes, they were arranged from the north side, with blocks Δ2, Δ169 and Δ4 found to be adjacent. From the block length, orthostate block Δ7 seemed to have been one of the 3 blocks used for the dividing wall of the opisthodomos. The exact location of the block could not be determined, but it was assigned to the north side based on the fact that the distance between the dowel holes on the top of the toichobate blocks was almost equal to the length of block Δ7.

With this, the arrangement of all the toichobate and orthostate blocks has been determined. The external dimensions of the cella are 6.149 m in width 14.289 m in length. The interior width of the cella was 5.175 m and was the same for all three rooms. The internal depths of the pronaos, naos and opisthodomos were 3.777 m, 6.732 m and 2.807 m respectively. Altogether, there were originally 37 toichobate blocks at the time of construction, but only 28 of these have been found. Similarly, only 9 of the original 21 orthostate blocks have been excavated at present. Thus 64 % of the toichobate and orthostate blocks have been found.

---

58 The naos side wall length was reconstructed from the measurements of the toichobate blocks placed on the north side. Where there were no blocks found, the average value of 0.960m was used. The exact measurements are as follows: 0.505 ＋0.960＋0.958＋0.968＋0.942＋0.961＋0.960＋0.478 = 6.732 m.

59 The length added by the toichobate blocks equals 5.175 m minus the length of the projecting part of the toichobate blocks for the intersection; that is, 5.175－0.414－0.415 = 4.346 m. Therefore we know that there were 5 toichobate blocks altogether.

Chapter 3   Reconstruction of the Temple

3-2-6   Wall blocks

Next, the wall blocks set on top of the orthostate were reconstructed. None of the excavated wall blocks are completely intact, so their original lengths are unknown. However, their approximate lengths and relative positions could be estimated from the dowel holes on top of the orthostate blocks. One clamp hole can be seen on each edge of the joint face of the wall blocks, so we know that the blocks were connected by a single clamp. There is also a dowel hole on one of the bottom edges of one joint face of the wall blocks. The same dowel hole was seen on the top of the orthostate blocks, meaning that the orthostate blocks and wall blocks were connected and affixed by a single dowel on one edge. Furthermore, from the location of the dowel holes and clamp holes on the top of the orthostate blocks, the block length of the wall blocks set on them was estimated as 0.880-0.884 m at the anta, 0.955-0.981 m at the side walls, and 0.853 m at the dividing wall of the opisthodomos. As these values were derived from the distances between the dowel holes, there is a possibility of error of some cm, but it can be seen that the lengths of the wall blocks were generally the same as those of the toichobate blocks underneath them.

In other words, the length of the wall blocks was found to be approximately 0.96 m for the side wall, 0.86 m for the dividing wall of the opisthodomos, and 0.88 m for the anta. Also, from the markings on the tops of the orthostate blocks for the dividing wall of the pronaos, smaller blocks of 0.495 m were found to have been used where the dividing wall connects with the side wall. This is similar to the length of the protruding part of the L-shaped toichobate blocks for the intersection. Judging from the top of orthostate block Δ144 for the intersection,

Table 3-4 Estimated length of wall blocks (m)

Block No.	Block length	Position
Δ6	0.884	Anta
Δ6~Δ144	0.967	Side wall
Δ144~	0.482	Side wall
~Δ19	0.500	Side wall
Δ19	0.981	Side wall
Δ19~	0.447	Side wall
Δ27~Δ22	0.967	Side wall
Δ22	0.880	Anta
Δ4+Δ568+Δ574+ΔX~	0.480	Side wall
~Δ7	0.437	Opisthodomus dividing wall
Δ7	0.853	Opisthodomus dividing wall
Δ7~	0.418	Opisthodomus dividing wall
Δ20	0.495	Pronaos dividing wall

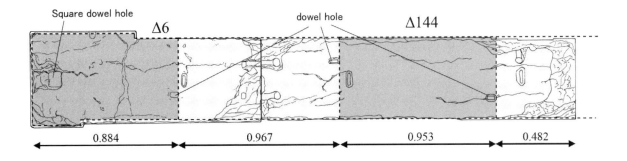

Fig. 3-13   Position of the orthostate blocks at the southwest corner of the cella wall.

the opisthodomos dividing wall blocks clearly do not protrude as far as the side wall of the naos; therefore, it is possible here too that smaller size blocks were used at the joint face of the intersection as at the dividing wall of the opisthodomos.

The top of wall block Δ105+Δ105α have a dowel hole and a lever hole, and the distance from the dowel hole to the edge of the joint face is 0.476 m, which is approximately half of the length of the side wall blocks. From this, it is known that the wall blocks were staggered so that the edges of the upper blocks fell on the centers of the lower blocks.

3-2-7 Order of placement of the blocks
1) Toichobate blocks

To clarify the order of placement of the toichobate blocks, the dowel holes on the bottom of the blocks were considered. From the observation of the bottom of the toichobate blocks, the dowel hole were set finally on one joint face of the blocks, after they were set exactly in the right position. Then the next adjacent blocks were set. There were dowel holes on the blocks for intersection on both the naos and the dividing wall sides. From this, we can tell that these blocks were set first, before the blocks of the dividing wall and of the naos side wall. In addition, the side wall blocks of the pronaos and the opisthodomos have dowel holes on the bottom which all face towards the naos. From this, it is understood that the pronaos and opisthodomos side wall blocks were set from the antae working towards the naos, and that the intersecting blocks were set afterwards.

Next we focused on the naos side wall and the dividing wall of the opisthodomos. As mentioned above, the blocks for intersection were set before those of the naos side wall and the opisthodomos dividing wall, so these blocks would have been set from the intersection blocks towards the inside, and the final block would have been dropped in place. Toichobate block Δ14 for the opisthodomos dividing wall has no dowel hole on the bottom, so it is believe that this was the final block dropped in place. The opisthodomos dividing wall toichobate would have been set from both north and south, and the center block was the one dropped in last. Similarly, the naos side wall toichobate would have been set both from east and west, and the center block dropped in place to finish it, but it was impossible to tell the location of this final block. Judging from the toichobate blocks that have already been located, it is surmised that the final block would have been either the first or second block from the east for the north wall, or the second or third block from the east on the south wall[60].

2) Orthostate blocks

To determine the order of placement of the orthostate blocks, the dowel holes and pry holes on top of the toichobate blocks were analyzed. When the orthostate blocks were set, workmen maneuvered to set the blocks exactly in the place using pries to push them. The pry holes, which were processed in advance on the top of the toichobate blocks, were also used to put the end of the pry. After setting the blocks at right position, then the dowels were set and the blocks were fixed. Thus, the observation of the dowel holes and pry holes on the top of the toichobate tells us the order of the placement of the orthostate blocks above them.

On top of the cella wall blocks for the pronaos, naos and opisthodomos, the pry holes are all located on the east side of the dowel holes. This means that the orthostate blocks were set from west to east. The intersection blocks were used to determine the detailed order of the orthostate blocks. Southwest intersection block Δ145 has dowel holes in two directions, at the

---

60 The bottom part of the block Δ575+Δ576+Δ579 and Δ15 are missing, so the dowel holes at the bottom could not be determined. Therefore, one of these two could have been the final block that was dropped in place at the end.

Chapter 3　Reconstruction of the Temple

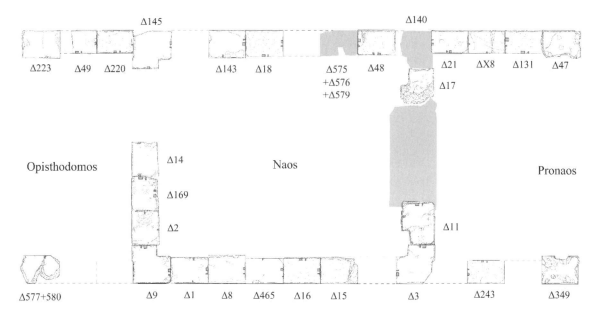

Fig. 3-14　Position of the toichobate blocks (looking up view).

north side and the east side, meaning that the orthostate block Δ144 above it was fixed in place from both directions. Therefore we know that this block must have been set before both of its adjacent block--the naos side wall block and the opisthodomos dividing wall block. Furthermore, dowel holes and pry holes can be seen on the surface of the opisthodomos dividing wall and the side wall of the northwest intersecting toichobate block Δ9. This means that the side wall on the north side was set in place from west to east after the opisthodomos dividing wall. Also, the southeast intersection toichobate block Δ140 has pry holes on the joint faces with the side wall and the pronaos dividing wall, from which we know that pronaos dividing wall block Δ20 was set after side wall block Δ19. Finally, no pry holes are seen on northeast intersection block Δ3, therefore with respect to the pronaos dividing wall on the north side, this block would have been dropped in place after the north side wall was completed.

3) Wall blocks above the orthostate

To decide the order of placement of the wall blocks above the orthostate blocks, the dowel holes and lever holes on the orthostate blocks were analyzed. The pry holes on the anta orthostate blocks corresponding to the dowel holes were all oriented towards the naos, indicating that the anta blocks were set in place first and then the wall blocks were set towards the direction of the naos side. That is, the side wall blocks would have been set from both direction from east to west and from west to east, with the final block dropped in from above to complete the row. Judging from the opisthodomos dividing wall blocks, the pry holes are all oriented towards the north; therefore these blocks must have been set from south to north, with the final block dropped in between the north wall and the opisthodomos dividing wall. Only a few orthostate blocks remain today, so it is impossible to determine exactly where the final wall block was. Finally, the lever holes on the pronaos dividing wall blocks are all on the south side, meaning that the blocks on the threshold side would have been set first, and then the intersecting block would have been dropped into place to complete the row.

3-2-8　Entrance to the pronaos

There was a uniquely shaped notch carved into the anta toichobate blocks Δ47 and Δ349 located at the edge of the pronaos entrance, most likely for an inside door.

Stylobate block Δ117+Δ118 has the same kind of cutaway part on the side, therefore

Fig. 3-15   Threshold block Δ130 for pronaos.   Fig. 3-16   Threshold block ΔX6 for pronaos.

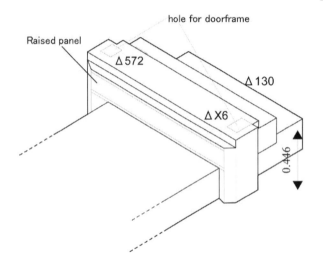

Fig. 3-17   Threshold for pronaos.

it would have supported a column at the entrance to the pronaos. On this block, the area on which the column was set is 0.177 m higher than the rest, and is square with one side being approximately 0.7 m. The cut-away portion are from two opposite sides and measures approximately 0.07 m in depth. Blocks Δ572 and ΔX6 have cut-away portions that correspond to this shape; therefore it is clear that they were connected to form the threshold to the pronaos. In addition block Δ130 has the same height and front width as the flooring and toichobate block, and like blocks Δ117+Δ118, there are remains of a higher level platform at the top. For these reasons, it is believed to have been used for the threshold of the pronaos. Using these blocks, the reconstruction is considered.

We begin with the northeast side of the anta. By setting blocks Δ349 and Δ117+Δ118 with their corresponding notches fit together, they not only correspond one another with the inside lines of their blocks, but also the front line of the anta block Δ349 corresponds to the front lines of the rise on block Δ117+Δ118 respectively block Δ349. In addition width of the inside corner pillar corresponds to the width of the stylobate top surface where the column was set. Therefore these two blocks were clearly made to correspond to each other. Next, from the shallowness of their cut-away portions, block ΔX6 and block Δ349 can be connected, and blocks Δ572 and Δ117+Δ118 with their deeper cut-away parts can also be joined (Fig. 3-18). In

Chapter 3   Reconstruction of the Temple

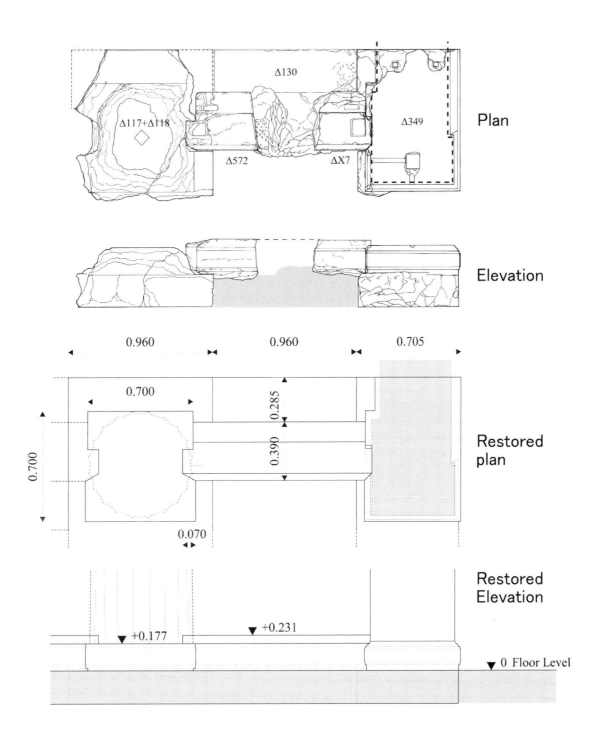

Fig. 3-18   Reconstructed threshold for pronaos.

consideration of the shape and dimensions of the blocks Δ130 (Fig. 3-15), Δ572 and ΔX6 (Fig. 3-16), all of the blocks fit together nicely, and it is believed that they formed one block originally. The height of the threshold blocks is 0.446 m, and the height of the top edge of the raised panel corresponds to the top surface for the column of block Δ117+Δ118. Therefore it is believed that the front side of block Δ117+Δ118 also had a raised panel on. As a result, the corresponding height of the threshold from the floor would have been 0.231 m, which is 5.4 cm higher than the top surface for the column. (Fig. 3-18) Similarly, the square top surface for the column is largely cut away by the notch, and the top width is only about 55 cm. An inner column drum block of 0.681 m was discovered, suggesting that the bottoms of the inner columns for the pronaos had notches to fix the end of the threshold block. The lower column diameter for the inner columns was then set as 0.681 m.

With this, all of the blocks have been positioned. Based on the shapes of toichobate block Δ47 for the anta on the southeast side and the other side of the block Δ117+Δ118, we can guess that there was a similar threshold at the center and the south side. The square holes at the ends of the threshold block show that there is a door jamb which was set along the column and the anta pillar. Inside of the doorframe, there are rectangular holes on either end which would have supported vertical axes for doors, which would have been metal latticed doors.

Another example of a temple in which the pronaos entrance doors were set in this way is the Temple of Aphaia at Aegina There were doors at the entrance to the pronaos and the east side outer colonnade at the Temple of Aphaia[61]. However, unlike the threshold at the Temple of Messene, it has only holes for door axes and bolts to lock the doors. There were no notches seen like those at the pronaos on toichobate blocks Δ223 and Δ577+Δ580 for the anta on the opisthodomos side. From this, it is assumed that there was no door on the opisthodomos side.

3-2-9 Relative height of the floor

From the condition of the toichobate blocks, we can tell that the floor levels were the same in the pteron, pronaos and opisthodomos, but the floor was at a higher level at the naos. The toichobate blocks at the cella wall of the naos measure 0.405 m in height, and are cut away on the inside top to a height of 0.080 m. This is believed to have been where the inside flooring blocks were set. None of the actual excavated blocks could be recognized as flooring blocks, so we estimated their thickness based on the relationships of the threshold blocks. The threshold blocks were set on top of the cut-away parts of toichobate blocks Δ11 and Δ17 for the pronaos dividing wall, and the level of cut-away part is the top of the inner joint face to naos flooring blocks, so in theory the back threshold level should have been the same with the naos floor level. The front and back threshold blocks were 0.400 m and 0.335 m in height respectively. The comparative difference of the naos floor level and the back threshold level is actually unknown. However, the back face of the threshold block has rough finishing, suggesting that it was a joint face, so flooring blocks were clearly set up to the top of the back of the threshold block. This shows that that the naos floor level and the back threshold level is equal. Thus, supposing that the pteron floor level is set as 0, the naos floor level would have been +0.335 m. Consequently, we know that the thickness of the naos flooring blocks would have been 0.231 m[62], and they would have been a little thicker than the flooring blocks of the pteron, which is 0.215-0.225 m in thickness.

3-2-10 Location of the cella walls

We have now decided the arrangement of the toichobate and orthostate blocks. Next, we determine the overall location of the cella itself of the temple. From considerations thus far, we know that the length of the cella wall was 14.289 m. This dimension is approximately equal to the sum of 7 spans of intercolumniation plus the lower column diameters, or external widths of the 7 spans, which is 14.248 m[63]. In general, the anta is usually located correspondingly to

---

61 There were three doors between the columns at the entrance to the pronaos and also at the east front colonnade at the Temple of Aphaia. See Bankel 1993, Tafel 54; Furtwängler 1906, Tafel 33. Furtwängler reconstructed the pronaos doors as grilled doors. The pronaos doors in the Temple of Messene must have been made in the same way.

62 The thickness of the flooring blocks used at the naos would have been equal to the relative height of the naos plus the exterior floor height, minus the height of the toichobate block for the naos up to the cutaway portion for the floor block, working out to $(0.335+0.221)-0.325 = 0.231$ m.

63 The intercolumniation is 1.920m, and the lower diameter is 0.808m, as will be explained later. Therefore, $1.920 \times 7 + 0.808 = 14.248$ m.

Chapter 3   Reconstruction of the Temple

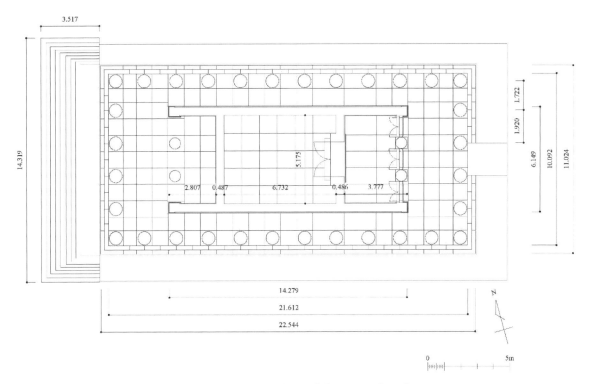

Fig. 3-19   Reconstructed plan of the Temple of Messene.

the columns, specifically across from the 3rd column from the corner[64]. Also, considering the location and size of the poros foundation for pteron pavement on the east side, it seems that the pteron width of the east side is equal to three pavement blocks. The Temple of Asklepios at Messene is also the same plan with the antae corresponding to the third columns from the corners[65]. The Temple of Athena Alea at Tegea, which is in Doric style and from the Hellenistic period of c.350 BC, has a similar type of floor plan[66]. Placing the end of the anta orthostate on the east side corresponding to the third column from the east on the east side of the temple, the end of the anta orthostate on the west side would also correspond to the third column from the west on the west side of the temple.

3-3   Reconstruction of the elevation
3-3-1   Reconstruction of the entablature
1) Architrave

None of the remaining entablature blocks were fully intact, but their lengths could be determined from the above analysis. We begin with the reconstruction of the length of the

---

64   The cella was generally set in relation to the colonnades, and examples of correspondence between the surface and central axis of the outer colonnade and the tip and central axis of the anta and the dividing walls of the naos and pronaos, etc., are often seen. In the present study, it is believed that the location of the foundation of the flooring blocks and the toichobate blocks for the pronaos of the anta was set near the third column from the east side and, based on the length of the inside wall of the inner court, that the column surface and the tip of the anta wall were adjoined. Similar examples of such temple construction are: Temple of Zeus Olympius at Acragas : Bell 1980, ILL. I.; Temple of Athena at Assos: Clarke 1902, fig. 3; Hephaesteion at Athens: Travlos 1971, fig. 335.; Temple of Apollo at Bassae: Cooper 1992, Plate 10.; Heraion at Paestum: Lloyd 1972, fig. 361.

65   Sioumpara 2011, Tafel 15.

66   Hill 1966, Pl. III and IV. In the Metroon at Olympia, the front line of the pronaos corresponds to the center between second and third column from the corner as well as the opisthodomos. .

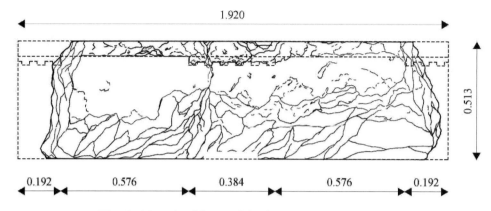

Fig. 3-20 Architrave block Δ85+Δ86.

longest of the remaining architrave blocks, block Δ85+Δ86. To perform the role of a beam placed on top of the columns, the architrave length would have to be based on the intercolumniation of the columns. This intercolumniation was calculated as above, so the length of the architrave would have been 1.920 m. In Doric style architraves, regulae are set in front at the top, with 6 guttae underneath them. These guttae are generally set corresponding to the triglyphs, with one in the center, and one half at each end of the blocks[67]. The regulae and guttae on block Δ85+Δ86 are badly damaged and the dimensions of each of the guttae are unclear, so their dimensions were reconstructed from those on block 166, on which they remain comparatively intact. The original reconstructed dimension was 0.384 m, which is appropriately equivalent to the front length of the triglyph[68]. The distance between the regulae calculated from this dimension works out to 0.576m[69]. Applying this dimension to block Δ85+Δ86, we find that the regulae at the ends of the block were located on the missing part. With this, the basic dimensions of the architrave were reconstructed. (Fig. 3-20)

Some blocks show the corner treatment of architrave. Δ166 with a square dowel hole and a groove for lead on top, and this shows that it is a corer block without 45° cut. One end of the architrave backer block Δ294, is cut at 45°, and also shows that it was used as a corner block.

2) Frieze

The triglyph and metopes at the temple of Messene were constructed from the same block, although no complete blocks of this type remain. Two triglyph blocks (Δ159, Δ160) on which the front length could be determined were excavated, but as block Δ159 is smaller than the external triglyph width to be discussed below, it is believed to have been used for the cella. Also, the front length of the triglyph on block Δ406 has a slightly shorter estimated triglyph length than the other blocks, which is relatively close to that of the block Δ159 for the cella. Therefore, the triglyph front width was decided as 0.383 m using block Δ279, which has the best preserved triglyph of the exterior (PL. 100). This value is considered appropriate as it is equivalent to the abovementioned front length of the regula and the length of the cornice mutules, to be discussed below.

---

67 Doric style orders generally use two metopes between each intercolumniation. As an exception, there are cases in which three metopes are used between an intercolumniation, but in this case it is clear that there were only two based on the length of block Δ85+Δ86. The regulae are set corresponding to the triglyph, so there would have been one in the center, and 1/2 each on either side at the edge. See the Temple of Athena Polias at Pergamon for an example of a Doric temple with three metopes. R. Bohn 1885.

68 From the previous section, the front length of the triglyph is 0.383m.

69 Subtract the front length of the regulae from half of the intercolumniation to obtain this value. That is, 1.920/2 - 0.384 = 0.576 m, which works out to be the same as the front length of the metope.

Chapter 3   Reconstruction of the Temple

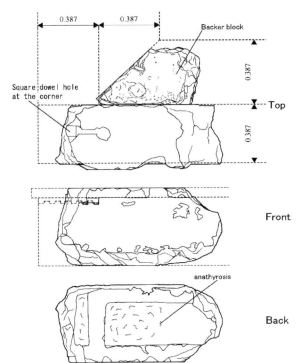

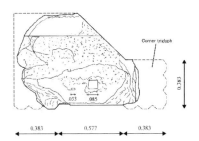

Fig. 3-22   Corner frieze block Δ293.

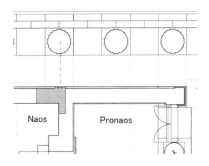

Fig. 3-21   Architrave block Δ166.   Fig. 3-23   Position of triglyph block Δ159.

The triglyph front length has been decided, so the length of the metopes can be determined from the intercolumniation dimension as follows:
Intercolumniation: 1.920 m
$2T + 2M = 1.920$ m (T: triglyph front length, M: metope front length)
$T = 0.383$ m therefore
$M = (1.920 - 0.383 \times 2) / 2 = 0.577$ m.

Next, block Δ293 (PL. 103) has a rectangular dowel hole on the top, the back of which is made at a 45° angle, so we can tell that it is a corner block. This block is in relatively good condition, and from it the frieze block height could be determined as 0.589 m and the depth was 0.565 m at the metopes and 0.607 m including the triglyph, with 0.170 m behind that in depth left over for the projecting part on which the ceiling block was set. Judging from the condition of corner triglyph block Δ273, corner frieze block Δ293 (Fig. 3-22, PL. 103) probably had a part on the front and side edges on which the triglyph was set.

The depth of the metopes on frieze block Δ159, as previously discussed, is approximately 10 cm smaller than on the other frieze blocks, and the block height of 0.578 m is also somewhat smaller. Therefore, this frieze block is believed to have been used at the cella wall. On the other hand, this block has markings of having been originally L-shaped. Therefore, we considered the possibility that Doric frieze with triglyphs and metopes might have been used at the side of the cella. As a result, block Δ159 with its width of 0.470 m was approximately the same as that of the cella walls, and the inner part of the L-shape may have been the protruding part that supported the naos walls. Although this is only conjecture, recent research has found that the Temple of Asklepios in the same city also had triglyphs at the cella side walls[70]. The temple is dated more than a century later than the Messene Temple and the use of the triglyphs at the cella side walls might have been one of the earliest example of the city.

---

70   Sioumpara 2010, pp. 14-15. Sioumpara 2011 Tafel 28-31,

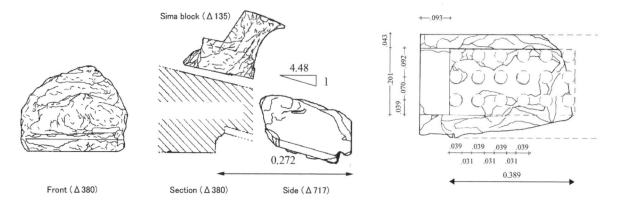

Fig. 3-24   Reconstruction of cornice and sima.

Fig. 3-25   Mutule of cornice block Δ717.

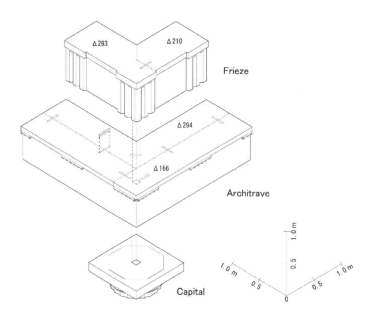

Fig. 3-26   System of entablature at the corner.

3) Cornice and sima

Only a few cornice and sima blocks were excavated, and none were completely intact. However, by considering each remaining block carefully, we were able to gain some information. On block Δ717 only a part of mutule with markings of guttae can be seen. From the dimensions of the existing part of the block, we can determine the original front length of the mutule, which was 0.389 m (Fig. 3-25, PL.106)[71]. We also know that the distance between mutules was 0.093 m from the block dimensions. Because the mutules were located corresponding to the triglyphs and in the center of the metopes, we also know that each intercolumniation corresponds to the length of 3 full mutules and 2 half-mutules. Calculating this from the reconstructed dimensions, we arrived at 1.928 m[72], which is approximately equal

---

71 From the actual measurements, the distance between the guttae and their measurements were the same; therefore 0.039 × 6 + 0.031 × 5 = 0.389 m.

72 To obtain this, the length of four mutules is added to the interior distance between the four, or 0.389 × 4 + 0.093 × 4 = 1.928 m.

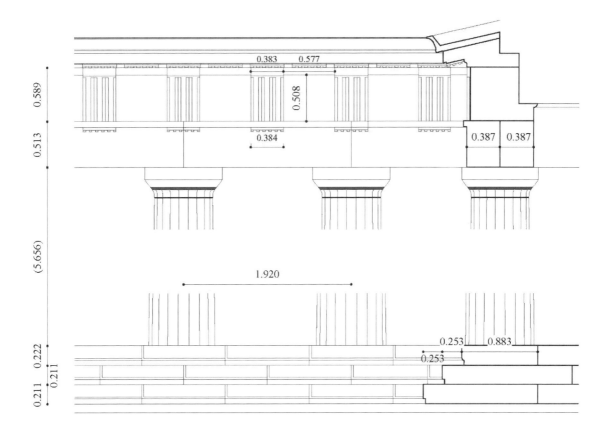

Fig. 3-27 Reconstruction of the order.

to the intercolumniation dimension with a slight error.

Additionally, block Δ380 is greatly weathered, but we can tell from it that the incline for the roof had a value of 1/4.48. This is the only block for which the incline could be determined, so this value was used in the reconstruction. Also part of the eave on block Δ380 is remaining, and from the above-mentioned block Δ717, the protrusion of the eave was determined as 0.2765 m. In addition from the slope of block Δ380, the height of the reconstructed cornice was found to be 0.175 m. The sima was greatly damaged, and it was impossible to tell anything about the decoration. However it is barely possible to determine the shape of the roof edge, so its intersection with the cornice block was reconstructed (Fig. 3-24).

4) Organization of the entablature

Thus far we have completed the reconstruction of the entablature blocks. The architrave was divided into front blocks and back blocks, which were joined by clamps. The front corners protruded on one side and the front and sides both used architraves with regula (Δ166). In contrast, the backer blocks were made up of two blocks cut at 45° angles and set together (Δ294). The corner at the front had a square dowel hole at the top, which connected to the frieze block above it. The frieze was constructed from one block only, which had a projecting part at the back to hold the ceiling. As for the corner, the cornice blocks were formed in the way for two triglyphs to meet together on sides and ends. The back part was cut at the 45° angle (Δ293), and the other adjacent corner block was set to fit this. The corner of the frieze block was affixed by a square dowel hole at the bottom (Fig. 3-26).

Very few of the cornice and sima blocks were excavated, and there are almost no markings. Therefore details of their placement could not be determined.

3-3-2 Peripteral columns

The lower column diameter could be determined from traces of the flutings remaining on top of stylobate block Δ43 (PLs. 17-1, 44) as 0.808 m[73]. The dimensions of the column capital were decided by using block Δ32, which was in better condition than the other column block excavated. The reconstructed dimensions were 0.689 m for the upper diameter (arris-arris), 0.882 m for the width of the abacus, and 0.332 m for the capital height. The column height was difficult to determine. The 25 column blocks remaining were measured, but all of these blocks greatly damaged and weathered, and the original dimensions could not be judged from any of them. Also the most of the column drums were lost and number of blocks excavated was fewer than the actual number of blocks that would have been required. Therefore the column height could not be reconstructed based on the remaining column drum blocks alone, and in the next section, we attempt to determine the column height by comparing it with other Doric style temples.

---

[73] Judging the lower column diameter based on the markings on the top of block Δ43, the radius from the center of the dowel hole to the arrises works out to 0.404 m. We doubled this value to obtain the diameter.

Chapter 4

Parallels and Comparative Study

This chapter will compare the Temple of Messene with other Doric style temples in order to determine its historical placement and significance. Prof. Themelis dates the Temple of Messene to around the end of the 4th century BC based on archeological survey results[74]. Here, we review the characteristics of Doric style temples from the 4th to 1st century BC (end of the Classical Era to the Hellenistic Era), in order to judge the characteristics of the Temple of Messene with respect to this time frame. We then estimate the date of construction based on the proportions of the order, and reconstruct the temple column height.

Data on Doric style temples used here for analyzing historical changes in proportions was collected based on research by Sioumpara[75], whose works include an overview of Doric style temples of that era, with addition by the authors of more recently discovered data. The temples under study were those with Doric orders dating from 400 BC to about 0 AD. The data set included 50 temples altogether, 41 of which are peristylar, and 23 examples of stoas and

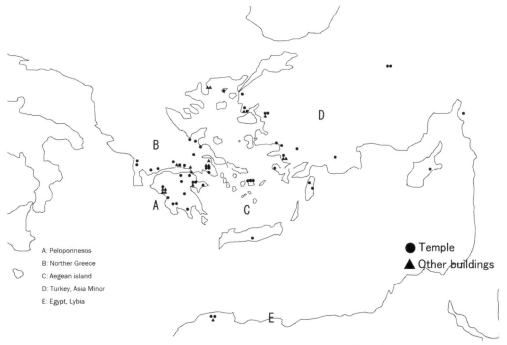

Fig. 4-1   Distribution of Doric peripteral temples (4th -1st cent. BC).

---

74   Themelis 2006, p. 43.
75   Sioumpara 2011, Tables 23-25. Sioumpara's study about Hellenistic Doric is thorough and the present study owes much to her study about the data of Doric temples which the authors could not get in Japan.

other buildings[76]. (PLs. 120, 121). The locations of the buildings were (A) the Peloponnesos, (B) Northern Greece (north of Attica), (C) islands in the Aegean Sea, (D) Turkey and Asia Minor, (E) Egypt and Libya. No Doric style peristylar temples from this era were found in Italy or Sicily, and although there were a few examples of Doric prostyle temples, none of these were well enough documented to obtain measurements, so they were omitted from this study.

4-1 Temple size

The size of the temples ranged from as little as less than 45 m^2 to over 6,000 m^2, and many different temple patterns were observed. However, it is generally believed that large Doric style temples disappeared from about the end of the 5th century BC[77].

Based on the relation between the temple dimensions and their columns, ancient Greek temples would be defined as temples measuring less than 350 m^2 at the stylobate level as small, temples measuring less than 1,000 m^2 as average, over 1,000 m^2 as large and over 10,000 m^2 as extra-large temples[78].

Applying these definitions to the present data, we find no examples of extra-large temples before the 4th century BC, and only 2 of the 41 peristylar temples can be classified as large temples. 17 are average-size temples, and 17 are small-size temples. However, one of the large temples, the Temple of Apollo at Delphi, was destroyed in a natural disaster in 373 BC and rebuilt thereafter[79], thus it cannot be considered to have been originally built in the 4th century BC. The stylobate length of the Temple of Apollo at Klaros is unknown, so the overall building length was used for analysis, and therefore, this temple may have actually been less than 1000 m^2 as well. It means that there would have been no large-size Doric style temples either built at that time. The majority of the temples were less than 500 m^2 in size, so the temples built in this period were clearly much smaller than those of earlier eras.

Among these, the Temple of Messene is classified as a small-size temple: the area ranks 6th from the smallest, and the front stylobate length is 5th from the smallest.

4-2 Doric order proportions

In this section the characteristics of Doric style order proportions from the 4th century BC onwards will be clarified. Vitruvius described how to decide these proportions in his *The Ten Books on Architecture*[80], but the proportions are not absolute but relative, and the actual values vary greatly and changed in actual use. Therefore we begin with characteristic proportions used at that time in order to clarify the architectural features of the Temple of Messene.

4-2-1 Column proportions

Column proportion relationships were analyzed using the values given below[81].

---

76 Insofar as possible, dimensions were gathered from note 1) above, and when additions were possible, these were made and the data revised.

For sample figures which could neither be found in reference materials or determined directly by measurement, dimensions given by E. P. Sioumpara (Siumpara 2011) were quoted directly. As a general rule, dimensions written or provided on blueprints were used, but in cases where there were no specific dimensions provided for details but there was an accurate scale bar, such as with the column capital profile, the scale bar was used to derive the measurements. Also, only those non-peristylar temples and other buildings for which detailed dimensions were available were used. Detailed references for the buildings are listed on Plates 120 and 121.

77 Dinsmoor 1975, p. 217.
78 Horiuchi 1979, pp. 123-124.
79 Dinsmoor 1975, p. 217.
80 Vitruvius 4. 3. 1-10
81 For the present analysis, the height of the amulet was included in the height of the echinus.

Chapter 4   Parallels and Comparative Study

Table 4-1 Size of Doric peripteral temples (4th -1st cent. BC).

	City	Temple	Columns	Intercolumn-iation (m)	Overall size (m)	Stylobate size (m)	Area (m²)
1	Kourno	Small temple	6x7	1.545	8.40x9.96	8.05x9.60	77
2	Demetrias	Agora temple	6x10	1.600	9.60x16.00	8.75x15.25	133
3	Athen	Kronos and Rhea	6x9	1.85	10.08x15.63		(158)
4	Emecik/ Alt Knidos	Apollon	6x11		11.60x21.11	10.20x19.70	201
5	Lepreon	Demeter	6x11	1.956	11.98x21.69	10.445x20.226	211
6	Messene	Messene temple	6x12	1.920	11.024x22.544	10.092x21.612	218
7	Aegae	NW Temple	6x12		11.40x19.34		(220)
8	Olympia	Metroon	6x11	2.010	11.88x21.93	10.62x20.67	220
9	Ptoioin	Apollon	6x13	1.868	11.65x24.72	9.85x22.93	226
10	Eretreia	Dionysos	6x11	2.00-2.07	12.45x23.05	10.70x21.35	228
11	Aigeira	unknown	6x11		11.82x20.40		(241)
12	Gortys	Asklepios	6x11	2.90	13.44x23.99	11.315x21.76	246
13	Kallithea	Zeus	6x11	2.184	12.38x23.33	11.46x22.38	256
14	Pergamon	Athena	6x10	2.367-2.371	13.02x22.52	12.27x21.77	267
15	Epidauros	Asklepios	6x11	2.258	13.20x24.45	12.03x23.28	280
16	Ephesos	Temple on the market	6x10	2.257-2.72	14.50x22.20		(322)
17	Messene	Asklepios	6x12	2.398-2.390	13.664x27.970	12.710x27.016	343
18	Kallio	unknown	5x10	2.94-3.04		12.55x28.22	354
19	Delos	Apollo (peripteral)	6x13	2.2905		12.47x28.53	356
20	Molykreion	Poseidon	6x13	2.45	14.254x31.416	12.87x30.032	386
21	Alexandreia Troas	unknown	6x11		14.50x29.60	14.11x27.40	387
22	Alabanda	Artemis/ Hekate	6x11			15.18x27.70	420
23	Xanthos	Letoon Temple B	6x11	2.590-2.580	27.97x15.07		421
24	Kalydon	Artemis	6x13	2.50	14.94x32.55	14.02x31.63	443
25	Troizen	Hippolytos or Asklepios?	6x11	2.887	17.365x31.783	15.045x29.463	443
26	Apollonia/ Kyrene	unknown	6x11	2.90	17.305x31.935	15.10x29.60	447
27	Ilion	Athena	6x12	2.877	16.40x35.70	15.13x32.39	490
28	Kos	Asklepios	6x11	3.050	18.075x33.280	15.965x31.170	498
29	Stratos	Zeus	6x11	3.160	18.32x34.12	16.64x32.44	540
30	Seleukeia/ Pieria	Isis-Aphrodite?	6x12		18.60x36.90	15.84x34.14	541
31	Rhodos	Appollo Pythios	6x11	3.72	22.25x40.90	19.80x38.45	761
32	Nemea	Zeus	6x12	3.745	21.88x44.448	20.085x42.549	855
33	Theben	Apollon	6x12	3.91	22.83x46.25	20.54x44.01	903
34	Tegea	Athena Alea	6x14	3.582-3.613	21.20x49.56	19.19x47.55	912
35	Klaros	Apollon	6x11		25.16x46.285		(1165)
36	Delphi	Apollo	6x15	4.138-4.083	23.82x60.32	21.68x58.18	1261
37	Pherai	Zeus Thaulios/ Ennodia-Hekate	6x12	2.743	15.81x?	14.44x?	?
38	Kassope	Aphrodite	6x10	1.800			?
39	Knidos	Apollon Karneios?	6x11				?
40	Lebadeia	Zeus Basileus	6x13				?
41	Sikyon	unknown	6x18				?

Column proportion data from 24 temples and 23 other buildings were used as reference (cf. PL. 122).

1) Abacus width to upper diameter (AbW/d)

This value represents the narrowness of the top of the column shaft to the abacus width. Prior to 300 BC, this value was concentrated between 1.3 and 1.4 for all types of buildings, but later both the range and value for this measurement decreased to between 1.25 and 1.3. Furthermore, the range became more scattered after 200 BC.

From this, we can see that with the passing of time, the proportion of the upper diameter to the abacus width gets smaller. This value is 1.280 for the Temple of Messene, which is less than 1.3. From this, it was estimated that the Temple of Messene column capitals were shaped according to the style of the period from 300 BC onwards.

2) Abacus width to column capital height (AbW/CH)

This value was generally between 2.5 and 3.0 before 300 BC, and most Temples of that era show a value of around 2.7. After this date, the values begin to spread out, becoming lower and higher. For the Temple of Messene, this value was 2.66. Several temples built after 300 BC have a similar value, so it is difficult to tell for certain, but this value can generally be often seen before or around 300 BC.

3) Abacus height to capital height (AbH/CH)

This value was generally between 0.4-0.45 before 300 BC, but there were two examples of a value below 4.0 in Peloponnesos. After 300 BC, values tended to creep below 0.4, and were distributed around 0.3-0.45. For the Temple of Messene, this value was 0.398, which is average.

4) Echinus height to abacus height (EH/AbH)

Before 300 BC, this value was concentrated around 0.9, and very few buildings showed a value over 1. After 300 BC, buildings with a value of more than 1 began to increase, with the echinus height becoming larger than the abacus height. However, there were still many buildings that had a value of around 0.9 as before. For the Temple of Messene, this value was 0.893, which is average.

5) Abacus width to lower column diameter (AbW/D)

In general this value is never below 1, so the abacus with is always larger than the lower diameter. The values do not show conspicuous tendency and the majority ranged from 1.0 to around 1.1., but after that they tended to increase and most values were higher than 1.05. For the Temple of Messene, it was 1.092, which is a little larger than the average.

6) Upper diameter to lower diameter (d/D)

This value represents the narrowing of the column. Before 300 BC, values under 0.8 were common, but later most of the values were over 0.8. That is, the columns showed a less of a tendency to narrow than before. This value is 0.852 at the Temple of Messene, which was higher than the others even after 300 BC. The Temple of Asklepios in the same city had a value of 0.860, which is almost the same as that of the Temple of Messene.

7) Column height to upper column diameter (H/D)

This value is often used in discussions on temple proportions. Vitruvius states that it should be designed to be 7[82], but in actuality this value varies greatly depending on the era. For example, the Temple of Zeus at Olympia built in the 5th century BC has a value of 4.72, and the Parthenon at Athens built in the latter 5th century BC has a value of 5.48. Here we observe that the value tended to increase as time went on. In actual temple construction, it tended to range between 5.5 and 6.5 prior to 300 BC, and most values were between 6.0 and 6.5. After this time, values higher than 6.5 became more common. From this, we can say that the columns tended to become slenderer with respect to the lower column diameter across the ages. On the other hand, for stoas and other buildings, values between 6.5 and 7.0 were common even before 300 BC, but many reached above 7.0 from 200 BC onwards, probably because the stoas were used for daily life in agoras and the slenderer proportion would be appropriate for citizen's

---

82   Vitruvius 4. 3. 4.

Chapter 4   Parallels and Comparative Study

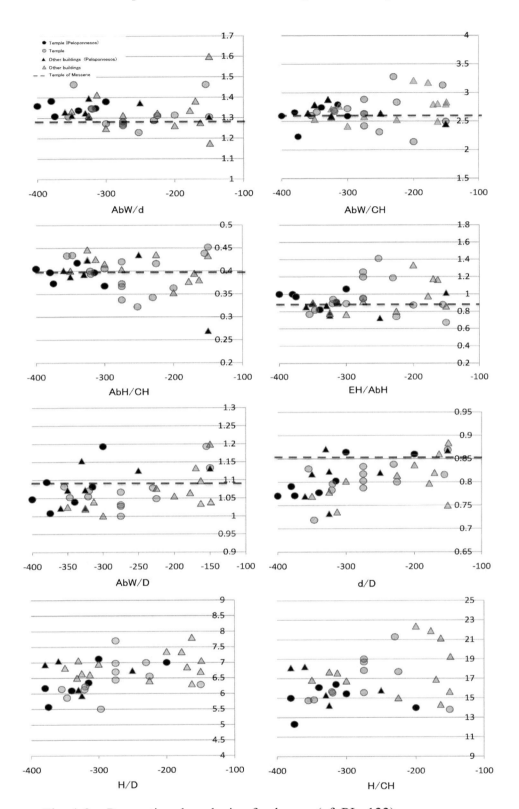

Fig. 4-2   Proportional analysis of columns (cf. PL. 122).

passage between columns. For the Temple of Messene, this value could not be calculated as the column height is unknown.

8) Proportion of capital height to column height (H/CH)

This value ranged between 15 and 17 before 300 BC, but higher values are seen thereafter, meaning that the capital tended to become smaller in proportion to the column. However, the earlier values seen before 300 BC can still be found from 200 BC on, thus such earlier proportions continued to be used as well. At the Temple of Messene, this value could not be determined as the column height is unknown.

9) Summary of column proportions

In general, many changes are seen in proportions after 300 BC. In the overall column proportions, the column tends to become much slenderer with the passing of time, and for temple buildings, the column height changed from 5.5-6.5 of the lower column diameter to values closer to 7. With respect to column capital proportions, values were generally the same before 300 BC, but began to diversify after this date, even though many buildings still showed the same earlier values. Therefore, we can say that there was more variation in the proportions with time. The proportions of abacus width to upper diameter and the capital height to overall column height become smaller. These changes are especially marked in stoas and other buildings. As a result, the capital came to stand out less with respect to the overall column, and became more of a simple and compact with the abacus like a thin plate and the echinus like a low truncated cone. However, as previously mentioned, the values tended to scatter more with the passing time. This phenomenon is difficult to explain, but once the order was established in Classical era, the Hellenistic architects' choice would have been to develop the proportional tendency or to return to the old proportion.

The overall values for the Temple of Messene generally coincide with the most common average values for buildings from before 300 BC, although the slenderness of the column and the narrowness of column necking have values similar to the period after 300 BC. However, as mentioned above, the column proportion values in general tend to scatter and become more diverse after 300 BC, so it was impossible to determine the date of the building from its proportions alone. If, as maintained by Themelis, the Temple of Messene dates to the end of the 4th century BC, we may surmise that it was perhaps closer to 300 BC than later.

4-2-2 Entablature proportions

Entablature proportions are calculated and analyzed based on the dimensions given in Table (3)-1~2[83] in the last page of the volume. The reference sample on which they are based includes 29 temples and 21 other buildings.

1) Frieze height to triglyph front width (FH/TW)

Before 250 BC, this proportion had a variety of values, generally between 1.4-1.7, but after this time, the range of values tended to be diminished somewhat to between 1.45-1.6. At the Temple of Messene, this value was 1.54, which is average. However, this proportion at the Temple of Asklepios at Messene was 1.67, which is quite high for a temple built around 200 BC.

2) Frieze height to metope front width (FH/MW)

For temple buildings built before 250 BC, proportions larger than 1 were conspicuous, and the values ranged between 1.0-1.2. In Peloponnesos, however, the values were closer to 1. After 250 BC, the proportions average less than 1 for a short time, but later tend to rise again

---

[83] In the present study sample, only a small amount of data was available for the cyma blocks. Therefore, the blocks up to the cornice, without the cyma, were considered as the entablature for the purposes of the present analysis.

Chapter 4   Parallels and Comparative Study

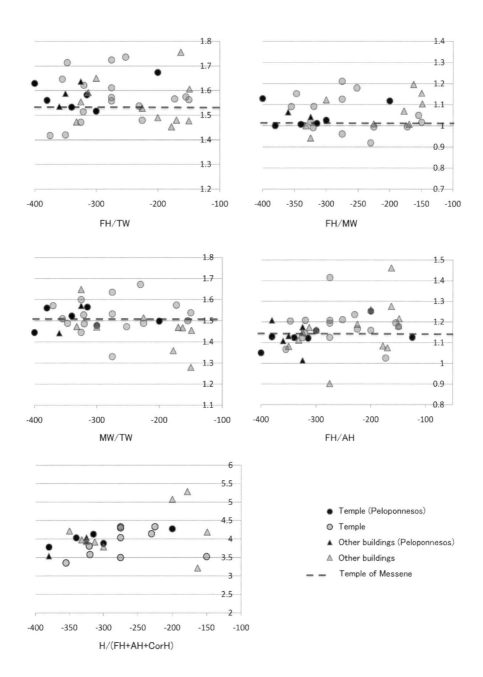

Fig. 4-3   Proportional analysis of entablature.

to around 1.0-1.1. That is, the originally elongated rectangular shape of the metope became squarer. However, this value for other buildings continued to tend to fall between 1.0-1.2 even after 250 BC. The value at the Temple of Messene was 1.021, which is commonly seen after 250 BC, but is also common before 250 BC in Peloponnesos. At the Temple of Asklepios in the same city, this value was 1.12, meaning that the shape of the metope was slightly more vertically rectangular than at the Temple of Messene.

3) Metope front width to triglyph front width (MW/TW)

Throughout the ages, this value has ranged between 1.4 and 1.6, averaging around

1.5[84]. However, the spread becomes more diverse between 300 and 200 BC. In buildings other than temples, values less than 1.5 were common after 200 BC. At the Temple of Messene, this value was 1.507, which is average. The Temple of Asklepios at Messene has a similar value.

4) Frieze height to architrave height (FH/AH)

This value ranged between 1.1-1.2 before 300 BC, and tended to be somewhat higher after that. However, there were also some exceptionally different values, and with only one exception the values were all above 1.0, meaning that the frieze was generally taller than the architrave. At the Temple of Messene, this value is 1.15, which is approximately equal to the median of the distribution. The Temple of Asklepios in the same city has a relatively large value of 1.25.

5) Column height to entablature height (H/FH+AH+CorH)

The column height to entablature height ratio is very often used in analysis of Doric style order proportions. Horiuchi used Dinsmoor's measurement data to discuss the relationship between the column height and entablature height from the archaic to Hellenistic era[85]. If in (H+FH+AH+CorH)/H, the value of H is over 2.0 as it was in the 6th century BC, the entablature on top of it would have measured over half of the column, making for a very unwieldy, top-heavy figure. However, this value becomes larger with the passing of time, meaning that the height of the entablature becomes increasingly smaller in proportion to the column height. Actual values range between 3.5 and 4.5 for most temples, with those from before 300 BC falling between 3.5 and 4.0 and later temples scattering between 4.0-4.5. Therefore we see that the value rises gradually with the passing of years. Other buildings also showed higher values from 200 BC on.

6) Summary of entablature proportions

Overall, these proportions did not show as much variation as for those of the column. The narrow triglyph tended to widen, and the frieze became taller with respect to the architrave, but in general these changes were difficult to determine clearly. However, the relationship between the entablature height and the column height ranged between 3.5 and 4.5 for temples, and this value increased with the passing of years, meaning that a clear tendency in the proportion of the entablature height to the overall order height from the column to the entablature could be determined. The values for the Temple of Messene were similar to those for temple structures in Peloponnesos prior to 300 BC. However, the diffusion of values generally became more scattered over time.

4-2-3 Column height of the Temple of Messene

This section attempts to restore the column height of the Temple of Messene based on the above analysis of proportions. Even though the proportions themselves did not indicate a

---

84 The proportions of triglyph, metope and frieze are mutually related. According to Vitruvius, width to height in triglyph is 1:1.5, width to height in metope 1:1, and width of triglyph to width of metope 1:1.5. That is, triglyph width is 1/5 of an intercolumniation, and metope width (= frieze height) is 1.5/5 of the same. See Vitruvius 4. 3. 4-5.

85 Horiuchi 1979, pp. 130-131. Here Horiuchi actually discusses the height of the order in relation to the column height; that is, (H+FH+AH+CorH) /H. For the present analysis, in order to express the relation more clearly, the column height was analyzed and expressed as a multiple of the entablature height. In his study, he found structures with a value of over 1.5 (corresponding to 2.0 in the present study) in the 6th century BC?, but from the end of the 6th century to the beginning of the 5th century BC, the values decreased to 1.4 (corresponding to 2.5 in the present study), and after the mid-4th century BC, further decreased to 1.25 (corresponding to 4.0). See Horiuchi 1979, p. 130, Fig. 5-1-20 for details. The present analysis used a higher number of samples, but the results derived were approximately the same.

Chapter 4   Parallels and Comparative Study

clear date for temple construction, they were all average values for temples built around 300 BC, and do not contradict Themelis' estimated dating based on his archeological observations of the late 4th century, that is, around 300 BC. The column height to lower column diameter (H/D) and the column height to entablature height (H/FH+AH+CorH), both representative of overall temple value tendencies, were used to determine the column height. It is assumed that the Temple of Messene was built around 300 BC, when the column height to lower column diameter proportions ranged from 5.5-6.5 and the column height to entablature proportions were 3.0-4.0. Reconstruction was analyzed using these values, the average value of the existing column drums (0.758 m, cf. Chapter 2 and Apendix) and the capital height of 0.332 m.

If were 5 drums in a column, the column height would be $0.758 \times 5 + 0.322 = 4.122$ m. This value is 5.10 times the lower column diameter (0.808 m), which is too low.

With 6 drums to a column, the same calculation method gives a column height of 4.880 m. This is 6.04 times the lower column diameter, which is an appropriate proportional value. It also works out to 3.82 times the height of the entablature (1.277 m), which is also appropriate.

Finally, with 7 drums in the column, the column height would be 5.638 m, which is 6.98 times the lower column diameter (clearly too high) and the 4.42 times the entablature height, which is a value unheard of around 300 BC. Therefore 7 drums considered inappropriate, and it was determined that the column had 6 drums, and the column height thereby reconstructed as 4.880 m.

However, only 24 column drums in approximately 190 in total were actually excavated, and those that did not have equal heights (Table 2-19), so there might be a large margin of error for this value. Even so, based on the present archeological remains we cannot hope for a more accurate estimate, so this value was used in the reconstruction of the column.

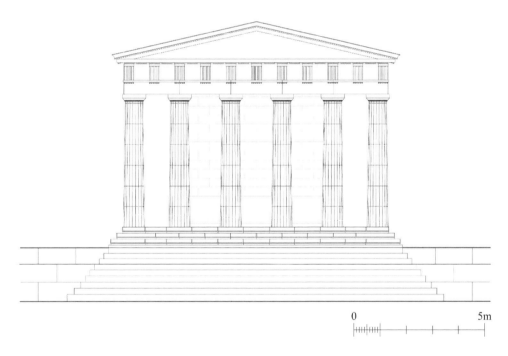

Fig. 4-4   Reconstruction of the west elevation of the Temple of Messene.

4-3 Comparison with the Temple of Asklepios at Messene

Finally, we compare the Temple of Messene with the Temple of Asklepios in the same city, which is also a Doric style temple. The Temple of Asklepios was built around 200 BC in the same peristylar style as the Temple of Messene.

4-3-1 Size and plan

Both temples have 6 × 12 columns in peristyle, and their cellas are both made up of three rooms: pronaos, naos and opisthodomus. Their sizes, based on stylobate length, are 343 m² for the Temple of Asklepios and 218 m² for the Temple of Messene, so the size of the Temple of Messene is approximately two thirds of the Temple of Asklepios. The antae of the cella walls are both located at the third column east-west and the second column north-south, so the plans are very similar. Comparing the relative sizes of the cellas, the naos length at the Temple of Asklepios is relatively shorter than at the Temple of Messene, and other two rooms, the pronaos and opisthodomus, are longer. Also, the Temple of Asklepios has a door at the south wall of the naos.

4-3-2 Comparison of the orders
1) Column proportions

The column capital of the Temple of Asklepios has not been restored, so the proportions cannot be compared directly. However, the proportion of column height and lower column diameter is 6.04 at Messene and 7.0 at the Temple of Asklepios, clearly showing the difference in era of construction. However, the proportion of the upper and lower diameters of the column (d/D) is very similar: 0.852 at the Temple of Messene and 0.860 at the Temple of Asklepios. That might be 6/7, so no change could be seen.

2) Entablature proportions

The metope and triglyph front lengths at the Temple of Asklepios and the Temple of Messene are almost the same (1.50m), but the frieze heights are all larger at the Temple of Asklepios, demonstrating that the frieze was narrower and taller there.

Table 4-2 Comparison of size and proportion with the Temple of Asklepios.

	Columns	Intercolumn-iation	Overall length	Stylobate length	Area (m)	Cella	Naos
Temple of Asklepios	6x12	2.398-2.390	13.664x27.970	12.710x27.016	343	7.855x17.774	6.355x7.287
Temple of Messene	6x12	1.920	11.024x22.544	10.092x21.612	218	6.149x14.289	5.175x6.732

	H/D	d/D	H/CH
Temple of Asklepios	7.000	0.860	14.000
Temple of Messene	6.040	0.853	14.700

	FH/TW	FH/MW	MW/TW	FH/AH	H/(FH+AH+CorH)
Temple of Asklepios	1.674	1.117	1.498	1.252	4.274
Temple of Messene	1.538	1.021	1.507	1.148	3.821

4-3-3 Ornament
1) Crepis, stylobate and orthostate

The relieving margin at the crepis and stylobate at the Temple of Messene and the vertical recessed joint on the only one edge of the sides are also found at the Temple of Asklepios. At the orthostate, the recessed joints at the bottom and sides were also seen at the Asklepion[86].

---

86 Sioumpara 2011, Tafeln 46-49, 109-127.

Chapter 4   Parallels and Comparative Study

Fig. 4-5   Toichobate and orthostate of the Temples of Messene (left) and the Temple of Asklepios (right).

2) Toichobate moulding

As previously discussed, moulding was used on the side of the toichobate at the Temple of Messene. This type of moulding is considered to have been rare in the Doric style, but it is also used at the Temple of Asklepios in an elegant manner that seems to have roots in the Ionic style[87].

3) Triglyph at the cella walls

The cella walls of the Temple of Asklepios also have metopes and triglyphs, which is very rare. However, such triglyphs may also have been present at the Temple of Messene, as discussed in Chapter 3 (See Chapter 3, Fig. 3-34).

4-3-4 Materials
1) Stone blocks

The stone blocks used at the Temple of Asklepios and the Temple of Messene were almost the same. The crepis, stylobate, toichobate, orthostate, threshold, cyma, etc. were all made of limestone, and the column drums and capitals, architrave, frieze, and cornice blocks were constructed of poros and finished with stucco. The architraves and capitals of the cella at the Temple of Asklepios were made of limestone, but no corresponding blocks could be found for the Temple of Messene, so the material could not be confirmed.

2) Condition and setting of the blocks

Differences can be seen in the setting of the blocks at the Temple of Asklepios and the Temple of Messene. For example, the toichobate blocks at the Temple of Messene are set at the same level as the flooring blocks, but these were set above the flooring in the Temple of Asklepios. For both structures, the naos is built higher than the pteron level, but the manner of setting the blocks is different. It is possible that the manner of setting used at the Temple of Asklepios was easier to use in conjunction with moulding.

In addition, the threshold at the Temple of Messene has a complicated shape, and its composite blocks and the orthostate blocks that adjoin it[88] cannot be seen at the Temple of Asklepios, which seems to have been built more simply.

---

87   Sioumpara 2011, Tafeln 84-108.
88   See pp. 331-33, 41-44.

4-3-5 Summary of the comparison with the Temple of Asklepios

From the above discussion, it was determined that the Temple of Asklepios and the Temple of Messene have many common points with respect to plan and decoration, and that the Temple of Asklepios was probably constructed with the Temple of Messene in mind. However, differences related to era of construction could also be seen: the column proportions of the Temple of Asklepios were clearly late Hellenistic, and the decorations seem to have been more influenced by the Ionic style than at the Temple of Messene. In addition, the general makeup of the corresponding blocks between the two buildings is similar, but the joint faces seem to be simpler and more functional at the Temple of Asklepios, for example with the threshold at the south entrance to the naos.

4-4 Details and date
4-4-1 Riser of crepis and stylobate

It is the tradition that a groove or grooves are cut at the bottom of crepis and stylobate to create shadows for architectural articulation especially in Peloponnesos[89]. There are many variations for the treatment of the risers of crepis and stylobate in Doric temples in Peloponnesos. Usually the risers had one or two grooves at the bottom of the risers for architectural articulation of risers and treads. The treatment may differ between stylobate and crepis in a single temple, and the lower crepis only may differ from stylobate and upper crepis in another temple. In the Temple of Messene, there is no crepis or stylobate in situ, and all their blocks were found demolished and scattered around the site. It is not possible to identify which course they belonged to. However, all the crepis blocks have a single groove at the bottom of the crepis risers, and it can be thought the single groove was worked all around the crepis. The raised panel was also worked on the risers and there seem to be a double groove at the bottom of the risers. The margin of the raised panel is lower than the groove. (Fig. 4-5, PLs. 16~18; 39~43)

In the Temple of Messene, the groove is 0.046 m in height and 0.019 m in depth, and the margin of the raised panel is 0.027 m in height and 0.003 m in depth. The margin of the raised panel was not worked all along the front faces of the blocks but only at the bottom and either the left or right side and there was no margin along the top of the blocks. The reason why

Fig. 4-6 Crepis Δ555 (left) and reconstructed stylobate (right).

---

89 Concerning the Doric order of the Peloponnesos, including treatment of the grooves at the bottom of the riser of crepis and stylobate, Coulton describes in detail. Coulton 1968, p.170.

Chapter 4   Parallels and Comparative Study

the vertical margin of the raised panel was worked on one of the sides may have been to avoid two vertical margins together along the vertical joint and make it look broader than the horizontal margins.

We could see that the treatment of crepis and stylobate in the Temple of Messene followed the tradition of Peloponnesos. As far as we see from the temples in and around Peloponessos in the fourth century, at the Temple of Zeus at Stratos, the single groove was cut only on the lower crepis, and the double groove on the upper crepis and stylobate, with raised panels above them. The margins of the raised panel are cut along all four sides of each block[90]. At the Temple of Athena Alea at Tegea, a single groove was cut on each crepis and double groove on the stylobate without raised panel[91]. At the Temple of Zeus at Nemea, double grooves were cut on each crepis and a triple groove on the stylobate, but there is no raised panel. At the Tholos at Delphi, there is cut a single groove on each crepis and double grooves on the stylobate, and there is no raised panel[92].

4-4-2 Orthostate

Of the excavated blocks, the orthostate blocks are the largest. There is a relieving margin or recessed joint along the bottom of the blocks with widths of 0.034-0.038 m. However, there seems to be no rule for the recessed joint, as far as we see from the blocks. In other words, some blocks have them on both right and left sides, some on only one side, and some have no recessed joints. In the Temple of Zeus at Stratos, there are two stepped grooves along the bottom and the margin is worked on them as if it forms a raised panel, but the margin goes straight to the next block without margin on the vertical joints[93]. The width of the orthostate at the pronaos and the opisthodomos decreases, probably corresponding to that of the anta pillar.

Fig. 4-7   Reconstructed orthostate Δ6 (left) and Δ144 (right).

4-4-3 Doric capital

Two Doric capitals (Δ32, ΔX1) were excavated and their profiles can be observed clearly, which provided an important evidence to date the building. The profile of the echinus is almost straight but a subtle outward curvature is easily identified. (Fig. 4-7, PLs. 35, 95~97) In that point, it bears a remarkable resemblance to the Temple of Zeus at Stratos and the Temple of Zeus at Nemea[94]. At the Tholos at Epidauros, dated to ca 350 BC, the profile of the echinus

---

90   Courby 1924, fig.6, pl. VII, VIII.
91   Dugas 1924, Pl. XXI-XXVI.
92   Charboneaux 1925, Ito 2004, Pl.100~103.
93   Courby 1924, Fig. 6, 20.
94   Hill 1966, Pl. XXVII, Courby 1924, Fig.11.

is almost straight and like a frustum of a cone[95]. The border line between abacus and echinus, which is preserved only partially, is grooved neither sharply nor deeply probably due to weathering of poros, but grooves with angles can be observed clearly between them.

In the Temple of Artemis (ca 300-270 BC) at Epidauros, the profile of the echinus is almost straight and it is nearly a frustum of a cone. In addition, the top of the echinus is not curved round but cut at a right angle to the abacus in a very simplified form[96]. The top of the echinus at the Temple of Messene is still curved round, suggesting that the temple can be dated earlier than the Temple of Artemis at Epidauros, that is, to the late 4th century BC. In the Tholos at Epidauros and also the Tholos at Delphi, the echinus profile is very straight but on the other hand, its top is round, forming a deep groove with the bottom of abacus.

The annulet is very weathered and remains only partially, however, three narrow grooves are observed. (Fig. 4-7) The profile of the annulet is not identified clearly due to weathering, but is at least not quadrant, which was normal from 5th to 4th century BC, but semicircular or quadrilateral.

Fig. 4-8   Profile of the Doric capital (Δ32).

4-4-4 Triglyph

Only some triglyphs are preserved but fragmentarily, and they are too damaged and weathered to be identified. The top of the triglyphs grooves is almost straight but seemingly only slightly curved upward, and inside of the top of the groove is hollowed inward. (PL. 38-2) The 'ear' at the both end of the groove, which is observed at the Stoa at Oropos[97], cannot be identified here.

---

95   Only fragments of Doric capitals are preserved. Sharp groove is observed between echinus and abacus. See Roux 1961, PL.42-2b. Fig.16, p.92. For elevational drawings, also see Cavvadias 1891, Pl.V.

96   Hill 1966, 10, Fig. 1. The profiles of six Doric capitals at the Temple of Asklepios, the Tholos at Epidauros, the South Stoa at Corinth, the Temple of Athena Alea at Tegea, the Temple of Zeus at Nemea and the Temple of Artemis at Epidauros are compared with drawings. It will help our understanding. However, all the profiles of their echinus are drawn as completely straight lines, and as far as we see the photographs, some of them seem to be only slightly bulging. For example, at Stratos, the echinus profile is not straight but slightly bulging. See Courby 1924, Fig. 11. In any case, the curve of the echinus is very slight and delicate, so, it is somewhat difficult to decide whether it is completely straight or slightly curved, and we should be very careful to see the drawings and photographs.

97   Coulton 1968, p.172.

Chapter 4   Parallels and Comparative Study

4-5 Mouldings
4-5-1 Cyma reversa of cornice soffit

The cornice block stands a little vertically on the frieze and the sloped eave protrudes from there. (PLs. 38-3, 105) Cyma reversa moulding is worked on the soffit at the border between the vertical and sloped parts. The moulding at the Temple of Messene bears very close similarity with those of other Hellenistic Doric temples like the Temple of Athena Alea at Tegea[98], the Temple of Zeus at Stratos[99] and the Temple of Zeus at Nemea[100], the Temple of Messene bear very close similarity with them. According to the sample collection by Shoe, the profile of the cornice soffit or the bottom part of the cornice is cyma reversa which balances well in form with the upper convex and lower concave parts[101]. The cornice soffit at the Temple of Messene has almost the same profile.

4-5-2 Sima

Only one sima block was excavated. The moulding is cavetto, the profile of which is curved gently outward without any sculptural ornament. (PLs. 38-5, 107) In the Temple of Zeus at Tegea and the Tholos at Epidauros, the sima profile is a straight line which stands vertically and is worked with ornamental sculpture and lion spout. At the Stoa at Oropos, the sima has a convex ovolo-type profile.

4-5-3 Cyma reversa on toichobate

Cyma reversa moulding is worked on the top of the toichobate at the Temple of Messene. The cyma reversa is all along the outer cella wall but is not worked inside the pronaos, naos or opisthodomos. Most of the cyma reversa moulding is broken because it is on the outer edge of the top. The dimensions of one well-preserved block (Δ349) is 0.028 m in height and 0.040 m in width, and at the antae 0.066 m in width. The total slope is gentle and less than 45°. (Fig. 4-9)

Ten examples of cyma reversa on the top of toichobate are reported in Shoe's collection[102]. The oldest one is the Temple of Hephaestos at Athens (450-440 BC)[103] and the newest is the building in Area B3 at Thera (3rd-2nd century BC)[104]. They spread throughout Attica, Peloponnesos, Phokis and Asia Minor, and examples in Peloponnesos can be seen at Tegea, Epidauros and Olympia. Four examples are observed inside and outside of the Temple of Zeus at Tegea.

The cyma reversa on the outer edge of the top of the cella toichobate at the Temple of Messene highly resembles that of the outer toichobate moulding of the cella at the Temple of Athena Alea at Tegea (350-330 BC). The latter is used independently but not combined with other mouldings, and the total slope is almost the same as that of the Temple of Messene[105]. The other three cyma reversa mouldings of the toichobate inside the cella at the Temple of Athena Alea are combined with other mouldings[106]. The Tholos at Epidauros has also well-balanced cyma reversa and the Philippeion at Olympia (336-335 BC) has a very similar profile

---

98 Dugas 1924, Pl. XLIV
99 Courby 1924, Fig.14-I
100 Hill 1966: Pl. XVI-B
101 Shoe 1936, PL. XXX, XXXI, XXXII
102 Shoe 1936, pp. 87-89, PL. XXXVII.
103 Penrose, Antiquity of Athens, p.53, pl.21, fig.34, Chap.I, pl.VII.
104 Thera III, p.145, fig.126-127.
105 Dugas 1924, Pl. XXI-XXVI.
106 The interior toichobate moulding is gorgeous, corresponding to the base moulding of the interior engaged column in Corinthian style, and quite different from the exterior usual moulding. Dugas 1924, Pl. XXI-XXVI.

Fig. 4-9 Cyma reversa on the top of toichobate (Δ47) and profile (Δ349).

as well[107]. All the cyma reversa profiles are used independently without any other mouldings except the three inner mouldings at the Temple of Athena Alea at Tegea. Observing these parallels, it might be safe to date the Temple of Messene to the second half of the 4th century BC.

4-5-4 Combination of cyma reversa and scotia of the threshold

At the bottom of the front side of the threshold at the naos entrance, there is a cyma reversa moulding. (Δ477, PL. 80) The front of the threshold is 0.400 m in height with a moulding of 0.144 m in total height including its vertical part. The total horizontal depth of the moulding is 0.065 m. The profiles continue from cyma reversa, scotia and vertical part with a raised panel from the top to the bottom. The cyma reversa is 0.028 m in height and 0.031 m in depth, and the scotia is 0.017 m in height and 0.022 m in depth, with a total ratio of the height to the depth of nearly 1:1. The vertical part at the bottom is 0.057 m in height. The combined part of cyma reversa and scotia is 0.052 in height and 0.057 m in horizontal depth.

In Shoe's moulding collection, there are introduced two examples of threshold in which the cyma reversa is used independently but not combined with the scotia[108]. However, we have two other examples of the combined mouldings: the interior platform of the Tholos at Delphi (dated to ca 370 BC by Roux) and the threshold of the Temple of Zeus at Stratos (dated ca 320)[109]. The profiles of both examples bear a close resemblance to that of the Temple of Messene, although they have shallow cavetto rather than deep scotia. In particular, at the latter temple, even the position of the moulding is exactly the same. At the contemporary Temple of Athena Alea at Tegea (350-330 BC), only a simple vertical face without moulding is observed at the front of the threshold[110].

There are five other examples of cyma reversa combined with cavetto or scotia, which are not exactly the same as that of the Temple of Messene but have another moulding added

---

107 Cavvadias 1893,
108 Shoe 1936, PL. XXXVII, no.5 for the Tholos at Delphi, and no.12 for the Temple of Zeus at Stratos.
109 The Temple of Zeus at Stratos has also the same moulding with cyma reversa at the front bottom of the threshold to the naos. The moulding is 0.063 m in height and 0.050m in horizontal distance. Although in Messene Temple, a raised panel can be observed on the vertical face below the moulding, at Stratos not. Courby/Picard 1924, fig.14, VI, fig.38.
110 Dugas 1924, Pl. LXIII-D.

Chapter 4   Parallels and Comparative Study

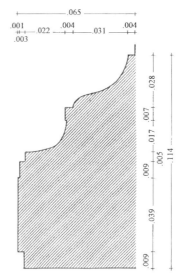

Fig. 4-10   Combination of Cyma reversa and scotia on the threshold.

together[111]. On the anta base of the Nereid Monumen at Xanthos (420-400 BC), a torus is added under the shallow cavetto. On the interior toichobate of the Temple of Athena Alea at Tegea (ca. 360), a large torus is added as well under the scotia. However, a largely protruding fillet is inserted between the cyma reversa and the scotia to make it look very different in appearance. On the toichobate of the Temple of Demeter at Pergamon(180-160 BC), scotia is deeply curved instead of shallow cavetto with a vertical flat face underneath. The base of the great frieze of the Altar of Zeus at Pergamon also has the combination of cyma reversa and scotia, but the curve of the cyma reversa is rather straight and that of scotia is extremely deep, making it look very different. The base moulding of a 'fragment of base' lying at southeast corner of the monument of granite at Delos resembles very closely to that of the Temple of Messene, but the date is unknown.

The discussion above can be summarized as follows. The combined moulding of cyma reversa and scotia which was used at the threshold of the Temple of Messene has the closest resemblance of profile at the interior of the Tholos at Delphi and at the threshold of the Temple of Zeus at Stratos. Especially, both its profile and position are exactly the same. Some other close examples with other mouldings can be seen at the Nereid Monument at Xanthos, 'fragment of base' at Delos, and the Temple of Athena Alea at Tegea. The combination of syma reversa and cavetto or scotia ranges from the second half of the 5th century BC to the 2nd century BC. However, the examples in and around Peloponnesos which bear close resemblance to that of the Temple of Messene, and date to after 369 BC when the town of Messene was founded, are limited to the threshold moulding of the Temple of Zeus at Stratos (350-340 BC), the toichobate moulding of the Temple of Athena Alea at Tegea.

4-6 Summary

From the architectural view point based on the study above, the subtly outward curved profile of echinus, combined moulding of the cyma reversa and cavetto at the front of the threshold of the naos might date to the second half of the 4th century. All other proportional analysis of the Temple also show the same time or late 4th century. This accords with the result of the study of the inscriptions found around the Temple. Considering that Themelis dated the

---

111   Shoe 1936, PL. XXXVII, no.6 for Nereid Monument, no.7 for Temple of Athena Alea, no.13 for Temple of Demeter at Pergamon, no.14 for the Altar of Zeus at Pergamon, and PL. XVIII no.15 for Fragment of Base lying at southeast corner of the monument of granite at Delos.

Temple of Messene late 4th century with the result of the study on the inscriptions, the temple is dated most probably to the last quarter of the 4th century BC.

Chapter 5

Summary and Conclusion

5-1 Summary

The Temple of Messene was a newly rediscovered Doric temple in the agora at Messene, which was reported already in the 2nd century AD together with some other temples by Pausanias. The architecture of the temple was clarified in our research and the results described in previous chapters. The temple must have been one of the most important temples at Messene as it was dedicated to Messene herself, the deified goddess of the town, and also as it was built almost in the center of the agora. In addition, architecturally, the temple was important and interesting because it is one of the examples of the 'last' Doric temples in the history of ancient Greek architecture, suggesting how the Doric temples ended. In this chapter, we summarize the results of our study and make some brief conclusions on the architecture of the Temple of Messene.

The site of the temple was almost empty except for a few foundation blocks of poros stone and rough ashlar in situ and a part of the west staircase. Our study revealed that the building which stood here was a Doric style temple with 6 columns on the front and 12 columns on the flanks from the study of blocks which were found demolished in and around the site. It measures 11.024 × 22.544 m at the lower crepis, and 10.093 × 21.625 m at the stylobate, which was a rather small scale for a Doric peripteral temple. The intercolumniation was calculated as 1.920 m and the corner intercolumniation as 1.7205 m.

The remaining foundation in situ includes poros blocks on the east side which supported the floor of the east pteron, and ones on the west side which were determined to be the foundation for the stylobate on the west side. The rough ashlar foundation blocks on the north and west sides are believed to have been the foundation of something similar to a stone-paved walkway around the temple platform.

The cella of the Temple of Messene was composed of pronaos, naos and opisthodomos. The outer width measured 6.149m and the length was 14.289m, and the width of each room measured 5.175m, with the inner depths of each room 3.777m, 6.732m, and 2.807m respectively. The front of the pronaos and opisthosmos was *di-style in antis*. The remaining traces on the antae and thresholds suggest that there were doors at the front. On the other hand, there is nothing to suggest that there were doors at the opisthodomos. The floor heights of the pteron and the pronaos were the same but that of the naos was 0.231 m higher.

The cella walls would have been aligned to the position of the peripteral colonnades as usual Doric temples. The center of the north and south cella walls would have approximately corresponded to the center axis of the second columns from the north and south corners respectively. Similarly, the edge of the anta toichobate would have corresponded to the edge of the 4th stylobate block from the corner, and the length of the toichobate at the inner court side wall was estimated to be equal to approx. 15 stylobate blocks. The edge of the anta orthostate would have corresponded to the face of the third column from the corner.

We succeeded in reconstructing the layout of the blocks used in the cella. Especially, the toichobate and orthostate blocks have holes for clumps and dowels on their top, and notches to support lever ends on the edges at the bottom. These marks could give information for corresponding adjacent blocks with their position, and we could place almost all the remaining blocks of toichobate and orthostate to their original position. The orthostate blocks were approx. twice as long as the corresponding toichobate blocks.

There were 37 toichobate blocks and 21 orthostate blocks altogether in the cella, 28 and 9 of which respectively were excavated. The toichobate blocks were set from the east and west antae towards the center, and the final block was dropped in at the side wall of the naos. This was probably done to use the final block in order to correct any error. On the other hand, the orthostate was probably set from the west towards the east, and there was no final block dropped into place. It is assumed that, as the orthostate blocks were large and heavy, it would probably have been ineffective to drop in a final block. As evidence for this, the wall blocks set on top of the orthostate were also set like the toichobate blocks from the east and west antae, with a final block dropped in at some point.

Concerning architectural proportions, it was found that although orders from the 3rd century and earlier had relatively stable proportions, later orders had widely scattered values and no clear changes could be confirmed. Even so, clear tendencies were found in the relationship between column height and lower column diameter as well as that between entablature height and column height. According to Themelis, the construction of the Temple of Messene dated to the end of the 4th century BC[112]; that is, to around 300 BC, so the height could be determined based on the proportional relationships between the excavated blocks. The column height was determined to be 4.880 m, which was 6.02 times the lower column diameter. In addition, the proportional relationships of the order at the Temple of Messene were found to be generally average for late 4th century BC temples.

From the viewpoint of architecture, the Temple of Messene could be dated roughly to the 2nd half of the 4th century based on study of the architectural ornamentation. Comparison with Doric temples after 369 BC when the Temple of Messene was built show close parallels to the Temple of Zeus at Stratos[113] and the Temple of Athena Alea at Tegea,[114] both of which are in Peloponnesos and dated to the 2nd half of the 4th century. In particular, the combined moulding of cyma reversa with scotia on the front of threshold to the naos in these temples is quite similar to that of the Temple of Messene. Considering that Themelis dated it to the late 4th century according to the study of the inscriptions on the stelae which were found around the temple, the Temple of Messene can be dated most probably to the last quarter of the 4th century BC.

We should also refer to the Doric Temple of Asklepios which was constructed approximately 100 years later than the Temple of Messene. The former has been preserved better than the latter and is in much better quality with its surrounding stoas, Bouleuterion and Ekklesiasterion, but its temple plan and architectural ornamentation were quite similar to and clearly patterned after the latter. Also, the toichobate moulding seen at the former temple was clearly inherited by the latter, and became even more refined. In many points, the former temple seems to have been built in a more sophisticated manner than the latter.

5-2 Hellenistic Doric temple in the agora

The Temple of Messene provides us with new valuable information in the history of

---

112 Themelis 2004, p. 41; Themelis 2006, p.30; Themelis 2012, p.44, Themelis 2012b, p.118.
113 Courby 1924, fig.14, VI, fig.38.
114 Dugas 1924, Pl. LXIII-D.

Chapter 5   Summary and Conclusion

Doric temples. The tradition of the Doric order still continued in Peloponnesos in the 4th century BC, and even a century longer as we see in the Temple of Asklepios in Messene. However, we might say that the architectural power of original Doric temples with simplicity and vigorousness seems to have weakened, as clearly seencla in their modest size, decorative tendency with mouldings on the toichobate, geison and threshold, etc. In particular, theslender proportion of their columns and smaller or lighter proportion of entablature to the height of column give us an elegant and graceful impression.

On the other hand, the Temple of Messene shows another aspect from the viewpoint of town or townscape planning. The temple was located almost in the center of the agora, in contrast to the most of the archaic and classical Doric temples which were located at acropolis. Why did they place the temple in the agora which has a secular function for civic but not sacred life? The Temple of Messene seems to have been treated as a symbol of the town probably with political meaning, although it is certainly a religious building. In fact, the simple rectangular building of the Bouleuterion from the 4th century BC was built[115] only 15 m away to the north of the Temple of Messene, facing south to it. The east wall of the Bouleuterion and the east front of the Temple of Messene are almost aligned and they seem to have been planned in coordination. Thus, the building of the Bouleuterion and the Temple of Messene in the agora must have been intentional from the beginning. The dedication of the temple to Messene, the deified goddess of the town, seems to have borne a political message of independence and glory of the town, but the discussion of the political background of the temple is beyond this study and we limit the discussion only to the building plan.

The idea of combining the religious function of a temple with a political function was inherited by and realized a century later in the Temple of Asklepios, where the Ekklesiasterion and Bouleuterion, both of which have political functions, were built into the surrounding stoas of the sanctuary and incorporated into the religious surroundings. Here, it is clear that the mixture of functions occurred, but this precedent had already been set by the Temple of Messene in the agora. During the 100 years or so before the Temple of Asklepios was built at the beginning of the 2nd century BC, the Doric Temple of Messene, which was built in the center of the agora, was probably the most important temple as a symbol of Messene, but its role seems to have been replaced thereafter by the newly built Temple of Asklepios which was surrounded by more gorgeous Corinthian stoas.

The Temple of Messene had a staircase with 9 steps along its west end. There is no other example of such a staircase added to Doric temples. Overall, the Messene agora was on a slope which differed in level from north to south by ca. 10 meters, and there was also a difference in the east-west land level in the area of the temple. Thus, the staircase is believed to have played a large role in making up for these differences. However, the addition of the west staircase to the temple would have also had something to do with the monumental layout of the temple. First of all, the temple look monumental with the high staircase when visitors look it up, and secondly the frontality of the temple can be emphasized. Staircases or crepis of 3 steps or more around temples are also seen in Ionic temples from the Hellenistic period in Asia Minor like the Temple of Artemis at Magnesia on the Maeander, etc[116]. They were built usually in flat sanctuaries which were surrounded by colonnaded stoas, and their higher staircases played a role to make them look more monumental, so the staircase at the Temple of Messene could have also shared partially this role with such Ionic temples already in the 4th century, although the staircase was added only to the west front and there is no surrounding colonnaded stoas.

Monumentalizing sanctuaries with central axis, symmetrical layout of the building,

---

115   Themelis 2010a, p.59. The Bouleuterion is a simple rectangular building which was enclosed by walls on its four sides and the roof was supported by twenty pillars inside.
116   Ito 2002, p.47ff. This can be seen in the Sanctuary of Artemis at Magnesia on the Maeander, the upper terrace at Sanctuary of Asklepios at Kos, and many Roman sanctuaries as that of Zeus at Aizanoi, and other Roman sanctuaries and agoras.

and frontality of the main building occurred in the 2nd century BC in Hellenistic period[117]. This type of planning was preceded by the Sanctuary of Asklepieion at Messene probably at the beginning of the same century[118]. However, the symptom of the monumentalizing can be seen even a century earlier in the higher west step of the Temple of Messene.

The agora in Messene may have been separated into two or three terraces from north to south and each terrace sustained by supporting walls to account for the level difference. In fact, such a wall of some 50 m in length was unearthed several meters north of the Bouleuterion.[119] In this topographical environment of the agora, it is not known how the Temple of Messene and the neighboring buildings were located, that is, how the size and location of the buildings were allocated with the space around them. The east front of the temple seems to be aligned to the north-south central axis of the agora, but not exactly. Neither the lines of the north and south sides of the temple, nor its east-west central axis seem to be decided proportionally to the size of the agora.

However, it might be true that a strong visual effect was intended in the layout of the temple in the agora. When the ancient Messenian citizens stood at the south edge of the agora on its north-south axis and looked up toward the north, the townscape of the agora must have been magnificent. The acropolis and Mt Ithomi which rise up to the sky, the gigantic two-storied North Stoa[120] with the length of 187.86 m at its foot with wings at its east and west ends, and the stoas which outlined the east and west edges of the gently sloped agora, all these would have created grandiose views of the agora. The Temple of Messene was observed in the almost center of the agora with the Bouleuterion against the background of this spectacular view. Thus, the temple played a role as one of the components of the agora rather than insisting on its own architectural existence. It is evident that the architects were starting to be conscious of 'space' for locating buildings to create dramatic views of the agora. These suggest that the Hellenistic symmetrical and axial planning of the sanctuaries in Asia Minor and the later Roman sanctuaries like Jupiter Sanctuary at Baalbek which followed them may have originated in the agora at Messene. To make such a conclusion, we will have to wait for results of further excavations in the agora.

---

117 See note no.116 above.
118 Sioumpara dates the Temple of Messene to the first decade of the 3rd century.
119 In the season of 2015, this supporting wall was excavated around 50 m from the north of the 'Meat Market' to the early Christian basilica.
120 Themelis 2003, p. 34, fig. 1; Themelis 2004, pp.29-47

Appendix:
Block Catalog

1. Crepis blocks

Δ50 (PL. 16-1, 39)

This block is diagonally broken, and the overall shape is unclear, but there is double-recessed joint at the bottom of two front faces at the corner, indicating that it was a cornerstone. The existing portion of the block measures 0.800 × 0.610 m at its greatest part, and the height is 0.208 m. The tread width can be determined from the surface marks, which are uniformly placed at 0.250 m from the side edges. A dowel of 0.610 × 0.610 m with a depth of 0.610 m was seen at the distance of 0.105 m from the bottom edge.

Δ52 (PL. 16-2, no illustration)

This block is cracked and broken into two parts, but they could be aligned along the crack to restore the original size of the block. The front length of the block is 0.958 m, depth is 0.409 m, and height is 0.212 m. Double-recessed joint is seen at the bottom of the front side, and there is also a recessed joint of 0.020 m in width at the front left edge. There are two clamp holes at the back edge of the top surface, and one clamp hole each at the joint surfaces. The tread width was determined from its surface finishing to be 0.260 m.

Δ59 (PL. 16-3, 40)

Due to severe damage, the original shape of this block is unclear, but the two sides are at almost perfect 45° angles, and due to this special shape the block was estimated to be a crepis cornerstone. A double-recessed joint can be seen at the bottom of the front face. Traces of two dowel holes 0.037 m in depth can be seen at the top, and a clamp mark 0.016 m in depth is found on the joint side, aligned 45° with respect to the front face. The tread width on the top face was 0.240 m.

Δ157 (PL. 16-4, no illustration)

The back part of this block is damaged, but the front remains fully intact. The length of the front is 0.958 m, depth is 0.397 m and height is 0.213 m. There is double-recessed joint at the bottom of the block front, and there is a recessed joint with the width of 0.024 m at the front left edge. There is a trace of a clamp hole on the top surface at the back. A pry notch was observed at the back of the bottom side near the center. The tread width was 0.263 m.

Δ181 (PL. 16-5, 41)

This block is almost completely intact. The front length is 0.802 m, depth 0.410 m and height 0.209 m. There is a double-recessed joint at the bottom of the front, and there is a vertical recessed joint with the width of 0.020 m at the front right edge. One clamp hole could be seen at each of the joint sides and at the back of the top surface. The tread width was 0.261 m.

Δ555 (PL. 16-6, 42)

Half of the right side of the block is missing, and the front length cannot be determined, but the depth is 0.400 m and the height is 0.214 m. There is a double recessed joint at the bottom of the front, and also a vertical recessed joint with the width of 0.024 m at the front left edge. A clamp hole is seen at the left edge and another at the back of the top surface. The tread width is 0.250 m.

Δ556 (PL. 16-7, 43)

This block is almost completely intact. The front length is 0.804 m, depth is 0.400 m and height is 0.206 m. There is a double-recessed joint at the bottom of the front, and there is a vertical recessed joint with the width of 0.024 m at the front right edge. Three clamp holes could be seen on the top: one at a joint side and two at the back. The tread width could not be determined due to weathering.

2. Stylobate blocks

Δ43 (PL. 17-1, 44)

The right and left sides are missing, so the front length cannot be determined. The front and back faces are partially observed. The depth is 0.885 m and height is 0.221 m. There is observed partially double-recessed joint on the front at the bottom. On the top, there is a square dowel hole for a column, measuring 0.089 × 0.087 m and 0.063 m in depth, located near the center at 45° to the side faces. Traces of round column fluting were found on the surface.

Δ56 (PL. 17-2, no illustration)

The block is broken in a triangular form with its frontal one third part missing. The other three side surfaces are partially remaining and were identified as joint faces. The block length from the front is 0.962 m and height is 0.223 m. The original block depth is unknown due to damage, but the existing part is 0.840 m at maximum. On the top, there is a dowel hole for supporting a column, measuring 0.085 × 0.080 m and 0.060 m in depth. It is located at 45° to the side faces.

Δ64+Δ161+Δ383 (PL. 16-3, 45)

Pieces of a stylobate block which did not support a column. The block was broken into three parts and pieced together after excavation. The front length is 0.960 m, depth is 0.880 m, and height is 0.218 m. There is double-recessed joint at the front bottom, and also a vertical recessed joint in width of 0.025 m at the front right edge. On the bottom, there is a dowel hole at the right edge and a clamp hole at the back edge.

Δ75 (PL. 17-4, no illustration).

Most of this block is missing due to damage. However, the traces of column flutes can still be seen at the top, showing that it was a stylobate block supporting a column. Only part of the front and left sides remain. The original size is unknown due to the damage, but the existing remains measure 0.58 × 0.54 m at maximum, and the height is 0.223 m. No dowel hole can be identified on the top due to breakage, but a dowel hole was observed on the left side of the bottom.

Δ96α+Δ96β (PL. 17-5, 46)

A corner stylobate block. The size of the block is 0.880 × 0.888 m and 0.222 m in height. Double-recessed joints on the bottom of two sides indicate that it was used in a corner. There are traces of column flutes on the top, as well as a dowel hole in the center to hold the column, measuring 0.085 × 0.080 m with a depth of 0.054 m. This dowel hole differs from those on other blocks in that it is parallel to the side line. On the bottom, two dowel holes and one pry support hole are identified on the joint face, and one square dowel hole which is 0.15 m inside from the front face, one each side with double-recessed joint.

Δ117+118 (PL. 17-6, 47)

Interior stylobate block of two broken pieces. Original size of which is impossible to determine due to damage. The height is 0.392 m. There are two notches, one on each side, which are believed to have been for doors or gates, and their front is cut at 45°. This notches are also seen on toichobate blocks for the anta, but their dimensions differ, so further analysis is needed. The front has a lowered horizontal surface of 0.215 m in height and 0.223 m in width, and there is observed another lowered surface on the left side, 0.130 m in width. It is possible that this lowered horizontal surface of 0.215 m in height was used around the central square part on which a column was set. A dowel hole to set the column is seen on the top, and a pry-support notch was found on the bottom at the front edge.

Δ130 (PL. 18-1, 48)

Stylobate block of the pronaos, of which back half is missing. The front measures 0.964 m, and the depth is unknown due to damage. The height is similarly unknown, but there is a lowered horizontal surface with a height of 0.217 m and a width of 0.290 m.

Δ147 (PL. 18-2, 49)

A stylobate block on which a column was set. Only a corner is missing. The front length is 0.961 m, depth is 0.884 m, and height is 0.222 m. Double-recessed joint is seen on the front at the bottom. There is a dowel hole for the column on the top in the center, measuring 0.078 × 0.074 m with a depth of 0.056 m. It is set at 45° with respect to the side faces. There are slight traces of column fluting. There are two dowel holes and pry-support notch on the bottom at the edges.

Δ267 (PL. 18-3, no illustration)

A stylobate block on which a column was set. Only one of the four sides is intact, and it is a joint face. The original block dimensions are unknown, but the present dimensions are 0.870×0.670 m with a height of 0.220 m. The top has a dowel hole in the center to hold the column, cut diagonally at 45° with respect to the side line, measuring 0.085 m square with a depth of 0.052 m.

Δ353 (PL. 18-4, no illustration).

A stylobate block on which a column was set. The double-recessed joint can be seen on the front bottom. The front, left, and back sides are partially preserved. The front length is unknown due to damage, but the present largest dimension is 0.890 m. The depth is 0.884 m, and the height is 0.221 m. The top has a dowel hole in the center to hold the column, cut diagonally at 45° with respect to the side line, measuring 0.080×0.077 m with a depth of 0.060 m.

Δ454 (PL. 18-5, no illustration)

A stylobate block on which a column was set. It is largely broken, and only a part of the front is preserved with double-recessed joint at the bottom. The present front length and depth are ca. 0.60 m and 0.69 m respectively, and the height is 0.220 m. The top has a dowel hole in the center to hold the column, cut diagonally at 45° with respect to the side line, measuring 0.090 m square with a depth of 0.054 m. A dowel hole was also seen on the bottom

0.120 m from the front edge, measuring 0.080 × 0.050 m with a depth of 0.039 m. Dowel holes on the bottom of stylobate blocks were seen only on this block and the abovementioned corner stylobate Δ96, thus these blocks with dowel holes on the bottom are believed to have been used to hold stylobate corners strongly in place.

Δ590 (PL. 18-6, no illustration).

A stylobate block on which a column was set. Two of the sides are only partially preserved, and are joint faces. The original length is unknown due to damage, but the present dimensions are approx. 0.70 × 0.70 m, and the height is 0.255 m. The top has a dowel hole in the center to hold the column, cut diagonally at 45° with respect to the side line, measuring 0.090 m square with a depth of 0.053 m.

Δ670 (PL. 19-1, no illustration).

A stylobate block on which a column was set. Two of the sides are only partially preserved, and are joint faces. The original length is unknown due to damage, but the present dimensions are 0.885×0.580 m, and the height is 0.222 m. The top has a dowel hole in the center to hold the column, set diagonally at 45° with respect to the side line, measuring 0.090 m square with a depth of 0.059 m.

ΔX4 (PL. 19-2, no illustration).

A stylobate block on which a column was set. Only one of the sides is partially preserved, and it is a joint face. The original length is unknown due to damage, but the present dimensions are approx. 0.70×0.55 m at most, and the height is 0.223 m. The top has a dowel hole in the center to hold the column, set diagonally at 45° with respect to the side line, measuring 0.090 m square with a depth of 0.043 m.

ΔX5 (PL. 19-3, no illustration).

A stylobate block that did not support a column. Only the front and back sides are partially preserved, and the front has a double-recessed joint at the bottom. The back is a joint face. The front length is unknown but presently 0.700 m, depth is 0.880 m and height is 0.240 m.

ΔX9 (PL. 19-4, no illustration).

A stylobate block on which a column was set. It is almost completely intact, and the front has a double-recessed joint. The front length is 0.956 m, depth is 0.881 m, and the height is 0.211 m, making it somewhat smaller than the other stylobate blocks. The top has a dowel hole to hold the column 0.440 m from the front and 0.470 m from the left side, set diagonally at 45° with respect to the side line and measuring 0.085 m square with a depth of 0.058 m. Although it was found a short distance away from the temple, it was determined to be a temple block due to its shape, and duly measured and recorded.

ΔX10 (PL. 19-5, no illustration).

A stylobate block on which a column was set. Only a part of one joint face is preserved. The original length is unknown due to damage, but the present dimensions are approx. 0.70×0.60 m at most, and the height is 0.224 m. The top has a dowel hole in the center 0.467 m from the side to hold the column, parallel with respect to the front line, measuring 0.100 m square. There are no dowel holes or pry holes on the bottom.

Appendix: Block Catalog

3. Flooring blocks

Δ55 (PL. 20-2, 50)

On this block, three of the sides remain. One of them is intact and the other two are a little broken at the same ends. The length of the undamaged side is 0.962 m. The other side, which is damaged, is 1.037 m and slightly longer than the stylobate blocks. The height is 0.217 m, and a dowel hole can be seen on the longer edge of the bottom.

ΔX2 (PL. 20-3, 51)

The height of this block is 0.225 m, and the size is 0.960 × 0.960 m. On one of the four sides, there is a part protruding 0.257 m from the corner, indicating that this was originally a special L-shaped block. However, the protruding portion is broken, so the complete dimensions are unknown. There is a dowel hole on the bottom edge.

4. Toichobate blocks

1) For the anta

Δ47 (PL. 21-1, 52)

This block is well preserved, but damaged a little on the anta part and the lower part of the inner side. The original size is unknown, but the present dimensions are at most 0.986 m in length, 0.701 m in width, and 0.405 m in height. The width of the finishing at the top on which the orthostate block was set is 0.522 m, but that on the anta part is unclear due to damage. The inner side has a cut about 0.20 m in width and 0.10 m in depth. The back part of this cut is right-angled but the front part is at 45°, and from this shape it seems to have been for a doorframe of the pronaos. There are two clamp holes on the top at the end, and a dowel hole of 0.010 m square and 0.035 m in depth at the anta part, as well as a lead groove to fix the dowel.

Δ223 (PL. 21-2, 53)

This block is greatly damaged and the size of the original is unknown. The size of the existing block is at most 0.983 m in length, 0.695 m in width and 0.392 m in height. The top and outer sides are missing, and the width of the finishing is unknown. Inner face is divided into the lower and upper parts, the upper is 0.154 m in height and recessed 0.066 m. There are two clamp holes on the top at the end, and a dowel hole on the anta part measuring 0.105 m square and 0.020 m deep, as well as a lead groove to fix the dowel. Another dowel hole was seen at the bottom inner edge.

Δ349 (PL. 21-3, 54)

The upper portion of this block is almost completely intact. It measures 0.705 m in width and 0.406 m in height. The bottom part is missing, so the original length is unknown, but the present block measures 0.972 m at maximum. The width of the surface finishing is 0.571 m on the anta end and 0.514 m on the other end. The inner side is cut in the middle similar to block Δ47, and the upper non-cut part is 0.221 m high and 0.054 m recessed. There are two clamp holes on the top and a dowel hole 0.096 m square and 0.040 m in depth to hold anta pillar, and a lead groove to attach the dowel.

Δ577+Δ580 (PL. 21-4, 55)

This block was broken in two large pieces which were re-adjoined, and the block as a whole measured 0.699 m in width and 0.403 m in height. The original length could not be determined due to breakage, but the present maximum length is 1.023 m. The damage is extensive and there is very little finishing left to see, but a trace of 90° angled moulding could be observed at the part believed to be the anta corner. From this, the block was determined to be a toichobate block for the anta. The width of the top finishing is impossible to determine due to damage. The upper part of the inner face is 0.224 m in height and recessed 0.076 m from the lower part. One clamp hole on the top, and one dowel hole on the bottom inside edge were observed.

2) L-shaped blocks for intersection
Δ3 (PL. 22-1, 56)

This block is preserved well, and measures 1.007×0.969 m and is 0.406 m in height. The finishing on the top is 0.529 m in width at the inner dividing wall and 0.490 m at the outer wall. The part inside the L is cut away to set the flooring; the cuts measure 0.114 m and 0.175 m in width and are 0.079 m deep. There are two clamp holes on the top of each tip of the L, and a clamp hole at the edge of the 45° angled joint face. On the bottom, there is one pry notch on each tip of the L.

Δ9 (PL. 22-2, 57)

This block is measures 1.005 × 0.964 m and is 0.400 m in height. The finishing on the tip of the L on the inner dividing wall side is unknown due to damage, but is 0.483 m on the outside wall side. The cut-away part of the inside of the L measures 0.147 m and 0.148 m in width and 0.071 m in height. There are one pry hole and two sets of two clamp holes which are set at right angles each other in the middle of the top. There are also two clamp holes on the joint faces at each tip and a corner of the L. On the bottom, there is one clamp hole and one pry hole on each tip of the L.

Δ140 (PL. 22-3, 58)

One end of the L shape is missing. The maximum size of the existing block is 0.933 × 0.833 m with a height of 0.404 m. The width of finishing at the top of the tip of the L is unknown. The cut on the inside of the L-shape is 0.180 m in width and 0.055 m in height. There are two clamp holes and on the top of the L tip and a pry hole at the inner corner of the L on the dividing wall side, and two clamp holes at the outer edge of the L. The bottom could not be measured.

Δ145 (PL. 22-4, 59)

This block measures 1.014 × 0.967 m with a height of 0.403 m. The finishing the top of the L tip was 0.506 m at the inner dividing wall and 0.486 m on the outer wall. The cut-away parts at the inside of the L-shape are 0.168 m and 0.185 m in width and 0.067 m in height. There is a set of one dowel hole and one pry hole on the top, and another dowel hole at right angles to it. The tips of the L have two clamp holes each, and one clamp hole is observed on the joint face at the corner of the L. There is also one clamp hole and one pry hole at each end of the L on the bottom

3) For the side wall of the naos
Δ1 (PL. 22-5, 60)

This block measures 0.960 m in length, 0.663 m in width and 0.403 m in height. The top finishing where the wall is set is 0.488 m in width. There is moulding and a raised panel on the outside surface, with a joint face below it. No vertical edges of the raised panel could be confirmed due to damage. There is a 0.110 m in width, 0.093 m in depth cut on the inside surface to set the flooring. Two clamp holes were seen at the joint face of each end on the top. On the bottom, there were three dowel holes; one at an end and one each at the inside and outside.

Appendix: Block Catalog

Δ8 (PL. 22-6, 61)

The length of the block is 0.958 m, with a width of 0.713 m and a height of 0.402 m. The top of the block is particularly severely damaged, and the width of the finishing on the surface is unknown. The outside has the same molding and raised panel as well as the others, but the vertical edges of the raised panel cannot be observed on this block. The cut-away part for the flooring measures 0.168 m in width and 0.105 m in depth. At the top, each edge of the joint face has two clamp holes and there are a set of two dowel holes and one pry hole in the center.

Δ15 (PL. 23-1, 62)

One end of this block was missing, but part of the missing portion was found and restored on the block. With the restoration, the original length of the block was 0.961 m, the width was 0.675 m and the height 0.408 m. The width of finishing at the top where the wall was set is 0.482 m. There is a molding and a course of raised panel without vertical recessed edge at each end on the outside, below which is a joint face.

The inside cut-away part for the flooring is 0.126 m in width and 0.085 m in depth. On the top, there are two clamp holes at one end, but one clamp hole on the other end due to damage. Three rectangular holes are arranged vertically in a row on the joint face. They must have been pry holes to maneuver the block at the exact position. No pry or dowel holes were seen on the bottom.

Δ16 (PL. 23-2, 63)

This block is almost completely intact. The length is 0.942 m, the width is 0.660 m and the height is 0.404 m. The width of finishing at the top is 0.484 m. The interior cut-away part for the flooring is 0.111 m in width and 0.075 m in depth. The exterior has moulding and a course of raised panel which has a vertical recessed edge at the right end. The lower half is a joint face with the floor. On the top, there are two clamp holes at each end, and a set of two dowel holes and one pry hole was seen in the middle. One set each of dowel and pry hole is also seen on the bottom at the inner edge and at one end.

Δ18 (PL. 23-3, 64)

This block is also preserved very well, and measures 0.957 m in length, 0.655 m in width and 0.405 m in height. The width of finishing at the top where the wall is set is 0.484 m. The interior cut-away part for the flooring measures 0.109 m in width and 0.073 m in depth. There is moulding and a raised panel on the outer side which has a vertical recessed edge at the right end as is shown on Δ16. The lower part is a joint face to the flooring. On the top, two clamp holes each could be seen at each edge. On the bottom, there was a set of a dowel hole and a pry notch at one end, and another set on the inside edge. On each vertical joint face at the end, there are observed a set of three rectangular pry holes which were set vertically in different levels to hold a pry end to maneuver the block.

Δ48 (PL. 23-4, 65)

This block is almost complete and measures 0.973 m (outside) and 0.984 m (inside) in length, 0.635 m in width and 0.405 m in height. The width of finishing at the top is 0.476 m. The interior cut-away part for the flooring measures 0.092 m in width and 0.067 m in depth. There is moulding and a raised panel on the outer side, below which is a joint face. The raised panel has a recessed edge at the right end. On top, two clamp holes are seen at each end, and there is a set of pry hole and two dowel holes in the center. On the bottom, there was a set of dowel hole and pry notch on the edge of the joint face at the end, and another set on the inside edge.

Δ143 (PL. 23-5, 66)
The top of this block is largely broken at its outer edge. The length of the block is 0.955 m, the width is 0.687 m, and the height is 0.401 m. The top moulding is missing and the width of top finishing is unknown, but we may guess that it was a toichobate block for the side wall of the naos from its size and form of the existing remains. At the top, there is one clamp hole on each end, and there are a set of two dowel holes and one pry hole in the center. The bottom has one pry notch and dowel hole on one end, as well as a dowel hole on the inside edge.

Δ465 (PL. 23-6, 67)
This block is missing a large portion of the top where clamp holes are usually seen. The length is 0.968 m, width is 0.632 m, and height is 0.403 m. The width of finishing at the top is 0.485 m. The cut-away part for the flooring on the inside is 0.077 m in width and 0.070 m in depth. There is moulding and a course of a raised panel on the outside, with a joint face below. The raised panel has no recess at the left edge and recessed joint at the right side edge is unknown due to damage. On the top, slight traces of two clamp holes are observed on each side of the joint face. There are two circular holes near the center, which from their shape seem to have been added later with a drill and have nothing to do with the actual construction. On the bottom, there is a pry notch at one edge of the joint face, and a dowel hole on the inside edge.

Δ575+Δ576 +Δ579 (PL. 24-1, 68)
The block is heavily damaged and the bottom half of the block is completely missing. The remaining block is broken into three pieces, which were joined together. The original height is unknown but the present height is at most 0.333 m, length is 0.963 m and width is 0.631 m. One side has moulding and a raised panel, and the opposite side has a cut-away portion for the flooring, which is 0.103 m in width and 0.082 m in depth. The width of finishing at the top where the wall was set is 0.481 m. On the top, there are two clamp holes at each edge of the joint face.

4) For dividing wall of the opisthodomos
Δ2 (PL. 24-2, 69)
This block is heavily damaged at the top, and the details of the outside portions are unknown. However, from the remaining width of the top and the block length, it is believed to be a toichobate block for the dividing wall of the opisthodomos. The block length is 0.858 m, width is 0.710 m and height is 0.410 m. The cut-away part for the flooring on the inside measures 0.206 m in width and 0.070 m in depth. At the top, there is one clamp hole at each edge of the joint face. The bottom shows one dowel hole each on the inside edge and on the edge of the joint face extending along the wall.

Δ14 (PL. 24-3, 70)
This block is 0.858 m in length, 0.690 m in width and 0.404 m in height. The width of finishing at the top is 0.527 m. The cut-away part on the inside for the flooring is 0.160 m in width and 0.072 m in depth. There is no joint face with anathyrosis underneath the cut-away part. On the outside, raised panel can be seen with a joint face underneath. The top has two clamp holes at each end of the joint face. There are also three rectangular pry holes set vertically in a row on each vertical joint face of the end. The lowest one of them is set at the bottom.

Δ169 (PL. 24-4, 71)
The top of this block is heavily damaged on both sides. It measures 0.860 m in length, 0.692 m in width, and 0.040 m in height. The width of finishing at the top where the wall was set is 0.512 m. The cut-away part on the inside for the flooring is 0.180 m wide and 0.076 m

deep. On the outside, raised panel can be seen with a joint face underneath. The top has one clamp hole on each end of the block, and there is a set of two dowel holes and one pry hole in the center. At the bottom, there is one set of pry notch and dowel hole each on the inside edge and the edge of the joint face at one end. There is another pry notch on the outside.

5) For the wall of the pronaos and opisthodomos
Δ21 (PL. 24-5, 72)

One of the inside corners of this block is cut slightly at 45°, indicating that the block adjoined a toichobate intersecting block. The length is 0.955 m, width is 0.585 m and height is 0.405 m. The width of the finishing on the top where the wall was set is 0.519 m. There is moulding and raised panel on the outside, with a joint face underneath. The inside also has smooth finishing and a joint face below it. Due to damage, it is impossible to tell whether it is a raised panel with smooth face or not without recess on the edge. On the top, there are two clamp holes on each end. There are also a set of two dowel holes and one pry hole in the center. At the bottom, there is a set of one dowel hole and one pry notch each at the inside edge and the end.

Δ49 (PL. 24-6, 73)

This block connects with a toichobate block of anta. Half of the block is broken away, so the original length is unknown. The length at present is at most 0.625 m. The width is 0.585 m and height is 0.405 m. The width of the finishing at the top cannot be determined due to damage. The outer edge has moulding and a raised panel with a joint face underneath. On the inside, a tiny trace of a raised panel is observed with a joint face below. Due to damage, it is impossible to tell whether there was a vertical recess at each end of the raised panel. At the top, there are two clamp holes at the end, and a channel for pouring lead could be seen. The channel is used to pour lead to a square dowel hole to fix anta blocks, and it is clear that this block connected to an anta toichobate block. At the bottom, there were two sets of one dowel hole and one pry notch each on the inner side and at the end.

Δ131 (PL. 25-1, 74)

This block connects to an anta block. It measures 0.954 m in length, 0.579 m in width, and 0.408 m in height. The inside surface is badly damaged at the top, and the width of the finishing at the top is impossible to determine. There is moulding and a raised panel on the outside face with a joint face underneath. The right edge of the raised panel has a vertical recess, and there is a partial cut in the center of the moulding. The raised panel at the inside face is missing due to damage. There are two clamp holes at each edge of the joint face, and a set of dowel holes and one lever hole in the center. A 0.094 m square dowel hole is also seen slightly to the inside of the center, and two lead pouring channels leading to it are seen extending from the outer and inner edges. From this, it could be determined that this block connected to an anta block. At the bottom, there is a dowel hole and pry notch each at the inside edge and the edge of an end.

Δ220 (PL. 25-2, 75)

This block connects to an intersecting block. It measures 0.949 m in length, 0.579 m in width and 0.401 m in height. The width of the finishing at the top where the wall was set is 0.510 m. The outer face has moulding and a raised panel with a joint face underneath. The inside face also has the raised panel without moulding and a joint face below. There is a vertical recess at the right edge of the inside raised panel. One of the inside edges is a slight cut-away at 45°, indicating that this block connected to a toichobate intersecting block. At the top, there are two clamp holes at each end. The bottom has two sets of one dowel hole and one pry notch each at the inside and the end.

Δ243 (PL. 25-3, 76)

This block is 0.976 m in length, 0.582 m in width and 0.403 m in height. The width of the finishing at the top where the wall was set is 0.512 m. The outside has moulding and a raised panel with a joint face underneath. The inside has a raised panel without moulding and a joint face underneath. Due to damage, no vertical recess is observed at the edge of the raised panel. On the top, there are two clamp holes at each end. At the bottom, there are two sets of one dowel hole and one pry notch each at the inside and the end.

ΔX8 (PL. 25-4, 77)

This block was broken in three pieces and joined together. It measures 0.963 m in length, 0.571 m in width, and 0.400 m in height. Due to extensive damage, the width of the finishing at the top is unknown. The raised panel inside is missing, but the moulding and the raised panel outside only partially remain. The bottom of each side is a joint face, and this shows that the block is considered to be for the side wall of the pronaos or opisthodomos. The top has one clamp hole at one end, and two clamp holes at the other end. The bottom has one dowel hole each at the inside and at one end.

6) For the dividing wall of the pronaos
Δ11 (PL. 25-5, 78)

This block measures 1.073 × 0.872 m with a height of 0.404 m. The width of the even finishing at the top where the orthostate is set is 0.526 m. The block is processed in an L shape, and the inside has a cut-away part for the flooring, which is 0.066 m in depth. There is a similar cut-away area on part of the outside of the L shape for the threshold measuring 0.242 m in width and 0.180 m in depth, and extending another 0.132 m at the front. The front face has a raised panel with recess along the top, bottom and right edges, below which is a joint face. There are two clamp holes at the end opposite the cut-away for threshold. On the bottom, there is one dowel hole and one pry notch at the side which connects to the threshold, and one dowel hole on the back side.

Δ17 (PL. 25-6, 79)

This block is damaged and the original dimensions are unknown. The present measurements are 0.0885 × 0.870 m with a height of 0.404 m. The width of the finishing at the top where the orthostate is set is 0.515 m. The block is L-shaped, and the inside of the L has a cut-away portion for the flooring, which measures 0.067 m in depth. Additionally, as with the L-shaped block (Δ11) described above, there is believed to have been a cut-away portion for the threshold, but that portion of the block is missing. There is observed a raised panel on the front surface, with a joint face below it. At the top, there are two clamp holes at the end opposite the threshold.

5. Threshold

1) Threshold of the entrance to the naos
Δ13+Δ133+Δ477+ΔX4, Δ119 (PL. 26-1, 26-2, 26-3, 80)

This block is a threshold block for the entrance to the naos. It was originally one large block but now it is made up of four different pieces (Δ13+133+477+X4) which compose approximately half of the original block including the edges. Another piece (Δ119) makes up approximately 1/4 of the entire block including the edges. About 1/4 of the center part is missing.

The block is made of limestone as well as most of the other blocks.

The height of the threshold block is 0.400 m. The front part is heavily damaged, but the section of the original block can be determined with slight traces of the original faces. Its front face has a vertical upper part with the height of 0.286 m and the bottom part are moulding part 0.114 m in height and 0.065 m in width. It is composed of mouldings of cyma-recta, scotia, and vertical raised panel.

The top is extremely weathered and also damaged. The inside part where the door was located is 0.065 m lower than the top. The present width is 0.300 m, but the original dimensions are unknown due to the weathering at the top. The inside vertical part has rough finishing and slants down 0.015 m with respect to the overall height. The sizes of the holes that hold the axis for the door are slightly different on the right and the left. The depth of the hole on the left side is 0.033 m and that on the right side is 0.029 m. The left door axis hole has a channel for pouring lead in order to fix the metal cup to set the pivot of the door. At the center of the threshold corresponding to the axis holes, there are two rectangular holes for the vertical door bolts that lock the doors. One of these is 0.075 × 0.065 m, and the other is 0.075 × 0.045 m. Both are 0.065 m in depth.

There are several complicated markings at the edges of both sides of the threshold block. Three rectangular dowel holes along each end of the threshold block are believed to have been used to fix the end of the orthostate of dividing wall to the threshold. There is a long and thin marking measuring 0.040 m in width and 0.022 m in depth, where the bottom of the vertical door jamb was dropped into. From the conditions of the markings, it is believed that the jambs of the entrance were made up of at least three parts corresponding to each of the sides: one on the pronaos side, one on the side of the main entrance and one inside the threshold. Also from these markings, it was estimated that the width of the effective opening of the doors was 2.030 m, the width of one door was 1.015 m, and the estimated overall length of the original threshold block was 2.955 m.

2) Threshold of the entrance to the pronaos
Δ572 (PL. 27-1, 81-2)

This block is believed to have been for the threshold of the entrance to the pronaos. It is missing one side and the bottom due to damage; thus it is impossible to tell the height and length of the overall block. At present, the block measures 0.273 m in height, 0.490 m in length and 0.390 m in width at most. The width of the top surface is 0.213 m and there is a parallel cut, 0.138 m in width and 0.054 m in depth, on the back of the top probably to set the door. The upper part of the front face is a raised panel with recessed edges on its top and bottom, but the lower part is unknown because it is missing. Additionally, the preserved end of the block protrudes 0.071 m at its front half and the front corner is cut off diagonally. From this shape, which corresponds to the notch on the inside of the toichobate block for the anta, we estimate that this block was for the threshold at the entrance to the pronaos. There is a dowel hole measuring 0.085 m square and 0.037 m in depth on the top at the end. And another dowel hole measuring 0.096 × 0.040 m and 0.029 m in depth is observed at the end of the lowered part on the back of the top.

ΔX6 (PL. 27-2, 81-1)

This is believed to have been a threshold block for the entrance to the pronaos. Due to damage, one of the sides and the bottom are missing and it is impossible to determine the height and length of the overall block. At present it measures at most 0.245 m in height, 0.396 m in length and 0.392 m in width. The width of the top is 0.214 m, and like block 572, the front has a raised panel with recessed joint at its top but the bottom edge is unknown due to damage. On the back of the top, there is also a horizontal surface or cut to set the door, 0.142 m in width and

0.055 m in depth. The end of the block protrudes 0.042 m, and its front corner cut diagonally. This diagonal cut would fit to the diagonal cut of the toichobate for the anta. From this shape we believe that this block was for the threshold of the pronaos. The top has a dowel hole at the end of the block measuring 0.085 × 0.149 m with a depth of 0.036 m. There is also a dowel hole on the back horizontal surface at the end. It measures 0.094 × 0.033 m with a depth of 0.033 m.

ΔX7 (PL. 27-3, No illustration)

Although the shape of this block differs somewhat in details, it is very similar to the overall shape of the other pronaos threshold blocks, so it is also believed to have been used for the threshold. Only a portion of two sides and the top remain. There is a horizontal surface 0.071 m below the top with a width of 0.110 m and rough finishing. A dowel hole measuring 0.060 × 0.028 m with a depth of 0.032 m can be seen at the top. Due to damage, the dimensions of the original block are unknown, but it presently measures at most 0.045 × 0.034 m, and the maximum height is 0.180 m.

6. Orthostate blocks

1) For the anta
Δ4+Δ568+Δ574+ΔX3 (PL. 28-1, 82)

The front part of the anta pillar is missing from this block, so the overall length is unclear. However the existing length is 1.410 m. The height is 0.964 m and the width of the wall part is 0.483 m at the top and 0.493 m at the bottom. The anta column is tapered, the width of which is 0.563 m at the top, and 0.573 m at the bottom. The exterior surfaces are slightly angled so that the top width of the block is 0.010 m smaller than the bottom. There is a square dowel hole in the center of the anta column at the top and a set of one pry hole and dowel hole near the center of the block. At the edge of the joint face, there are two clamp holes. Something that looks like a clamp hole can also be seen on the inside of the anta part. At the bottom, there is a square hole in the center of the anta which measures 0.095 × 0.080 m, with a depth of 0.035 m. There is also a square dowel hole measuring 0.081 m with a depth of 0.038 m near the vertical joint face. At the bottom of the wall part, there is a recessed joints on both outer and inner sides.

Δ6 (PL. 28-2, 83)

This block is in almost perfect condition. The height of the block is 0.959 m and the length is 1.384 m at the bottom and 1.376 m at the top. The width of the wall side is 0.488 m at the bottom and 0.485 m at the top. The anta widths are as follows.

Anta column front width: 0.562 m at the bottom, 0.552 m at the top.
Anta column outside width: 0.316 m at the bottom, 0.308 m at the top.
Anta column inside width: 0.637 m at the bottom, 0.629 m at the top.

A deep recessed joint can be seen at the bottom on the outside, but the inside is damaged at the bottom, so it is unclear whether there is a recessed joint or not. There is one dowel hole at the top in the center of the anta column, which measures 0.085 × 0.067 m, with a depth of 0.037 m. There is also a set of a dowel hole and pry hole near the center of the block, and two clamp holes at the edge of the joint face side. On the bottom, there are two square dowel holes; one in the center of anta column, which measures 0.093 × 0.088 m, with a depth of 0.038 m and another near the joint face, which measures 0.085 × 0.077 m, with a depth of 0.038 m.

Δ22 (PL. 28-3, 84)

The bottom inside of this block is severely damaged. The block measures 0.962 m in height and 1.390 m in length at the bottom and 1.383 m in length at the top. The width of the bottom cannot be determined due to damage, but the top width of the wall is 0.483 m. The widths at the anta column are as follows:

Anta front width: 0.572 m at the bottom, 0.558 m at the top.
Anta outside width: 0.323 m at the bottom, 0.316 m at the top.
Anta inside width: 0.625 m at the bottom, 0.615 m at the top.

There is a deep recessed joint at the bottom of the outside surface, but due to damage a recessed joint at the inside surface cannot be identified. A dowel hole measuring 0.066 × 0.081 m with a depth of 0.035 m is seen on the top of the anta part in the center. There is also one dowel hole and one pry hole near the center of the block, and two clamp holes at the edge of the joint face. At the bottom, there is a dowel hole measuring 0.090 × 0.093 m at the anta part.

Δ40+45 (PL. 28-4, 85)

This block is broken into two pieces: Δ40 which includes the anta part and Δ45 which is the wall part. The inside part is broken away. The block measures 0.965 m in height, 1.390 m in length at the bottom and 1.377 m in length at the top. The width of the wall part is impossible to tell due to damage.

Anta column front width: 0.577 m at the bottom, 0.557 m at the top.
Anta column outside width: 0.325 m at the bottom, 0.312 m at the top.
Anta column inside width: unclear due to damage.

The anta column front width is slanted 0.010 m both at the outside and the inside. The front face of the anta is angled 0.013 m from the front towards the back with respect to the height. In other words, the front, inner and outer sides of the anta all angled towards the center with an angle of 0.010 m to the height. One rectangular dowel hole with a groove for pouring lead from the front face was seen on the top in the center of the anta part. There was also a pry hole near the center of the block and a clamp hole on the joint face side. The bottom could not be measured.

2) For the intersection

Δ19 (PL. 28-5, 86)

This block is 1.920 m in length and the width is 0.483 m at the top and 0.484 m at the bottom. The height is 0.962 m. There is anathyrosis at a point approximately 0.55 m from the edge on the inside, which is the joint face. A recessed joints are found at the bottom and left edge of the outside face. At the top, there are two sets of one dowel hole and pry hole. There are also observed two clamp holes at one end and one clamp hole at the other end, also two clamp holes at the edge of the joint face that extends towards the inside.

Δ144 (PL. 28-6, 87)

This block measures 1.904 m in length, 0.477 m in width and 0.955 m in height. There is anathyrosis at a point 0.131 m from the edge of the inside face, and below this a dowel hole can be seen. Recessed joints are observed at the far edge from the anathyrosis and at the bottom of the inside face. On the outside face, recessed joints can also be seen at the remaining left side edge and at the bottom. On the top, there are two sets of one dowel hole and one pry hole each at the top, two clamp holes at one end, and one clamp hole at the joint face extending along the inside.

3) For the wall of the pronaos and the opisthodomos
Δ27 (PL. 29-1, 88)

Part of this block was missing, but the missing portion was found and the original block was almost completely restored to its full condition. The length of the restored block was 1.924 m, the width was 0.447 m at the top and 0.485 m at the bottom, and the height was 0.966 m. On both the inside and outside faces, there are recessed joints at the bottom and on the sides. On the top, there is a dowel hole near one end and a set of a dowel and pry hole near the other end, as well as two clamp holes on each end.

4) For the dividing wall of the pronaos
Δ20 (PL. 29-2, 89)

Whole face of one side of the block is missing, and one of the joint faces is completely missing on this block, so the original length is unknown. The height is 0.965 m, and the present length and width are 1.240 m and 0.402 m respectively. There are recessed joints measuring 0.037 m in width at the bottom and at one side. These are believed to have been on the outside. There is also cut-away part at the right corner of the bottom, measuring 0.206 m in height at a point 1.110 m from the joint face. At the top, there are two clamp holes at an end, as well as a set of one dowel hole and one pry hole in the center.

5) For the dividing wall of the opisthodomos
Δ7 (PL. 29-3, 90)

The block is almost complete except the a little broken corners, and measures 1.708 m in length and 0.480 m in width at the top, and 0.487 m in width at the bottom. The height was 0.953 m. A recessed joint can be seen at the bottom of the exterior side only. Due to the fact that the outside surface was cut at an angle, the width at the top is 0.007 m smaller than the width at the bottom. At the top, two sets of one dowel hole and one pry hole can be seen, and there are also two clamps holes on each end. At the bottom there is one pry notch in the center of the inside face.

6) For the wall of the naos
No block for the side wall of the naos was found.

7) Unidentified block
Δ98+Δ98a (PL. 29-4, 91)

Part of the block is missing. This block measured 0.484 m in width at the top and 0.490 m in width at the bottom, and was 0.969 m in height. Due to damage the original length of the block could not be determined, but the present length is 1.529 m. There is a recessed joint 0.039 m tall at the bottom of one side only, and this side was believed to have been on the outside. The block is inclined toward inside; outside face 0.006 m and inside face 0.005 m with respect to the height. At the top, two clamp holes can be seen at the remaining end, and a set of one dowel hole and one clamp hole can be seen. A pry notch can also be seen on the bottom at the edge of the inside face in the center. From this, this block is believed to have been for the inside wall of the naos or for the dividing wall of the opisthodomos. However it cannot be determined for sure, as the original length of the block is unknown.

7. Wall blocks
Δ68 (PL. 29-5, 92)

This block measures 0.473 m in width and 0.332 m in height. Due to damage, the length of the original block is unknown, but the existing block is 0.545 m in length at most. At the top, there is a dowel hole and one clamp hole in the center, and one clamp hole can be seen at the edge of the vertical joint face. There was also a pry hole on the vertical joint face and a pry notch can be seen at its bottom.

Δ105+105a (PL. 29-6, 93)

This block measures 0.471 m in width and 0.331 m in height. Due to damage the original length is unknown, but the present length is 0.756 m at most. One clamp hole was seen at the edge of the vertical joint face at the top and a set of one dowel hole and one pry hole were seen in the center.

8. Column drums

Δ127 (PL. 32-1, 94)

This block measures 0.780 m in height and the top diameter is 0.754 m at the arrises and 0.712 m at the flutings. The bottom diameter is 0.776 m at the arrises and 0.734 m at the flutings. There is a dowel hole at the top in the center measuring 0.100 m on one side and 0.072 m in depth. In the center of this dowel hole, there is another dowel hole cut diagonally at 45°, measuring 0.045 m on one side and 0.052 m in depth. At the bottom, there is also a dowel hole cut at 45°, similar to that at the top.

9. Column capitals

Δ32 (PL. 35-1, 95)

Although the overall shape of this block is recognizable, it is badly weathered and the flutings are almost completely gone. The annulets remains only partially. The top of the abacus measures 0.882 × 0.882 m, and the overall height is 0.332 m. The heights of the abacus, echinus, and annulets are 0.128 m, 0.088 m, and 0.030 m respectively. There are 22 flutes. The upper column diameter is 0.689 m at the arrises and 0.655 m at the bottom of flutes. There is a dowel hole at the bottom measuring 0.080 × 0.085 m, with a depth of 0.072 m. At the top there is an octagonal bedding to set the architrave, which is 0.004 m in height. In the center of the top there is a dowel hole measuring 0.053 m on one side and 0.063 m in depth. There also is a rectangular dowel hole on each side of this hole.

ΛX1 (PL. 35-2, 96, 97)

The weathering of this block is extreme and the details are almost completely missing. The top of the abacus is 0.885 × 0.885 m and the overall height is 0.342 m. The abacus, echinus, and annulet heights are 0.136 m, 0.084 m, and 0.031 m respectively. There are 20 flutes. The upper column diameter is 0.676 m at the arrises and 0.648 m at the bottom of flutes. At the bottom, a dowel hole was seen in the center measuring 0.085 × 0.075 m and 0.059 m in depth. Inside this dowel hole, there was another rectangular hole measuring 0.052 × 0.041 m and 0.106 m in depth from the surface. This was a stepped dowel hole. On top of the abacus, there is an octagonal bedding to set the architrave, which measures 0.004 m in height. In the center there is a dowel hole measuring 0.065 × 0.062 m with a depth of 0.043 m. Within this dowel hole there is another dowel hole measuring 0.050 × 0.046 m with a depth of 0.061 m from the surface. On either side of this dowel hole, one rectangular dowel hole could also be seen.

10. Architrave blocks
Δ85+Δ86 (PL. 36-1, 98)

The overall length of this block is unknown due to damage. The height is 0.514 m and the present length is 1.783 m. The present width, which seems to be almost equal to the original width, at the top is 0.421 m and the width at the bottom is 0.385 m. The height of the taenia is 0.066 m and the depth is 0.036 m. At the top, there is a dowel hole in the center and three clamp holes at the edge of the back. The reconstructed dimensions of the reglae are length 0.375 m, height 0.030 m. The diameter of the guttae is 0.030 m and the height is 0.017 m.

Δ166 (PL. 36-2, 99)

The original length of this block is unknown due to damage. The height is 0.511 m and the present length is 1.060 m. The width is 0.475 m at the top and 0.389 m at the bottom. The height of the taenia is 0.065 m, and the width is 0.036 m. On the front surface, fragments of stucco can be confirmed. At the top is a square dowel hole which measures 0.070 m on one side with a depth of 0.038 m. The height of the regla is 0.044 m and the width is 0.036 m. The diameter of the guttae is 0.035 m. The axial distance of guttae is 0.06 m and the height is 0.016m.

Δ294 (PL. 36-3, 100)

The original length and width of this block are unknown due to damage. The present height is 0.514 m and length is 0.653 m. The present width is 0.375 m. Because this block is a simple block with no guttae or taenia, and its height is the same as that of the architrave, it is believed to have been a backer block of architrave. Only one of the edges remains intact and it is cut at 45°, so it was probably used at the corner of the architrave. A clamp hole is seen on the top of the 45° angled part.

11. Frieze blocks
Δ107 (PL. 37-1, No illustration)

The block is severely broken and the upper half is missing, and a portion of the triglyph is remaining. The overall size is unclear due to damage, but the present length is 0.942 m, the depth 0.668 m, and the height 0.36 m. The part at the back on which the ceiling was set is partially remaining, the height of which is 0.190 m. The back part of the metope is also remaining, and from this we know the depth of the metope part to be 0.565 m.

Δ159 (PL. 37-2, 101)

This block is a fragmentary block, and has part of the triglyph and metope. The part of the triglyph remains at the front, but the right side and back part corresponding to the triglyph are missing. The left side of the triglyph is a vertical joint face. The original length and depth of the block are unknown, but the present measurements are 0.630 m and 0.580 m respectively at most. The top face is weathered and rough finishing, and both the top and bottom faces are partially remaining. The overall height is 0.578 m. One triglyph unit measures 0.115 m to 0.128 m, and the front length of the whole triglyph is 0.369 m. The depth from the metope to the back face is 0.470 m. Part of the back extends out at a right angle with respect to the triglyph. The width of the protruding part is 0.235 m. The original length of the protruding part is unknown due to damage, but at present it extends 0.073 m. On the part of the block that does not protrude, some processing markings are left for setting the ceiling. No dowel holes or clamp holes are seen on the top.

Appendix: Block Catalog

Δ210 (PL. 37-3, No illustration)

This is a corner triglyph block. The front and bottom of this block are greatly damaged, so the original heights of the triglyph and the block are both unknown. The present length is 0.900 m and the height is 0.536 m. At the back there are some processing marks for setting the ceiling. Also, there is a cut-away part at 45° on one of the sides, and one clamp hole in the center. There is a rectangular dowel hole on the top, and near the 45° cutaway part there is a square dowel hole measuring 0.080 m.

Δ279 (PL. 37-4, 102-1)

This block is an important triglyph fragment with an extended corner part at the front and on one of the sides. The present block measures 0.335 m in height and 0.403 m in width. A unit of the triglyph were 0.129 m to 0.131 m in width. On the bottom is a square dowel hole measuring 0.066 m with a depth of 0.036 m.

Δ293 (PL. 37-5, 103)

This is a fragmentary frieze block with triglyph and metope. The front part has many scratches at the bottom made by a tractor. The damage is extensive, but the top and bottom, and also the 45° angled joint face, are partially preserved, making it a very important block. Parts of the triglyph can be found at the front left edge. The present overall length is 1.060 m and the width is 0.776 m. The height is 0.589 m. The width of the metope part is 0.565 m, and a unit of the triglyph is about 0.130 m in width, so the overall triglyph width was 0.390 m. The crowning at the top of the front was 0.080 m in height. On the back at the bottom, there is a section to set the ceiling measuring 0.170 m in width and 0.193 m in height. Much of the back right edge is cut away at 45°, meaning that it connected to another corner frieze block which was cut at 45°. The width of the protruding part on the right edge is 0.365 m. From these dimension and shape, it is believed this block had two triglyphs which met on the external corner of the frieze as well as block Δ279. On the top, there is a dowel hole measuring 0.085 m × 0.072 m with a depth of 0.047 m.

Δ406 (PL. 38-1, 104)

This is a frieze block on which parts of the triglyph and metope remain. It is heavily damaged, and only the top front and one side partially remain. The present height, length and width are 0.516 m, 0.711 m and 0.597 m respectively. The top and bottom of the front triglyph are missing but their overall shape clearly remains. The length of the triglyphs is 0.375 m. On the top there is a dowel hole and a pry hole.

Δ773 (PL. 38-2, 102-2)

This is a small fragment of the triglyph, used at the edge of a frieze block. The present size is 0.241 m × 0.303 m, and the height is 0.391 m.

12. Cornice blocks

Δ380 (PL. 38-3, 105)

This block is a fragment and is heavily damaged. The overall dimensions are unknown. However, it is the only cornice block that shows the angle of the roof, so it is a very important piece. There is a rise at a position about 0.040 m from the bottom, and there is cyma reversa moulding about 0.022 m above this. The protruding part is 0.0275 m. The mutules are almost completely missing but the internal distance between them measures 0.098 m. The ceiling slope is 1/4.48.

Δ717 (PL. 38-4, 106)

This fragment is part of the cornice geison, on which mutule and some guttae could be recognized. The horizontal width of the mutule is 0.201 m, and the height is 0.024 m. The internal distance between them is 0.093 m. Due to damage, their length could not be confirmed. The diameter of the guttae is 0.039 m and the distance between them (measured from the inside) was 0.031 m, but the height could not be confirmed.

13. Sima blocks
Δ135 (PL. 38-5, 135)

This block measures 0.653 m in length and 0.124 m in height. The width is unknown due to damage but at present the maximum width is 0.310 m. The rise part outside the building is curved and extends far outward, and the tip is damaged. The inside is straight and slanted. Seen from the outside, the right edge of the inside has a notch. A clamp hole can also be seen at the outside edge of the top.

Bibliography

Abbreviations

AA: Archäologischer Anzeiger
AJA: American Journal of Archaeology
AM: Mitteilungen des Deutschen Archäologischen Instituts, Athenische Abteilung
BCH: Bulletin de Correspondence Hellénique
BSA: Annual of the British School at Athens
Ergon: Έργον της εν Αθήναις Αρχαιολογικής Εταιρείας
IstMitt: Mitteilungen des Deutschen Archäologischen Instituts, Istanbüler Abteilung
Prakt: Πρακτικά της εν Αθήναις Αρχαιολογικής Εταιρείας
Pausanias: Pausanias, *Description of Greece,* Jones, W. H. S. Jones, H. A. Ormerod (trans.): Loeb Classical Library, Cambridge/Mass., 1977.
Vitruvius: Vitruvius. *The Ten Books on Architecture*, M. H. Morgan (trans.), New York, 1980

Adler 1966: F. Adler, W. Dörpfeld, F. Graeber and P. Graef, *Die Baudenkmäler von Olympia,* textband II, Amsterdam, 1966. Rep. (Die Ergebnisse der von Deutschen Reich veranstalteten Ausgrabung, edit. E. Curtius and F. Adler. Originally published in Berlin in 1890-1897)
Allen 1911: G. Allen and L. D. Caskey, "The East Stoa in the Asclepieum at Athens", *AJA* 15, 1911, pp. 32-43.
Bacon 1921: F. H. Bacon, J. T. Clarke and R. Koldewey, *Investigations at Assos 1881-3*, Cambridge/Mass., 1921.
Bankel 1993: H. Bankel, *Der Spätarchaische Tempel der Aphaia*, Berlin, 1993,
Bell 1980 : M. Bell, "Stylobate and Roof in the Olympieion at Akragas", *AJA* 84, 1980, pp. 359-372.
Berges 2000: D. Berges and N. Tuna, "Das Apollonheiligtum von Emecik. Bericht über die Ausgrabungen 1998 und 1999", mit Einem Beitrag von Regina Attula, *IstMitt* 50, 2000, pp. 171-214
Birtachas 2008: Π. Μπίρταχα, *Μεσσήνη: Το Ωδείο και το Ανατολικό Πρόπυλο του Ασκληπιείου*, Athens, 2008.
Bohn 1885: R. Bohn, *Das Heiligtum der Athena Polias Nike-phoros: Altertümer von Pergamon,* Bd. 2, Berlin, 1885.
Bohn 1889: R. Born, *Altertümer von Aegae*, Berlin, 1889
Böhringer 1937: E. Böhringer and F. Krauss, *Das Temenos für den Herrscherkult: Altertümer von Pergamon,* Bd. 9, Berlin, 1937
Broneer 1954: O. Broneer, *The South Stoa and its Roman Successors: Corinth; Results of Excavations;* Vol.1, Pt. 4, Princeton, 1954
Charboneaux 1925: T. H. Charboneaux, *La Tholos; Fouilles de Delphe II, Text*, Paris, 1925
Clarke 1902: J. T. Clarke, F. H. Bacon and R. Koldewey, *Investigations at Assos*, London, 1902.
Cooper 1992: F. A. Cooper, *The Temple of Apollo Bassitas,* vol. IV, Princeton, 1992.

Coulton 1964: J. J. Coulton, "The stoa by the Harbour at Perachora", *BSA* 59, 1964, pp. 100-131.

Coulton 1968: J. J. Coulton, "The Stoa at the Amphiaraion, Oropos", *BSA* 63, 1968, pp. 147-183.

Coulton 1976: J. J. Coulton, *The Architectural Development of the Greek Stoa*, Oxford, 1976.

Coulton 1977: J. J. Coulton, *Greeek Architects at Work - Problems of Structure and Design*, London, 1977.

Coulton 2002: J. J. Coulton, "Why build Doric? The Choice of Orders in Hellenistic Architecture", Symposium for International Collaborative Studies on Ancient Messene (J. Ito ed.), Kumamoto University Architectural Mission to Greece, pp. 49-55, 2008.

Courby 1924: F. Courby and Ch. Picard, *Recherches Archéologiques à Stratos d'Acarnanie*, Paris, 1924.

Dinsmoor 1910: W. B. Dinsmoor, "The Choragic Monument of Nicias", *AJA* 14, 1919, pp. 459-484.

Dinsmoor 1941: W. B. Dinsmoor, "Observation on the Hephaisteion", *Hesperia*, Supplement V, 1941, pp. 1-171.

Dinsmoor 1975: W. B. Dinsmoor, *The Architecture of Ancient Greece*, New York, 1975.

Döerpfeld 1902: W. Dörpfeld, "Die 1900-1901 in Pergamon Gefundene Bauwerk (Tafel I-VI), *AM* 27, 1902, pp. 10-43.

Dugas 1924: C. Dugas, J. Berchmans and M. Clemmensen, *Le Sanctuaire d'Aléa Athéna à Tegée au 4 Siècle*, Paris, 1924.

Dyggve 1948: E. Dyggve, *Das Laphrion der Tempelbezirk von Kalydon*, Kopenhagen, 1948.

Dyggve 1960: E. Dyggve, *Le sanctuaire d' Athena Lindia et l'architecture Lindienne.* (Fouilles et recherches III 1), Lindos, 1960.

Furtwängler 1906 : A. Furtwängler, *Aegina: Das Heiligtum der Aphaia*, Band 1-2, München, 1906.

Ginouvès 1956: R. Ginouvès, "Note sur quelques relations numériques dans la construction des fondations de temples grecs", *BCH* 80, 1956, pp. 104-117.

Ginouvès 1992: R. Ginouvès and R. Martin, *Dictionnaire Methodique de l'Architecture Grecque et Romanine II*, Paris, 1992.

Goodchild 1971: R. G. Goodchild, *Kyrene und Apollonia*, Zürich, 1971.

Hayashida 2013: N. Hayashida, R. Yoshitake and J. Ito, *Architectural Study of the Asklepieion at Ancient Messene*, (J. Ito ed.), Fukuoka, 2013.

Hill 1966: B.W. Hill, L. T. Lands and C. K. Williams, *The Temple of Zeus at Nemea*, New Jersey, 1966.

Höpfner 1969: W. Höpfner, "Zum Entwurf des Athena-Tempels in Ilion", *AM* 84, 1969, pp. 165-181.

Ito 2002: *Theory and Practice of Site Planning in Classical Sanctuaries*, Fukuoka, 2002.

Ito 2004: J. Ito and Y. Hayashida, K. Horiuchi, Y. Okada, K. Hoshi, T. Katsumata, A. N. Ota, *New Measurement and Observation of the Treasury of Massaliotes, the Doric Treasury and the Tholos in the Sanctuary of Athena Pronaia at Delphi*, Fukuoka, 2004.

Lacoste 1920: M. H. Lacoste, *La Terrasse du Temple : Fouilles de Delphes,* Tome 2, fasc. 1, Paris, 1920.

Lechat 1895: H. Lechat and A. Defrasse, *Epidaure*, Paris, 1895.

Lehmann 1969: P. W. Lehmann, *The Hieron: Samothrace,* Vol. 3, Pt.1-3 (1-2; Text and Plates 3), London, 1969.

Lloyd 1972: S. Lloyd, H.W. Müller, R. Martin, *Architettura Mediterraneana Preromana*, Venice, 1972.

Love 1970: I. C. Love, "A Preliminary Report of the Excavations at Knidos", 1969, *AJA* 74, 1969, pp. 149-155.

Luraghi 2008: *The Ancient Messenians; Constructions of Ethnicity and Memory*, Cambridge/Mass., 2008.

Kawärau 1914: G. Kawärau and A. Rhem, *Das Delphinion in Milet: Milet,* Bd.1, Heft 3, Berlin, 1914.

Knackfuss 1908: H. Knackfuss, *Das Rathaus von Milet: Milet,* Bd.1, Heft 2, Berlin, 1908.

Knell 1971: H. Knell, "Eine beobachtung am Asklepiostempel in Epidauros", *AA* 83, 1971, pp. 206-210.

Knell 1973: H. Knell, "Der Artemistempel in Kalydon und der Poseidontempel in Molykreion", *AA* 85, 1973, pp. 448-461.

Knell 1978: H. Knell, Troizen, "Temple des Hippolytos", *AA* 90, 1978, pp. 397-406.

Knell 1983: H. Knell, "Lepreon der Tempel der Demeter", *AM* 98, 1983, pp. 113-147.

Martin 1959: R. Martin, *L'agora. Études Thasiennes VI*, Paris, 1959.

Martin 1965: R. Martin, *Manuel d'architecture grecque* 1, *Matériaux et techniques*, Paris, 1965.

Martin 1974: R. Martin, *Greek Architecture: Architecture of Crete, Greece, and the Greek World*, New York, 1974.

Marzolff 1976: P. Marzolff, *Der Tempel auf der Agora*, in V. Milojcic and D. Theocharis, *Demetrias I*, Bonn, 1976.

Mertens 1984: D. Mertens, *Der Tempel von Segesta und die Dorische Tempelbaukunst des Griechischen Westens in Klassischer Zeit*, Sonderschriften, Bd.6, Mainz am Rhein, 1984.

Metzger 1979: H. Metzger, *La Stèle Trilingue du Letoon: Fouilles de Xanthos,* Tome 6, Paris, 1979.

Müth-Herda 2007 : Müth-Herda, S., *Eigene Wege: topographie und Stadtplan von Messene in spätklassischer und hellnistischer Zeit*, Rahtens, 2007. (Originally published as a dissertaion in 2005 in Berlin.)

Norman 1984: N. J. Norman, "The Temple of Athena at Tegea", *AJA* 88, 1984, pp. 169-194.

Orlandos 1978: A. K. Orlandos, *The Architecture of the Parthenon*, Athen, 1978.

Robert 1952: F. Robert, *Trois Sanctuaires sur le Rivage Occidental : L'Exploration Archéologique de Délos,* Fasc.20, Paris, 1952.

Schazmann 1932: P. Schazmann, *Asklepieion. Baubeschreibung und Baugeschichte*, Berlin, 1932.

Shoe 1936: L.T. Shoe, *Profiles of Greek Mouldings*, Cambridge/Mass., 1936.

Sioumpara 2006: E. P. Sioumpara, *Der Asklepiostempel von Messene auf der Peloponnes*, Dissertation at Free University of Berlin, Berlin, 2006.

Sioumpara 2010: E. P. Sioumpara, "Innovations on Doric Hellenistic Temple-Architecture: The case of Asclepius Temple at Messene of the Peloponesos", International Symposium for Ancient Messene and Phigalia, (edit. J. Ito), Kyoto, 2010, pp. 11-19.

Sioumpara 2011: E. P. *Sioumpara, Der Asklepios-tempel von Messene auf der Peloponnes*, (Athenaia 1), München, 2011 (Dissertation which was submitted to Free University of Berlin in 2006. See Sioumpara 2006. All the notes on her book here are from for the publication in 2011.)

Stucchi 1965: S. Stucchi, *L'Agora di Cirene 1; I Lati Nord ed Est della Platea Inferiore*, Roma, 1965.

Stucchi 1975: S. Stucchi, *Architettura Cirenaica*, Roma, 1975.

Themelis 2002. P. Themelis, "Ανασκαφή Μεσσηνής", *Prakt* 2002, pp. 34-46.

Themelis 2003: P. Themelis, "Ανασκαφή Μεσσηνής", *Prakt* 2003, pp. 25-44.

Themelis 2004: P. Themelis, "Ανασκαφή Μεσσηνής", *Prakt* 2004, pp. 29-47.

Themelis 2005: P. Themelis, "Ανασκαφή Μεσσηνής", *Prakt* 2005, pp. 29-47.

Themelis 2006: P. Themelis, "Ανασκαφή Μεσσηνής", *Prakt* 2006, pp. 49-52.

Themelis 2007: P. Themelis, "Ανασκαφή Μεσσηνής", *Prakt* 2007, pp. 509-528.

Themelis 2008: P. Themelis, "Ανασκαφή Μεσσηνής", *Prakt* 2008, pp. 31-50.
Themelis 2009: P. Themelis, "Ανασκαφή Μεσσηνής", *Prakt* 2009, pp. 61-98.
Themelis 2009/2010: P. Themelis, "Ancient Messene; An Important Site in SW Peloponnese", *AAIA Bulletin*, 2009-2010, pp. 28-37.
Themelis 2010a: P. G. Themelis, "Ανασκαφή Μεσσηνής", *Prak* 2010, pp. 61-98, pp. 53-64.
Themelis 2010b: P. G. Themelis, "Die Agora von Messene", Neue Forschungen zu griechischen Städten und Heiligtümern. H. Frielinghaus/J.Stoszeck, ed. Festschrift für Burkhardt Wesenberg zum 65. Geburtstag, pp. 105-125.
Themelis 2011: P. G. Themelis, "Ανασκαφή Μεσσηνής", *Prakt* 2011, pp. 35-40.
Themelis 2012a: P. G. Themelis, "Ανασκαφή Μεσσηνής", *Prakt* 2012, pp. 53-61.
Themelis 2012b: P. G. Themelis, "The Agora of Messene" (Chankowski,V.,/ Karvosnos, P., eds), *Tout vendre, tout acheter. Structures et équipements des marchés antiques*, Scripta Antica 42, Bordeaux, 2012, pp. 35-45.
Tomlinson 1983: R. A.Tomlinson, *Epidauros*, Austin, 1983.
Travlos 1971: I. Travlos, *Pictorial Dictionary of Ancient Athens*, New York, 1971.
Will 1955: E. Will, *L'Exploration Archéologique de Délos,* Fasc.22 ; *Le Dôdékathéon*, Paris, 1955.
Winter 1983: J. E. Winter and F. E. Winter, "The date of temples near Kourno in Lakonia", *AJA* 87, 1983, pp. 3-10.

List of Figures

Fig. 2-1 Location of Messene.
Fig. 2-2 Location of the Temple of Messene at the Agora.
Fig. 2-3 Section of the Agora.
Fig. 2-4 Site of the Temple of Messene.
Fig. 3-1 Reconstruction of the corner of the stylobate.
Fig. 3-2 Reconstruction of the peristyle plan and east-west section.
Fig. 3-3 Plan of the cella wall and toichobate block types.
Fig. 3-4 Threshold and dividing wall of the pronaos.
Fig. 3-5 Position of the blocks for threshold and dividing wall of the pronaos.
Fig. 3-6 Position of block Δ20 for dividing wall of the pronaos.
Fig. 3-7 Reconstruction of the south side wall of the pronaos.
Fig. 3-8 Reconstruction of the opisthodomos side wall of the southwest cella.
Fig. 3-9 Combination patterns of toichobate blocks of naos side wall.
Fig. 3-10 Position of the toichobate blocks on the naos side wall.
Fig. 3-11 Position of the toichobate blocks of the cella wall.
Fig. 3-12 Position of the orthostate blocks of the cella wall.
Fig. 3-13 Position of the orthostate blocks at the southwest corner of the cella wall.
Fig. 3-14 Position of the toichobate blocks (looking up view).
Fig. 3-15 Threshold block Δ130 for pronaos.
Fig. 3-16 Threshold block ΔX6 for pronaos.
Fig. 3-17 Threshold for pronaos.
Fig. 3-18 Reconstructed threshold for pronaos.
Fig. 3-19 Reconstructed plan of the Temple of Messene.
Fig. 3-20 Architrave block Δ85+Δ86.
Fig. 3-21 Architrave block Δ166.
Fig. 3-22 Corner frieze block Δ293.

Fig. 3-23 Position of triglyph block Δ159.
Fig. 3-24 Reconstruction of cornice and sima.
Fig. 3-25 Mutule of cornice block Δ717.
Fig. 3-26 System of entablature at the corner.
Fig. 3-27 Reconstruction of the order.
Fig. 4-1 Distribution of Doric peripteral temples (4th – 1st cent. BC).
Fig. 4-2 Proportional analysis of columns (cf. PL.122).
Fig. 4-3 Proportional analysis of entablature.
Fig. 4-4 Reconstruction of the west elevation of the Temple of Messene.
Fig. 4-5 Toichobate and orthostate of the Temples of Messene (left) and the Temple of Asklepios (right).
Fig. 4-6 Crepis Δ555 (left) and reconstructed stylobate (right).
Fig. 4-7 Reconstructed orthostate Δ6 (left) and Δ144 (right).
Fig. 4-8 Profile of the Doric capital (Δ32).
Fig. 4-9 Cyma reversa on the top of toichobate (Δ47) and profile (Δ349).
Fig. 4-10 Combination of Cyma reversa and scotia on the threshold.

Contributors: Society of Messenian Archaeological Studies; Fig. 2-2; N. Yasui: Figs. 2-1, 2-3, 2-4, 3-1~3-3, 3-5~3-14, 3-17~3-27; J. Ito. 3-4, 3-15, 3-16, English translation.

List of Tables

Table 2-1 Dimensions of crepis blocks (m).
Table 2-2 Dimensions of stylobate blocks (m).
Table 2-3 Dimensions of inner stylobate blocks (m).
Table 2-4 Dimensions of floor paving blocks (m).
Table 2-5 Dimensions of toichobate blocks for antae (m).
Table 2-6 Dimensions of toichobate L-shaped blocks for intersection (m).
Table 2-7 Dimensions of toichobate blocks for the naos side wall (m).
Table 2-8 Dimensions of toichobate blocks for opisthodomos dividing wall (m).
Table 2-9 Dimensions of toichobate blocks for pronaos and opisthodomos side walls (m).
Table 2-10 Dimensions of toichobate blocks for pronaos dividing walls (m).
Table 2-11 Dimensions of orthostate blocks for antae (m).
Table 2-12 Dimensions of orthostate blocks for intersection (m).
Table 2-13 Dimensions of orthostate blocks for pronaos side walls (m).
Table 2-14 Dimensions of orthostate blocks for pronaos dividing wall (m).
Table 2-15 Dimensions of orthostate blocks for opisthodomos dividing wall (m).
Table 2-16 Dimensions of unidentified orthostate block (m).
Table 2-17 Dimensions of orthostate block (m).
Table 2-18 Average block length (m).
Table 2-19 Dimensions for column drums (m).
Table 3-1 Dimensions of normal stylobate blocks (m).
Table 3-2 Length of toichobate blocks (m).
Table 3-3 Dimensions of flooring blocks (m).
Table 3-4 Estimated length of wall blocks (m).
Table 4-1 Size of Doric peripteral temples (4th -1st cent. BC).
Table 4-2 Comparison of size and proportion with the Temple of Asklepios.

Contributors: All the tables were made by N. Yasui. English translation by J. Ito.

PLATES

LIST OF PLATES

Photographs

1
    Temple of Messene, as excavated. Overview (Courtesy of Society of Messenian Archaeological Studies)

2
1. Temple of Messene. View from the northwest.
2. Temple of Messene. View from the east.

3
1. West staircase. View from the west.
2. West staircase. View from the southwest.

4
1. Foundation of the west staircase. View from the south.
2. East front. View from the south.

5
1. East front. View from the west.
2. East front. View from the southeast.

6
1. Foundation blocks of poros for the east pteron.
2. Foundation of the slope on the east front of the Temple.

7
1. North side of the Temple. Foundation of rubble masonry.
2. South side of the Temple. Bedrock for pteron foundation.

8
1. Temple of Messene. View from the northwest after reconstruction.
2. Temple of Messene. View from the southeast after reconstruction

9
1. Temple of Messene. View from the west after reconstruction.
2. Temple of Messene. View from the east after reconstruction.

10
1. Opisthodomos with separating wall after reconstruction. View from the west.
2. Pronaos with threshold to the naos after reconstruction. View from the east.

11
1. Opisthodomos. View from the southwest after reconstruction.
2. Pronaos. View from the northeast after reconstruction.

12
1. South cella wall after reconstruction.
2. Northeast corner of the colonnade after reconstruction.

13
1. Threshold of the naos.
2. View from the southwest with the neighboring building.

14
1. Colonnade of the building to the west of the Temple of Messene.
2. Colonnade and inside of the building to the west of the Temple of Messene.

15
1. Treasury to the south of the Temple of Messene.
2. Arsinoe Fountain at the northwest corner of the agora.

16
1. Crepis block, Δ50.
2. Crepis block, Δ52.
3. Crepis block, Δ59.
4. Crepis block, Δ157.
5. Crepis block, Δ181.
6. Crepis block, Δ555.
7. Crepis block, Δ556.

17
1. Stylobate block, Δ43.
2. Stylobate block, Δ56.
3. Stylobate block, Δ64+Δ161+Δ383.
4. Stylobate block, Δ75.
5. Stylobate block, Δ96a+b.
6. Stylobate block, Δ117+Δ118.

18
1. Stylobate block, Δ130.
2. Stylobate block, Δ147.
3. Stylobate block, Δ267.
4. Stylobate block, Δ353.
5. Stylobate block, Δ454.
6. Stylobate block, Δ590

19
1. Stylobate block, Δ670.
2. Stylobate block, ΔX4.
3. Stylobate block, ΔX5.
4. Stylobate block, ΔX9.
5. Stylobate block, ΔX10.

20
1. Trace of column fluting on the stylobate block, Δ43.
2. Floor pavement block, Δ55.
3. Floor pavement block, ΔX2.

21
1. Toichobate block for anta, Δ47.
2. Toichobate block for anta, Δ223.
3. Toichobate block for anta, Δ349.
4. Toichobate block for anta, Δ577+Δ580.
5. Cyma reversa moulding. Toichobate block, Δ47.

22
1. Toichobate L-shaped block for intersection, Δ3.
2. Toichobate L-shaped block for intersection, Δ9.
3. Toichobate L-shaped block for intersection, Δ140.
4. Toichobate L-shaped block for intersection, Δ145.
5. Toichobate L-shaped block for intersection, Δ1.
6. Toichobate L-shaped block for intersection, Δ8.

23
1. Toichobate block for naos side wall, Δ15.
2. Toichobate block for naos side wall, Δ16.
3. Toichobate block for naos side wall, Δ18.
4. Toichobate block for naos side wall, Δ48.
5. Toichobate block for naos side wall, Δ143.
6. Toichobate block for naos side wall, Δ465.

24
1. Toichobate block for naos side wall, Δ575+Δ576+Δ579.
2. Toichobate block for opisthodomos separating wall, Δ2.
3. Toichobate block for opisthodomos separating wall, Δ14.
4. Toichobate block for opisthodomos separating wall, Δ169.
5. Toichobate block for pronaos south wall, Δ21.
6. Toichobate block for opisthodomos south wall, Δ49.

25
1. Toichobate block for pronaos south wall, Δ131.
2. Toichobate block for opisthodomos south wall, Δ220.

List of Plates

   3. Toichobate block for pronaos north wall, Δ243.
   4. Toichobate block for pronaos south wall, ΔX8.
   5. Toichobate L-shaped block for pronaos separating wall, Δ11.
   6. Toichobate L-shaped block for pronaos separating wall, Δ17.

26
   1. Threshold block, Δ13+Δ133+Δ477+ΔX4, Δ119.
   2. Threshold block details. North end.
   3. Threshold block details. South end.

27
   1. Threshold block, Δ572.
   2. Threshold block, ΔX6.
   3. Threshold block, ΔX7.

28
   1. Orthostate block for anta, Δ4+Δ568+Δ574+ΔX3.
   2. Orthostate block for anta, Δ6.
   3. Orthostate block for anta, Δ22.
   4. Orthostate block for anta, Δ40+Δ45.
   5. Orthostate block for intersection, Δ19.
   6. Orthostate block for intersection, Δ144.

29
   1. Orthostate block for pronaos side wall, Δ27.
   2. Orthostate block for pronaos separating wall, Δ20.
   3. Orthostate block for opisthodomos separating wall, Δ7.
   4. Orthostate block, Δ98+Δ98a.
   5. Wall block, Δ68.
   6. Wall block, Δ105+105α.

30
   1. Column drum, Δ61.
   2. Column drum, Δ62.
   3. Column drum, Δ63.
   4. Column drum, Δ67.
   5. Column drum, Δ84.
   6. Column drum, Δ87.

31
   1. Column drum, Δ88.
   2. Column drum, Δ111.
   3. Column drum, Δ121.
   4. Column drum, Δ122.
   5. Column drum, Δ124.
   6. Column drum, Δ126.

32
   1. Column drum, Δ127.
   2. Column drum, Δ128.
   3. Column drum, Δ148.
   4. Column drum, Δ149.
   5. Column drum, Δ150.
   6. Column drum, Δ165.

33
   1. Column drum, Δ167.
   2. Column drum, Δ168.
   3. Column drum, Δ190.
   4. Column drum, Δ191.
   5. Column drum, Δ193.
   6. Column drum, Δ653.

34
   1. Top of column drum, Δ129c.
   2. Dowel hole on the side of a column drum, unnumbered.
   3. Remains of stucco, Δ127.

35
   1. Doric capital, Δ32.
   2. Doric capital, ΔX1.
   3. Top of Doric capital, ΔX1.
   4. Doric capital details, Δ32.

36
   1. Architrave block, Δ85+Δ86.
   2. Architrave block, Δ166.
   3. Architrave backer block, Δ294.

37
   1. Frieze block, Δ107.
   2. Frieze block, Δ159.
   3. Frieze block, Δ210.
   4. Frieze block, Δ279.
   5. Frieze block, Δ293.

38
1. Frieze block, Δ406.
2. Frieze block, Δ773.
3. Cornice block, Δ380.
4. Cornice block, Δ717.
5. Sima block, Δ135.

Contributores for photographs: Ito took almost all the photographs except a few one taken by N. Yasui.

Drawings

39	Crepis block, Δ50.	64	Toichobate block for naos side wall, Δ18.
40	Crepis block, Δ59.	65	Toichobate block for naos side wall, Δ48.
41	Crepis block, Δ181.	66	Toichobate block for naos side wall, Δ143.
42	Crepis block, Δ555.	67	Toichobate block for naos side wall, Δ465.
43	Crepis block, Δ556.	68	Toichobate block for naos side wall, Δ575+Δ576+Δ579.
44	Stylobate block, Δ43.	69	Toichobate block for opisthodomos separating wall, Δ2.
45	Stylobate block, Δ64+Δ161+Δ383.	70	Toichobate block for opisthodomos separating wall, 14.
46	Stylobate block, Δ96a+b.	71	Toichobate block for opisthodomos separating wall, Δ169.
47	Stylobate block, Δ117+Δ118.	72	Toichobate block for pronaos side wall, Δ21.
48	Stylobate block, Δ130.	73	Toichobate block for opisthodomos side wall, Δ49.
49	Stylobate block, Δ147.	74	Toichobate block for pronaos side wall, Δ131.
50	Flooring block, Δ55.	75	Toichobate block for pisthodomos side wall, Δ220.
51	Flooring block, ΔX2.	76	Toichobate block for pronaos side wall, Δ243.
52	Toichobate block for anta, Δ47.	77	Toichobate block for pronaos side wall, ΔX8.
53	Toichobate block for anta, Δ223	78	Toichobate L-shaped block for pronaos separating wall, Δ11.
54	Toichobate block for anta, Δ349.	79	Toichobate L-shaped block for pronaos separating wall, Δ17.
55	Toichobate block for anta, Δ577+Δ580.	80	Threshold block,
56	Toichobate L-shaped block for intersection, Δ3.		
57	Toichobate L-shaped block for intersection, Δ9.		
58	Toichobate L-shaped block for intersection, Δ140.		
59	Toichobate L-shaped block for intersection, Δ145.		
60	Toichobate block for naos side wall, Δ1.		
61	Toichobate block for naos side wall, Δ8.		
62	Toichobate block for naos side wall, Δ15.		
63	Toichobate block for naos side wall, Δ16.		

List of Plates

Δ13+Δ133+Δ477+ΔX4, Δ119.
81 Threshold block, Δ572, ΔX6.
82 Orthostate block for anta, Δ4+Δ568+Δ574+ΔX3.
83 Orthostate block for anta, Δ6.
84 Orthostate block for anta, Δ22.
85 Orthostate block for anta, Δ40+Δ45.
86 Orthostate block for intersection, Δ19.
87 Orthostate block for intersection, Δ144.
88 Orthostate block for pronaos side wall, Δ27.
89 Orthostate block for pronaos separating wall, Δ20.
90 Orthostate block for opisthodomos separating wall, Δ7.
91 Orthostate block, Δ98+Δ98a.
92 Wall block, Δ68.
93 Wall block, Δ105+Δ105α.
94 Column drum, Δ127.
95 Doric capital, Δ32.
96 Doric capital, ΔX1.
97 Doric capital, restored, ΔX1.
98 Architrave block, Δ85+Δ86.
99 Architrave block, Δ166.
100 Architrave block, Δ294.
101 Frieze block, Δ159.
102 Frieze block, Δ279, Δ773.
103 Frieze block, Δ293.
104 Frieze block, Δ406.
105 Cornice block, 380.
106 Cornice block, Δ717.
107 Sima block, Δ135.
108 General plan of ancient Messene. *(Courtesy of the Society of Messenian Archaeological Studies.)*
109 Central part of ancient Messene. *(Courtesy of the Society of Messenian Archaeological Studies.)*
110 Plan of Temple of Messene, as excavated in 2003. *(Courtesy of the Society of Messenian Archaeological Studies.)*
111 Plan of Temple of Messene, as cleaned in 2007.
112 Reconstructed plan of Temple of Messene, superimposed on the plan as excavated.
113 Sections of temple platform.
114 Reconstructed plan of Temple of Messene.
115 Reconstructed elevations of Temple of Messene.
116 Placement of toichobate blocks.
117 Placement of toichobate blocks. (from the bottom looking-up)
118 Placement of orthostate blocks.
119 Details of Doric order.
120 Doric temples from 4th to 1st century BC.
121 Other Doric buildings except temples 4th to 1st Century BC.
122 Column proportions of Doric temples and buildings referenced.
123 Entablature proportions of Doric temples and other buildings referenced.

Contributors for drawings: J. Ito, 39, 45, 47, 55, 65, 80, 94, 103; N. Yasui, 49, 62, 63, 75, 81, 83, 86, 88, 91, 85+86, 98, 100, 105; R. Hayashida 107; R. Yoshitake 61, 64, 67, 72, 76, 82, 105; M. Kunitake 42, 51, 66, 69, 70, 71; A. Kato 41, 56, 79, 89, 93; Y. Kameyama 48, 50, 53, 58, 59, 74, 87, 92; S. Sueyasu 40, 52, 57, 60, 78, 90, 102; I. Koyanagi 44, 46, 84, 85, 95, 99, 106; Y. Kasho 96, 97; K. Kimoto 104; K. Ogawa, 54; S. Sokunthy 77; S. Nakanomaru 68; T. Totake 43.

Plates

PLATE 1

1. Temple of Messene, as escavated. Overview. (Courtesy of Society for Messenian Archaeological Studies.)

PLATE 2

1. Temple of Messene. View from the northwest.

2. Temple of Messene. View from the east.

Plates

PLATE 3

1. West staircase. View from the west.

2. West staircase. View from the southwest.

PLATE 4

1. Foundation of west staircase. View from the south.

2. East front. View fron the south.

1. East front. View from the west.

2. East front. View from the southeast.

1. Foundation blocks of poros at the east pteron.

2. Foundation of the slope on the east front of the Temple.

PLATE 7

1. North side of the Temple. Foundation of rubble masonry.

2. South side of the Temple. Bedrock for pteron foundation.

PLATE 8

1. Temple of Messene. View from the northwest after reconstruction.

2. Temple of Messene. View from the southeast after reconstruction.

Plates

PLATE 9

1. Temple of Messene. View from the west after reconstruction.

2. Temple of Messene. View from the east after reconstruction.

1. Opisthodomos with separating wall. View from the west after reconstruction.

2. Pronaos with threshold to the naos. View from the east after reconstruction.

Plates

PLATE 11

1. Opisthodomos. View from the southwest after reconstruction.

2. Pronaos. View fron the northeast after reconstruction.

PLATE 12

1. South cella wall after reconstruction.

2. Northeast corner of the colonnade after reconstruction.

PLATE 13

1. Threshold of the naos.

2. View from the southwest with the neighboring building.

PLATE 14

1. Colonnade of the building to the west of the Temple of Messene.

2. Colonnade and inside of the building to the west of the Temple of Messene.

1. Treasury to the south of the Temple of Messene.

2. Arsinoe Fountain at the northwest corner of the agora.

PLATE 16

1. Crepis block, Δ50.

2. Crepis block, Δ52.

3. Crepis block, Δ59.

4. Crepis block, Δ157.

5. Crepis block, Δ181.

6. Crepis block, Δ555.

7. Crepis block, Δ556.

Plates

PLATE 17

1. Stylobate block, Δ43.

2. Stylobate block, Δ56.

3. Stylobate block, Δ64+Δ161+Δ383.

4. Stylobate block, Δ75.

5. Stylobate block, Δ96a+b.

6. Stylobate block, Δ117+Δ118.

PLATE 18

1. Stylobate block, Δ130.

2. Stylobate block, Δ147.

3. Stylobate block, Δ267.

4. Stylobate block, Δ353.

5. Stylobate block, Δ454.

6. Stylobate block, Δ590.

Plates

PLATE 19

1. Stylobate block, Δ670.

2. Stylobate block, ΔX4.

3. Stylobate block, ΔX5.

4. Stylobate block, ΔX9.

5. Stylobate block, ΔX10.

PLATE 20

1. Traces of column fluting on the stylobate block, Δ43.

2. Floor pavement block, Δ55.

3. Floor pavement block, ΔX2.

Plates

PLATE 21

1. Toichobate block for anta, Δ47.

2. Toichobate block for anta, Δ223.

3. Toichobate block for anta, Δ349.

4. Toichobate block for anta, Δ577+Δ580.

5. Cyma reversa moulding. Toichobate block, Δ47.

PLATE 22

1. Toichobate L-shaped block for intersection, Δ3.

2. Toichobate L-shaped block for intersection, Δ9.

3. Toichobate L-shaped block for intersection, Δ140.

4. Toichobate L-shaped block for intersection, Δ145.

5. Toichobate L-shaped block for intersection, Δ1.

6. Toichobate L-shaped block for intersection, Δ8.

PLATE 23

1. Toichobate block for naos side wall, Δ15.

2. Toichobate block for naos side wall, Δ16.

3. Toichobate block for naos side wall, Δ18.

4. Toichobate block for naos side wall, Δ48.

5. Toichobate block for naos side wall, Δ143.

6. Toichobate block for naos side wall, Δ465.

PLATE 24

1. Toichobate block for naos side wall, Δ575+Δ576+Δ579.

2. Toichobate block for opisthodomos separating wall, Δ2.

3. Toichobate block for opisthodomos separating wall, Δ14.

4. Toichobate block for opisthodomos separating wall, Δ169.

5. Toichobate block for pronaos south wall, Δ21.

6. Toichobate block for opisthodomos south wall, Δ49.

PLATE 25

1. Toichobate block for pronaos south wall, Δ131.

2. Toichobate block for opisthodomos south wall, Δ220.

3. Toichobate block for pronaos north wall, Δ243.

4. Toichobate block for pronaoss south wall, ΔX8.

5. Toichobate L-shaped block for pronaos separating wall, Δ11.

6. Toichobate L-shaped block for pronaos separating wall, Δ17.

PLATE 26

1. Threshold block, Δ13+Δ133+Δ477+ΔX4, Δ119.

2. Thrshold block details. North end.

3. Thrshold block details. South end.

Plates

PLATE 27

1. Threshold block, Δ572.

2. Threshold block, ΔX6.

3. Threshold block, ΔX7.

PLATE 28

1. Orthostate block for anta, Δ4+Δ568+Δ574+ΔX3.

2. Orthostate block for anta, Δ6.

3. Orthostate block for anta, Δ22.

4. Orthostate block for anta, Δ40+Δ45.

5. Orthostate block for intersection, Δ19.

6. Orthostate block for intersection, Δ144.

Plates

PLATE 29

1. Orthostate block for pronaos side wall, Δ27.

2. Orthostate block for pronaos separating wall, Δ20.

3. Orthostate block for opisthodomos separating wall, Δ7.

4. Orthostate block, Δ98+Δ98a.

5. Wall block, Δ68.

6. Wall block, 105+Δ105α.

PLATE 30

1. Column drum, Δ61.

2. Column drum, Δ62.

3. Column drum, Δ63.

4. Column drum, Δ67.

5. Column drum, Δ84.

6. Column drum, Δ87.

Plates

PLATE 31

1. Column drum, Δ88.

2. Column drum, Δ111.

3. Column drum, Δ121.

4. Column drum, Δ122.

5. Column drum, Δ124.

6. Column drum, Δ126.

PLATE 32

1. Column drum, Δ127.

2. Column drum, Δ128.

3. Column drum, Δ148.

4. Column drum, Δ149.

5. Column drum, Δ150.

6. Column drum, Δ165.

Plates

PLATE 33

1. Column drum, Δ167.

2. Column drum, Δ168.

3. Column drum, Δ190.

4. Column drum, Δ191.

5. Column drum, Δ193.

6. Column drum, Δ653.

PLATE 34

1. Top of column drum, Δ129c.

2. Dowel hole on the side of a column drum, unnumbered.

3. Remains of stucco, Δ127.

Plates

PLATE 35

1. Doric capital, Δ32.

2. Doric capital, ΔX1.

3. Top of Doric capital, ΔX1.

4. Doric capital details, Δ32.

PLATE 36

1. Architrave block, Δ85+Δ86.

2. Architrave block, Δ166.

3. Architrave block, Δ294.

Plates

PLATE 37

1. Frieze block, Δ107.

2. Frieze block, Δ159.

3. Frieze block, Δ210.

4. Frieze block, Δ279.

5. Frieze block, Δ293.

PLATE 38

1. Frieze block, Δ406.

2. Triglyph block, Δ773.

3. Cornice block, Δ380.

4. Cornice block, Δ717.

5. Syma block, Δ135.

PLATE 39

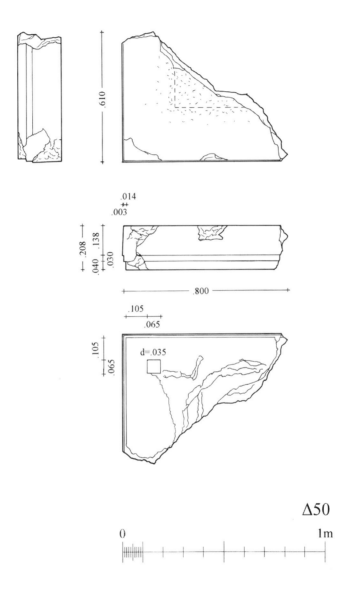

Crepis block, Δ50.

PLATE 40

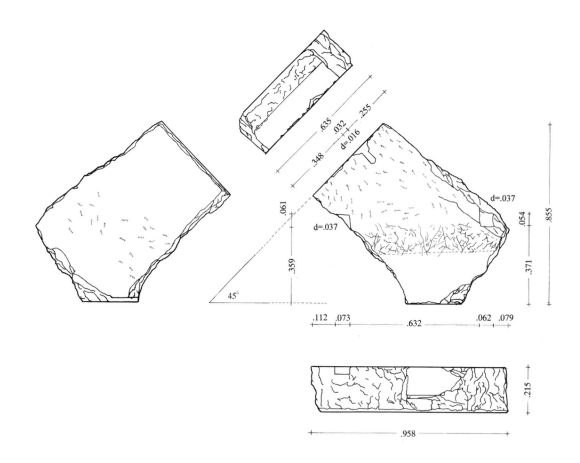

Crepis block, Δ59.

Plates

PLATE 41

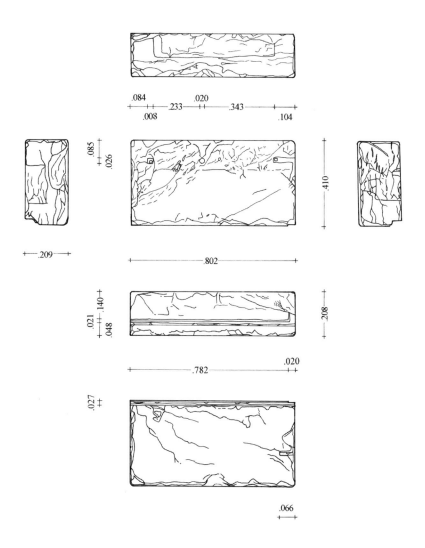

Crepis block, Δ181.

PLATE 42

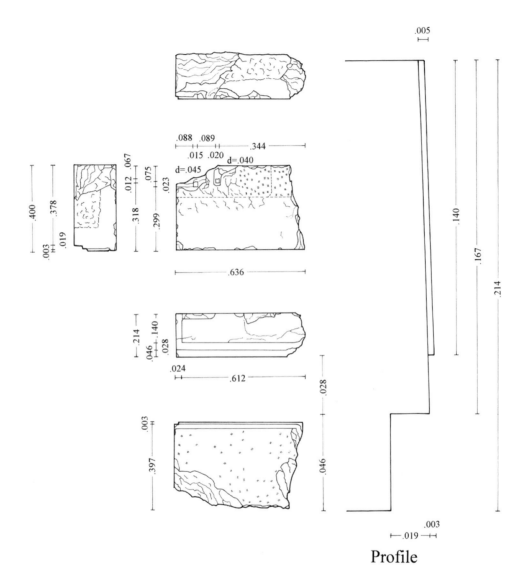

Profile

Crepis block, Δ555.

Plates

PLATE 43

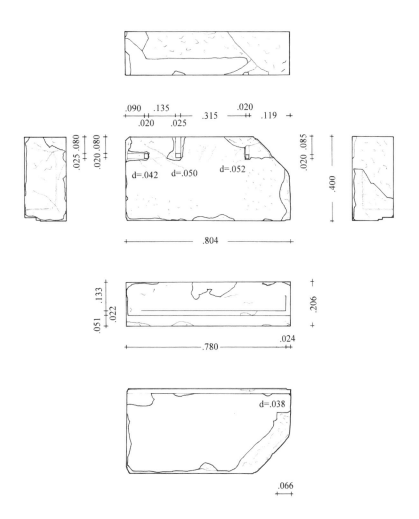

Crepis block, Δ556.

PLATE 44

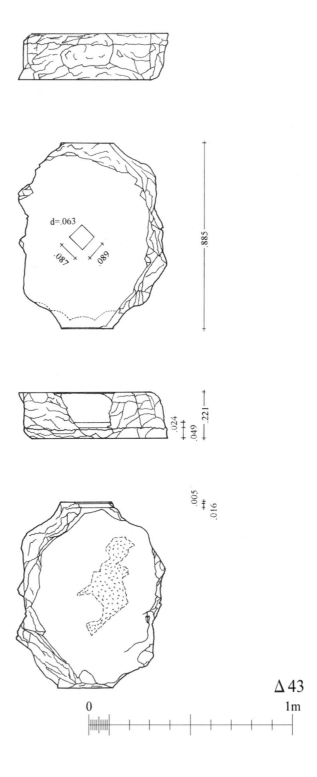

Stylobate block, Δ43.

Plates

PLATE 45

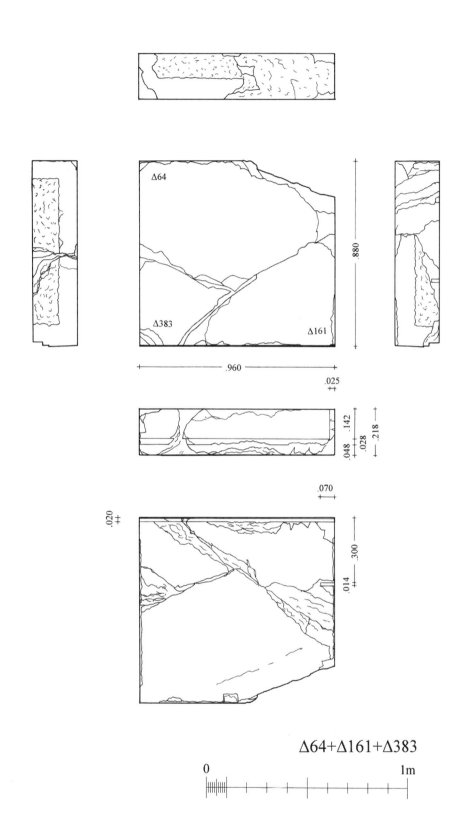

Stylobate block, Δ64+Δ161+Δ383.

PLATE 46

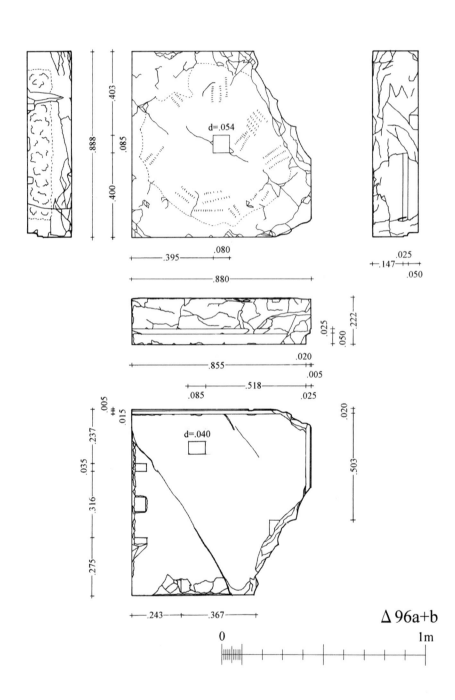

Stylobate block, Δ96a+b.

Plates

PLATE 47

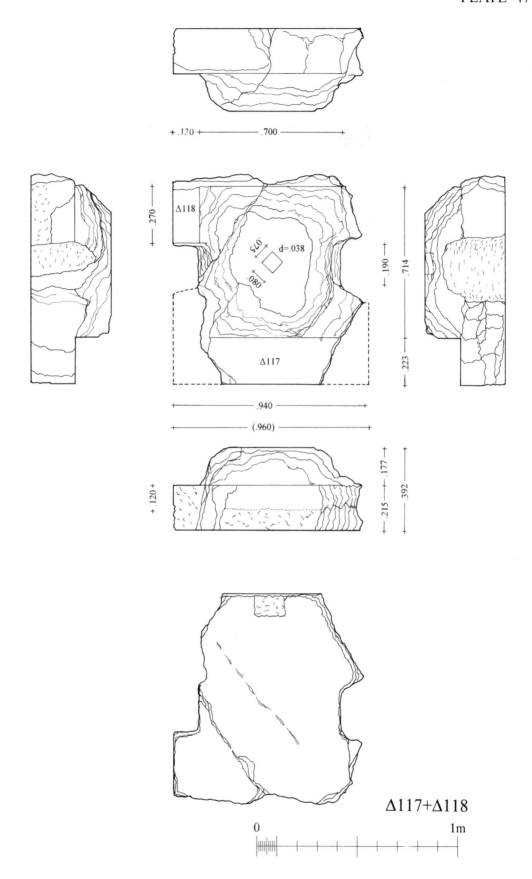

Stylobate block, Δ117+Δ118.

PLATE 48

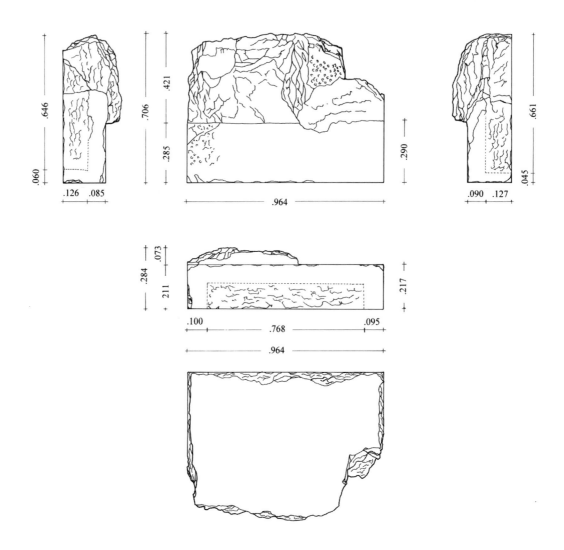

Stylobate block, Δ130.

Plates

PLATE 49

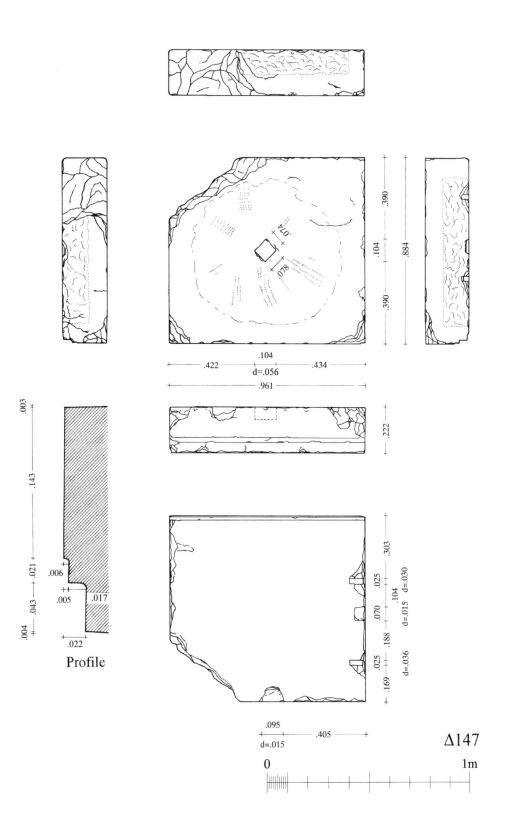

Stylobate block, Δ147.

PLATE 50

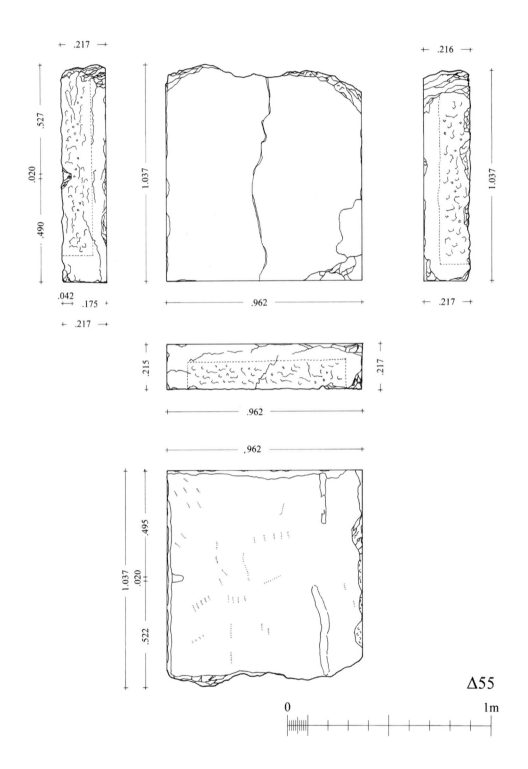

Flooring block, Δ55.

PLATE 51

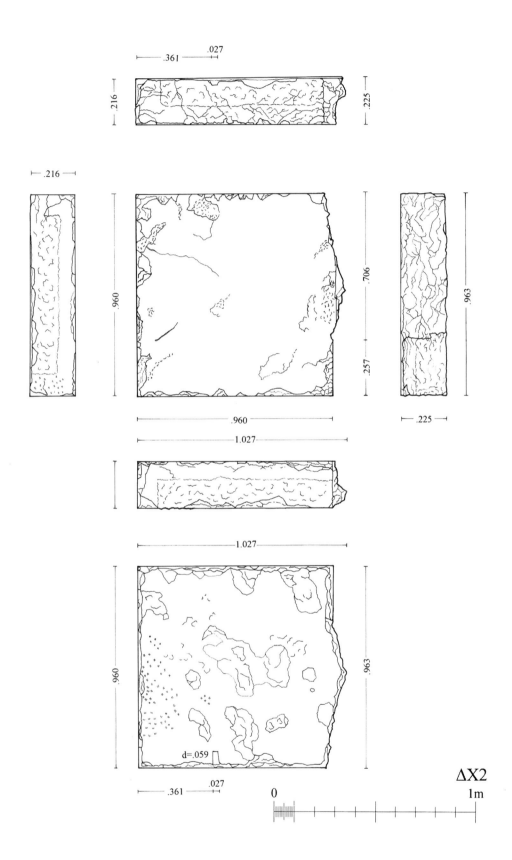

Flooring block, ΔX2.

PLATE 52

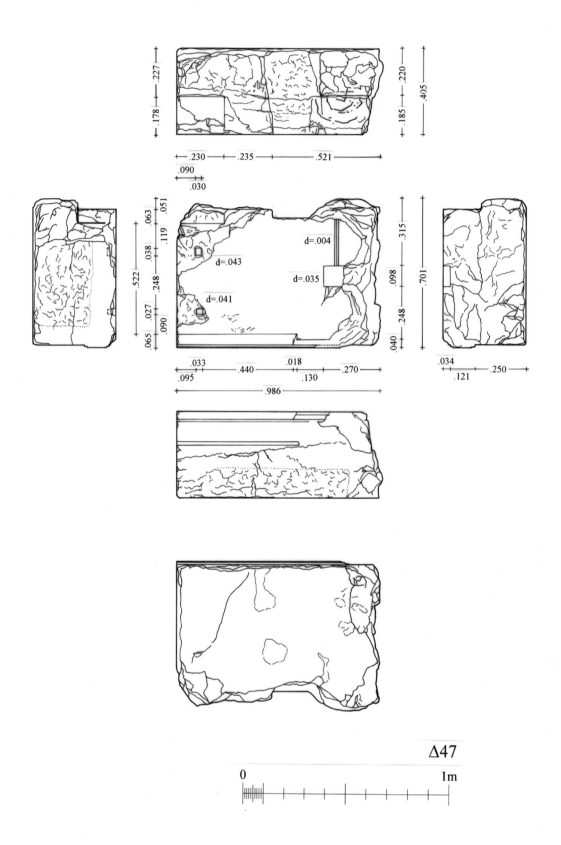

Toichobate block for anta, Δ47.

PLATE 53

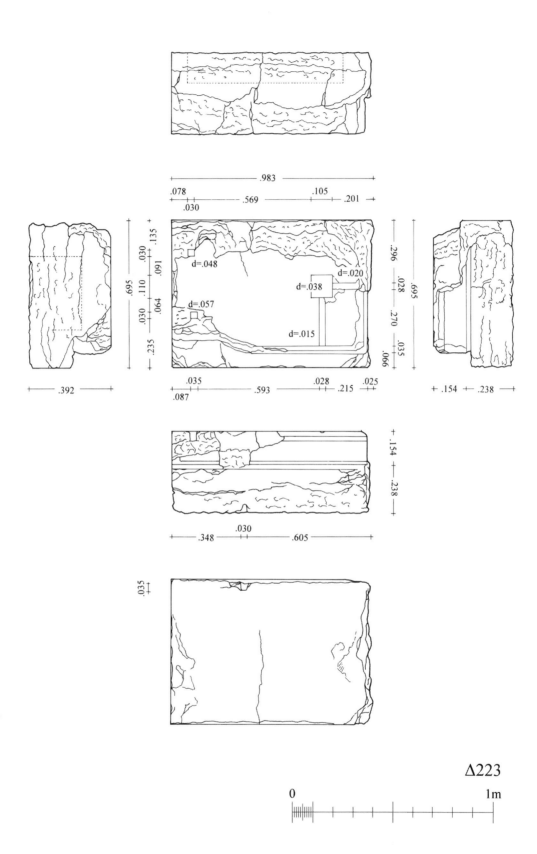

Δ223

Toichobate block for anta, Δ223.

PLATE 54

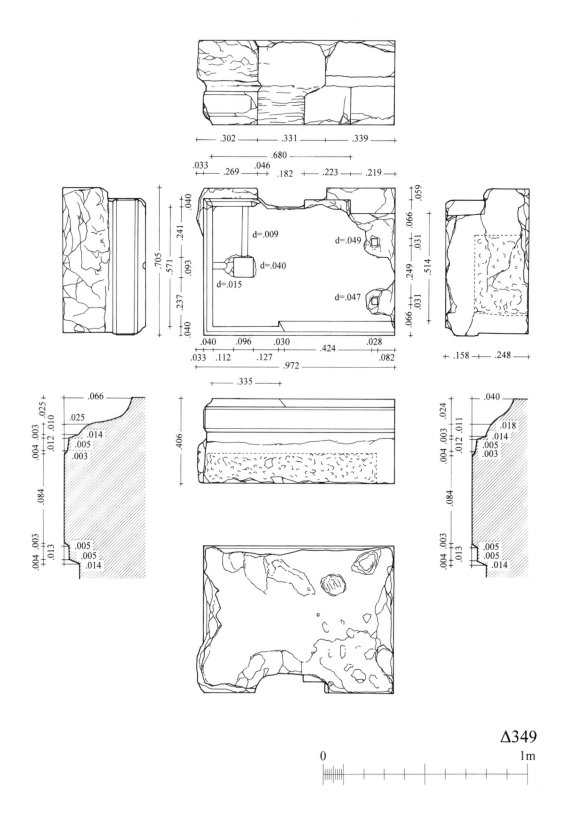

Δ349

Toichobate block for anta, Δ349.

PLATE 55

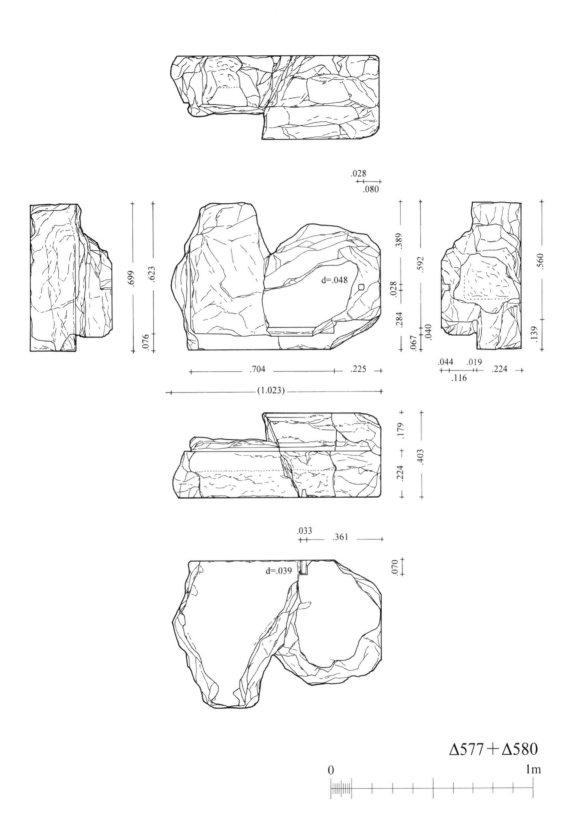

Δ577+Δ580

Toichobate block for anta, Δ577+Δ580.

PLATE 56

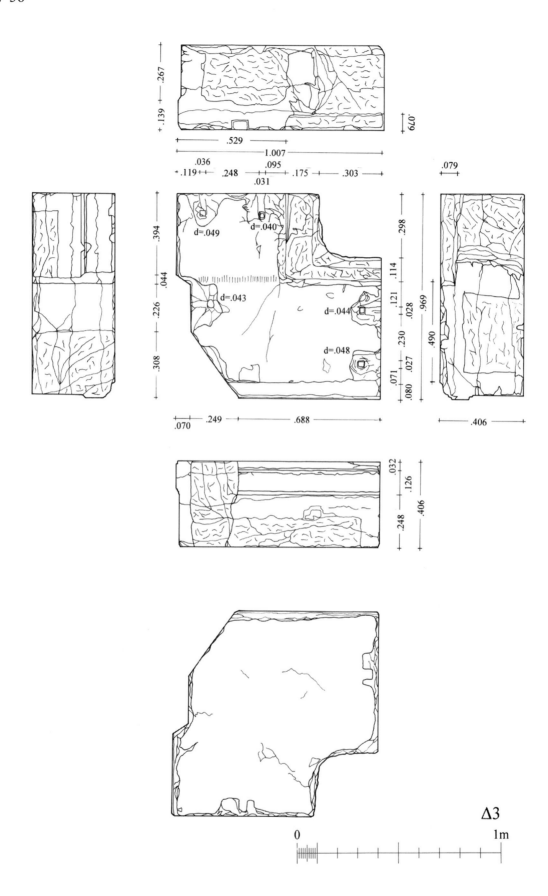

Toichobate L-shaped block for intersection, Δ3.

Plates

PLATE 57

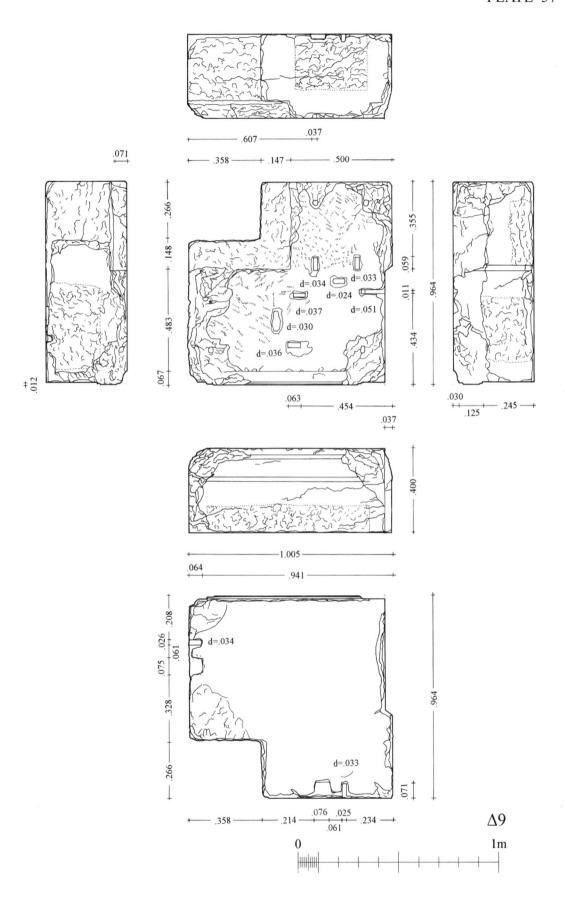

Toichobate L-shaped block for intersection, Δ9.

PLATE 58

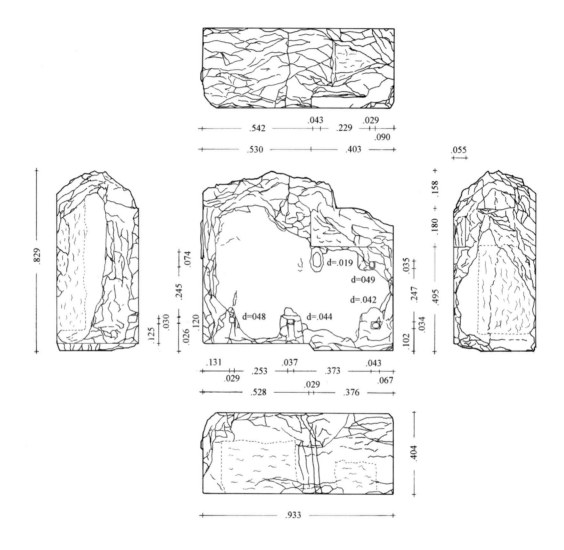

Toichobate L-shaped block for intersection, Δ140.

PLATE 59

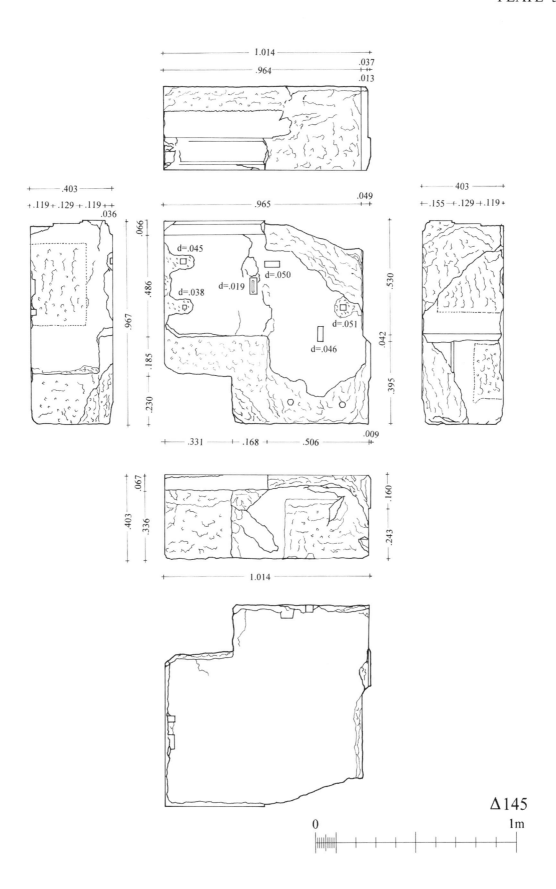

Toichobate L-shaped block for intersection, Δ145.

PLATE 60

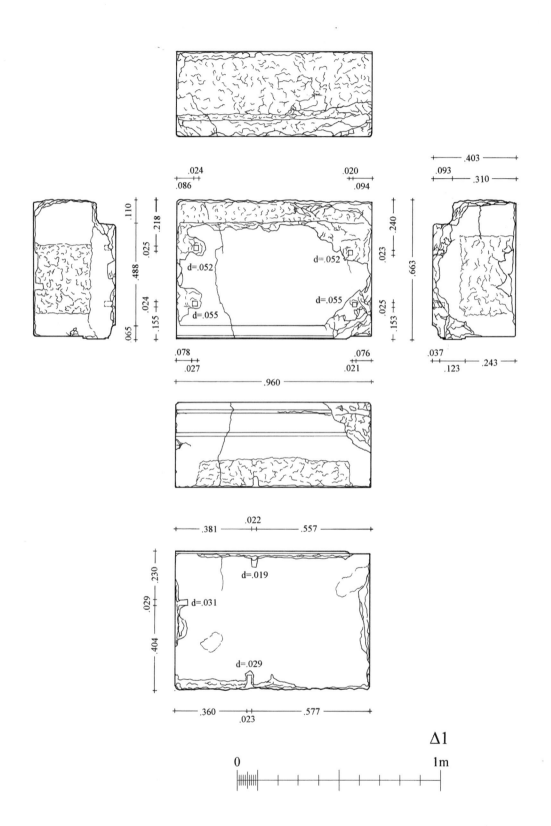

Toichobate block for naos side wall, Δ1.

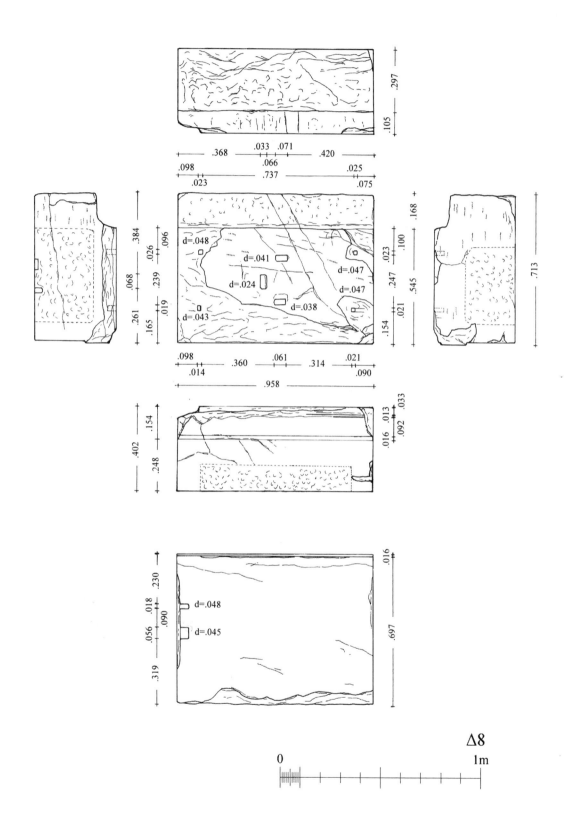

Toichobate block for naos side wall, Δ8.

PLATE 62

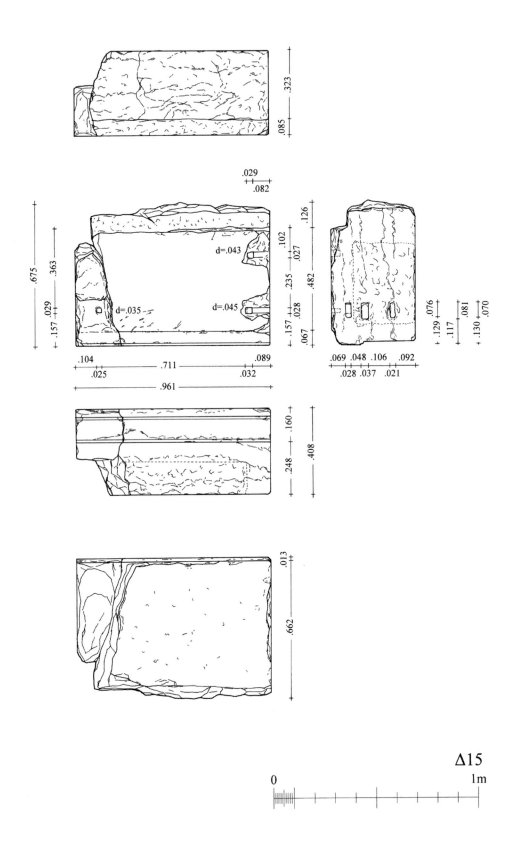

Toichobate block for naos side wall, Δ15.

Plates

PLATE 63

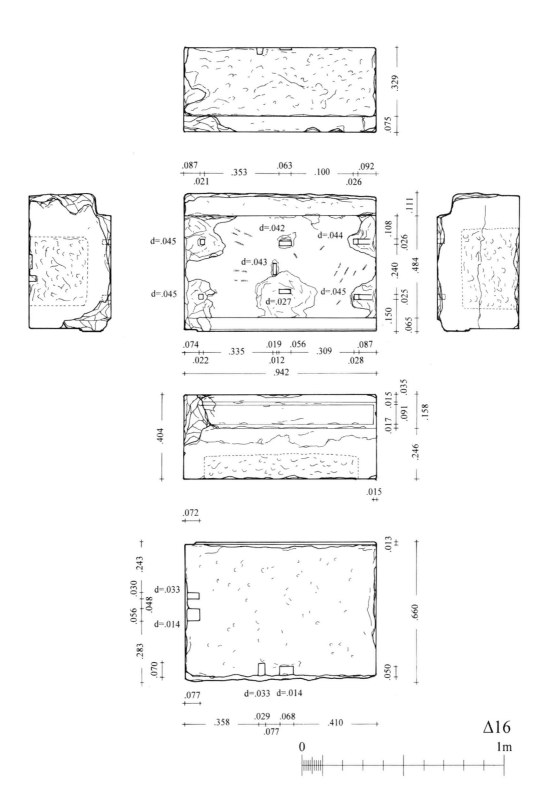

Toichobate block for naos side wall, Δ16.

PLATE 64

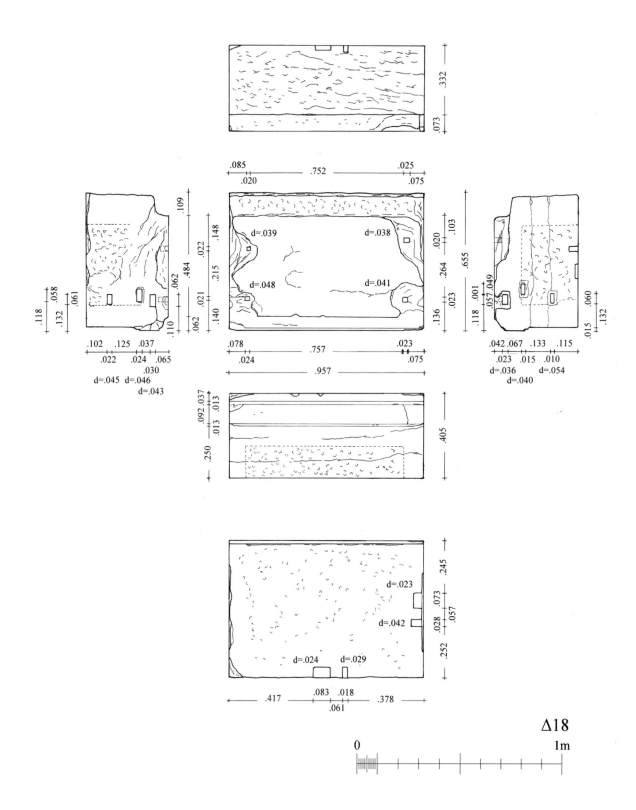

Toichobate block for naos side wall, Δ18.

Plates

PLATE 65

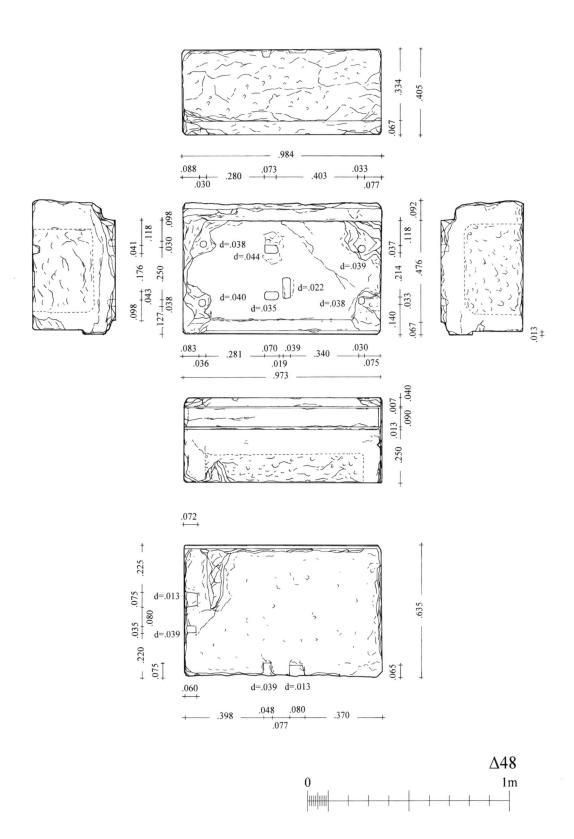

Toichobate block for naos side wall, Δ48.

PLATE 66

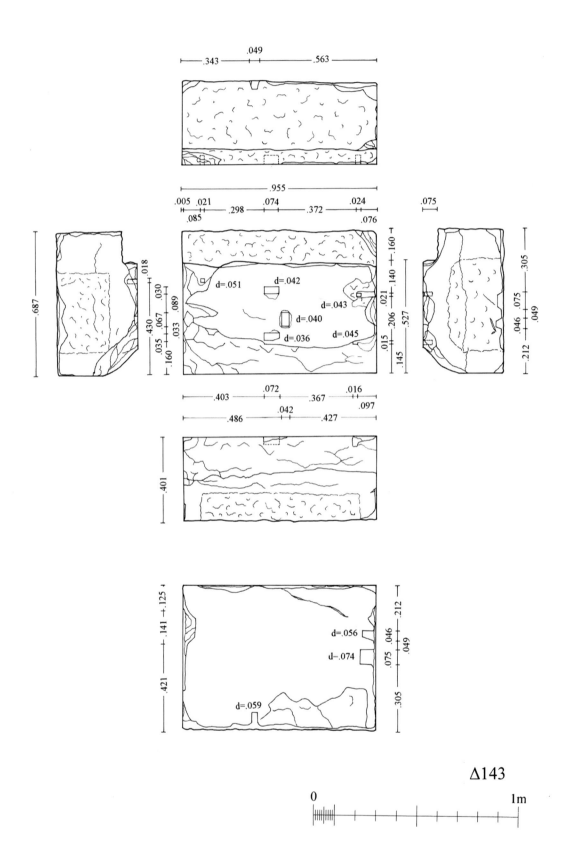

Δ143

Toichobate block for naos side wall, Δ143.

Plates

PLATE 67

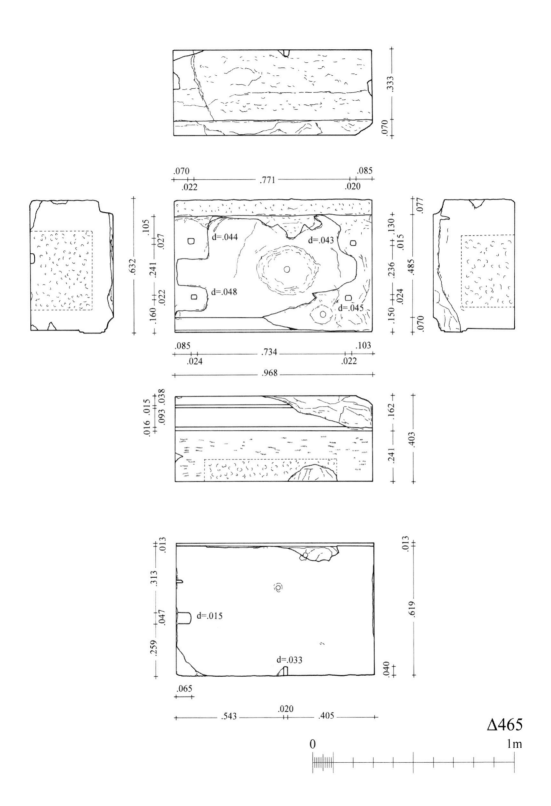

Toichobate block for naos side wall, Δ465.

PLATE 68

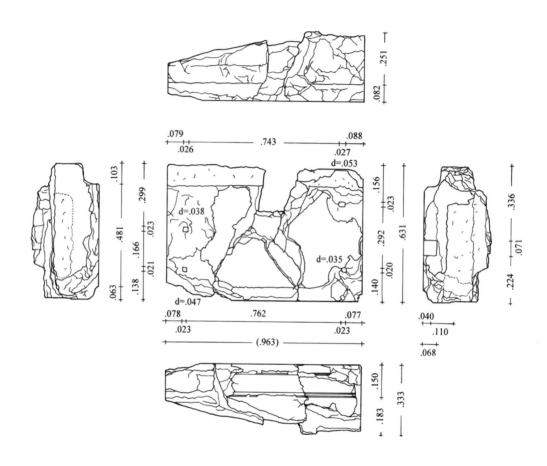

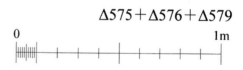

Toichobate block for naos side wall, Δ575+Δ576+Δ579.

PLATE 69

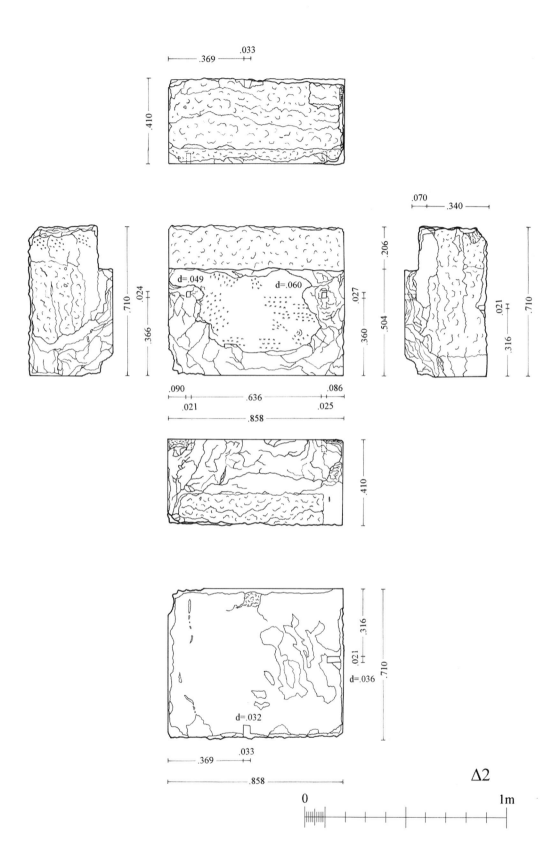

Toichobate block for opisthodomos separating wall, Δ2.

PLATE 70

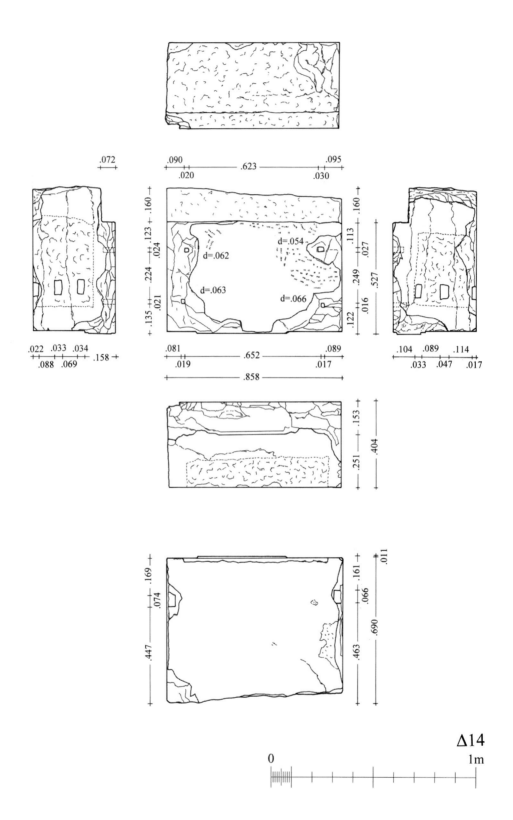

Toichobate block for opisthodomos separating wall, Δ14.

Plates

PLATE 71

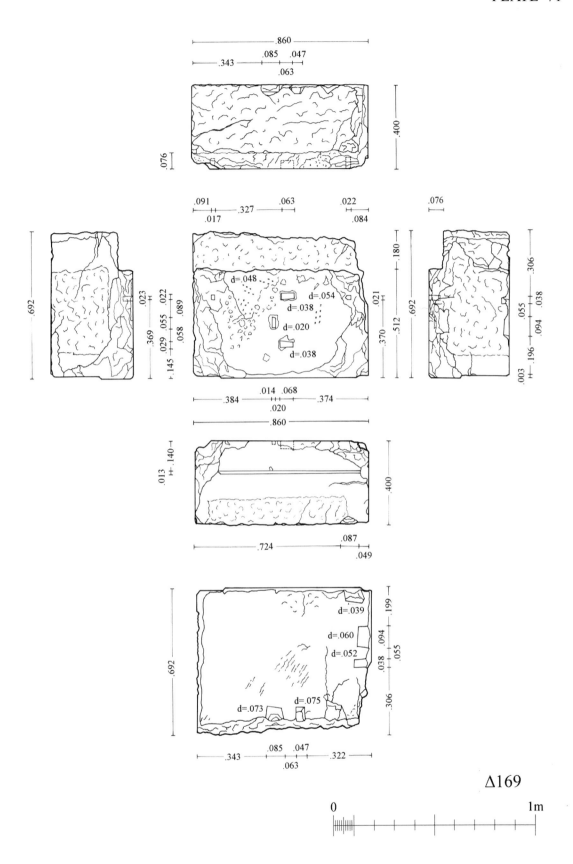

Δ169

Toichobate block for opisthodomos separating wall, Δ169.

PLATE 72

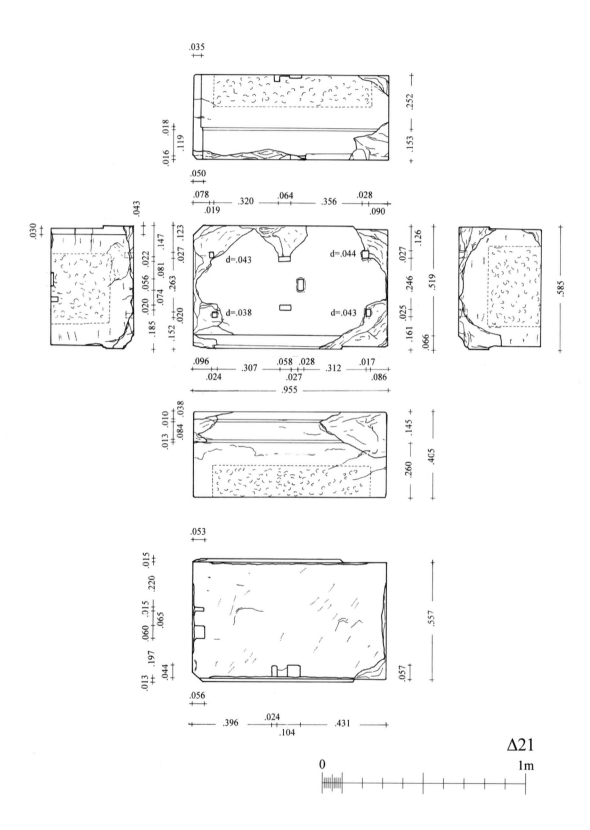

Toichobate block for pronaos side wall, Δ21.

Plates

PLATE 73

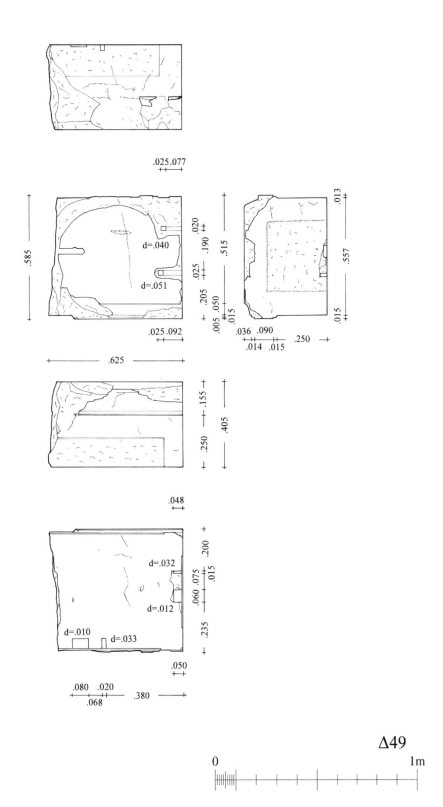

Toichobate block for opisthodomos side wall, Δ49.

PLATE 74

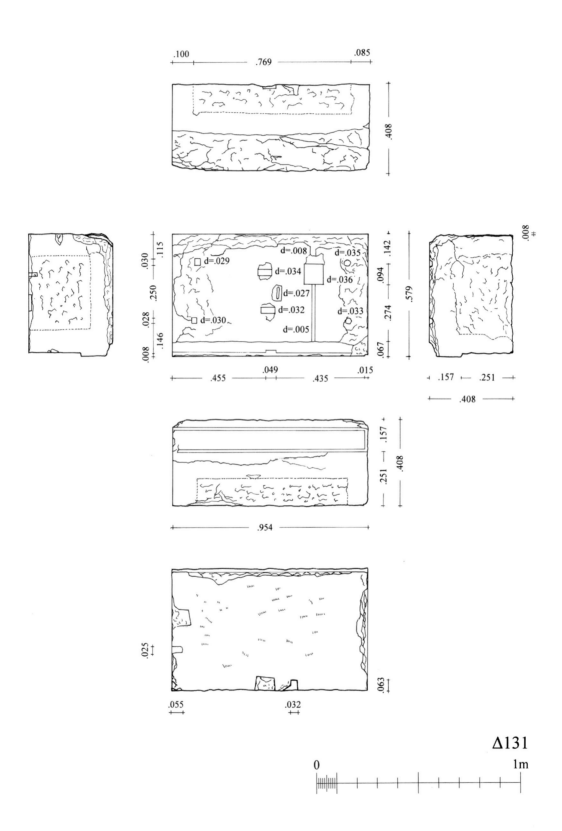

Toichobate block for pronaos side wall, Δ131.

PLATE 75

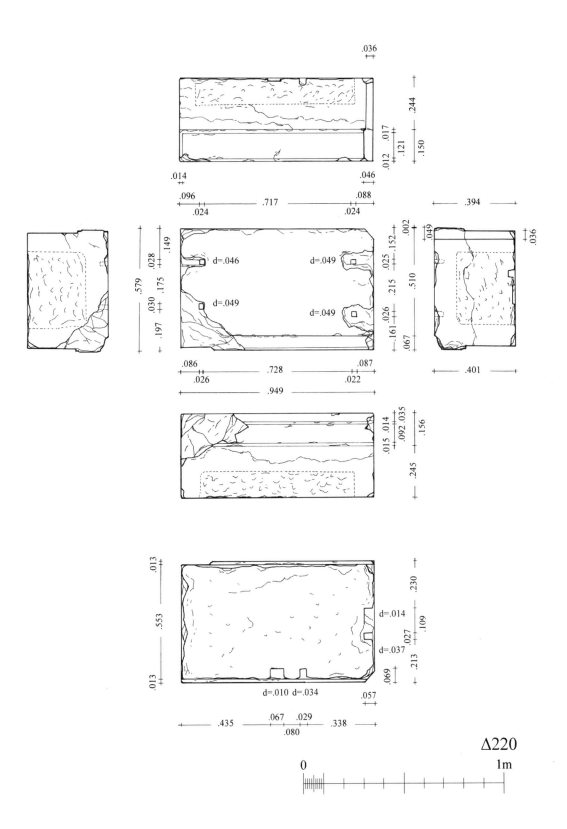

Toichobate block for opisthodomos side wall, Δ220.

PLATE 76

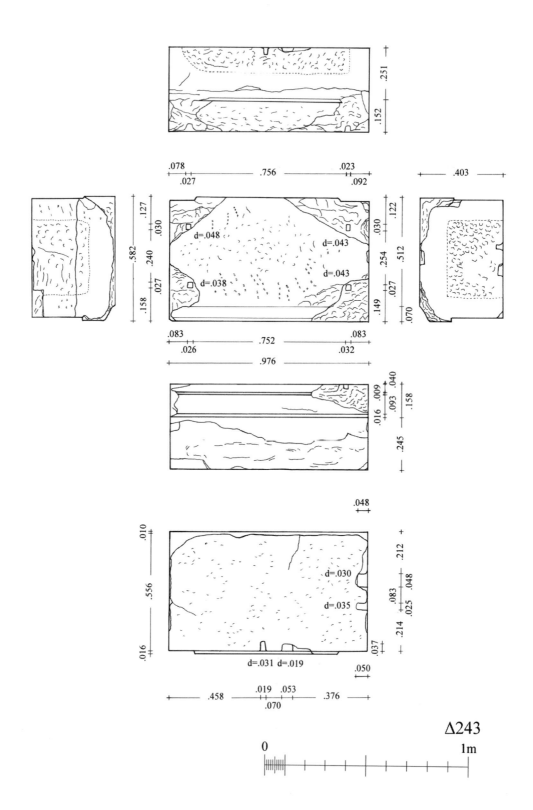

Toichobate block for pronaos side wall, Δ243.

PLATE 77

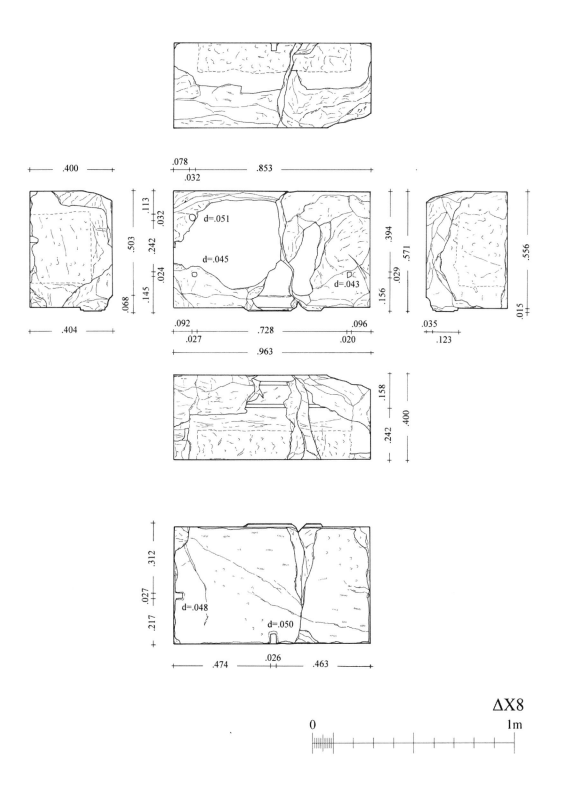

Toichobate block for pronaos side wall, ΔX8.

PLATE 78

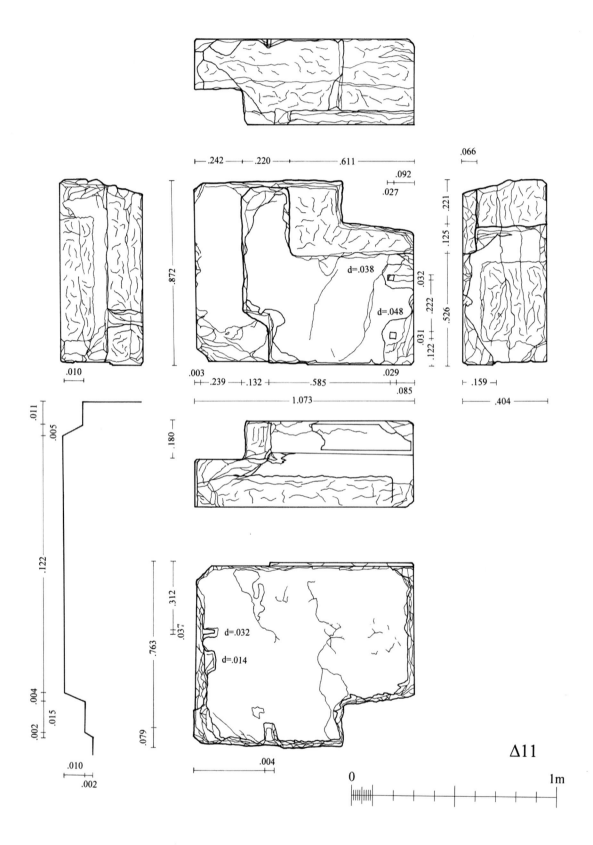

Toichobate L-shaped block for pronaos sepating wall, Δ11.

PLATE 79

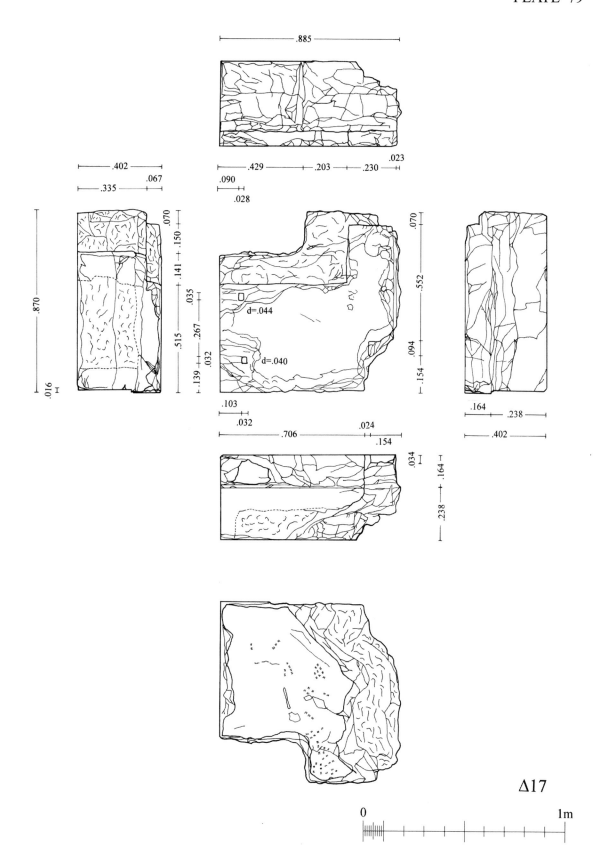

Toichobate L-shaped block for pronaos sepating wall, Δ17.

PLATE 80

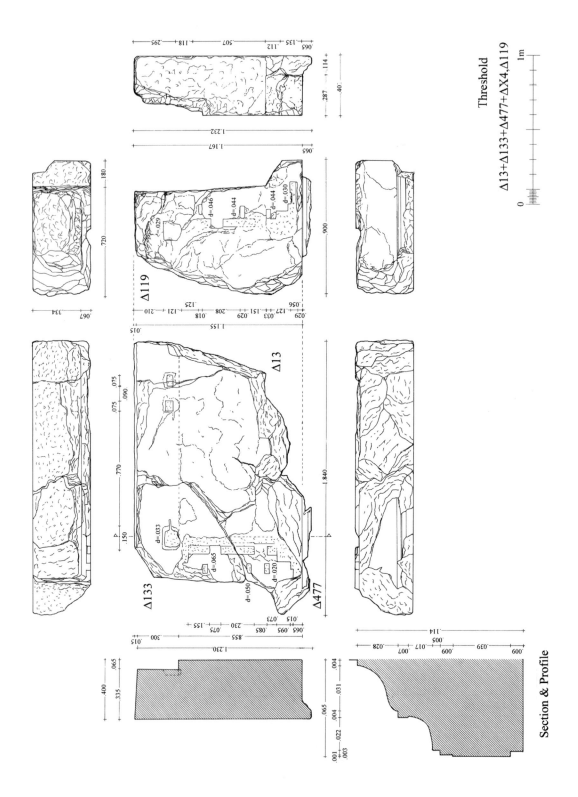

Threshold block Δ13+Δ133+Δ477+ΔX4, Δ119.

PLATE 81

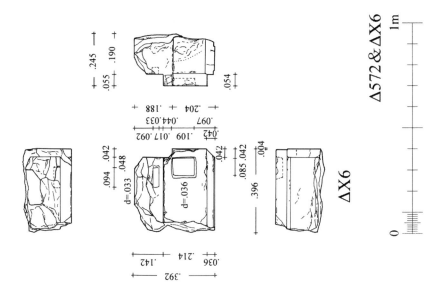

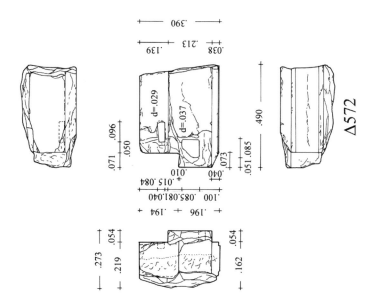

Threshold block Δ572, ΔX6.

PLATE 82

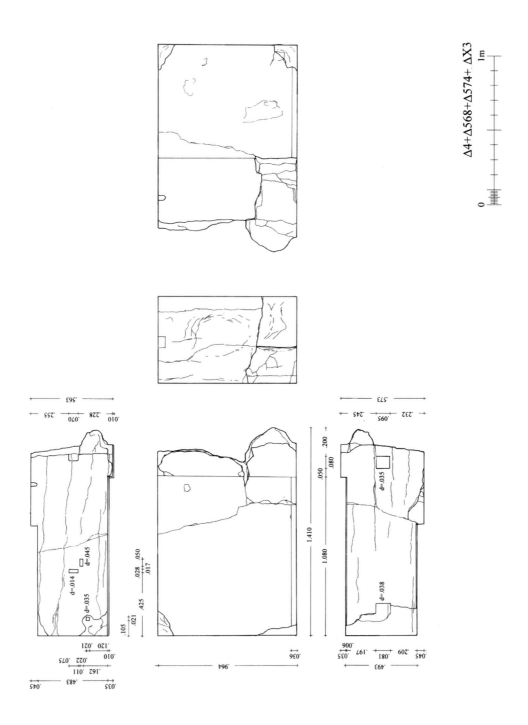

Orthostate block for anta, Δ4+Δ568+Δ574+ΔX3.

PLATE 83

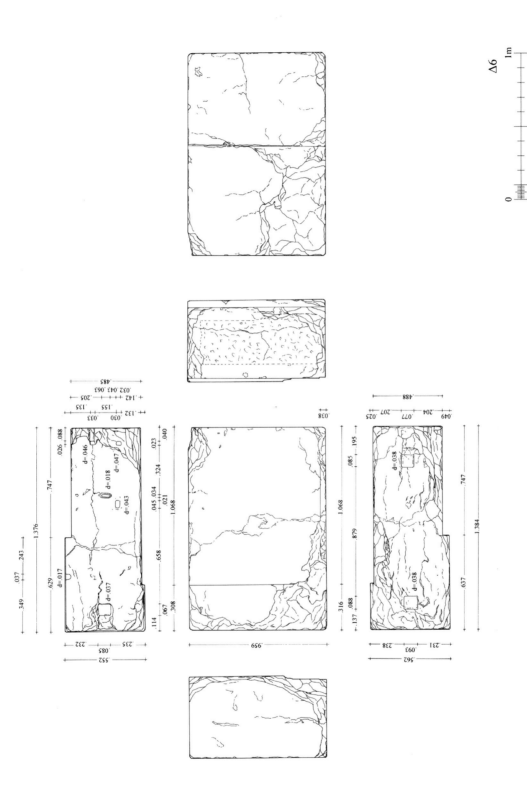

Orthostate block for anta, Δ6.

PLATE 84

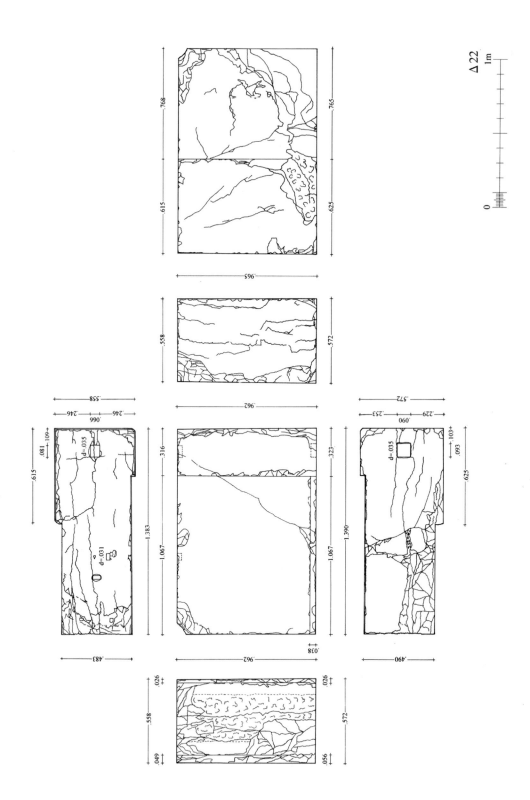

Orthostate block for anta, Δ22.

Plates

PLATE 85

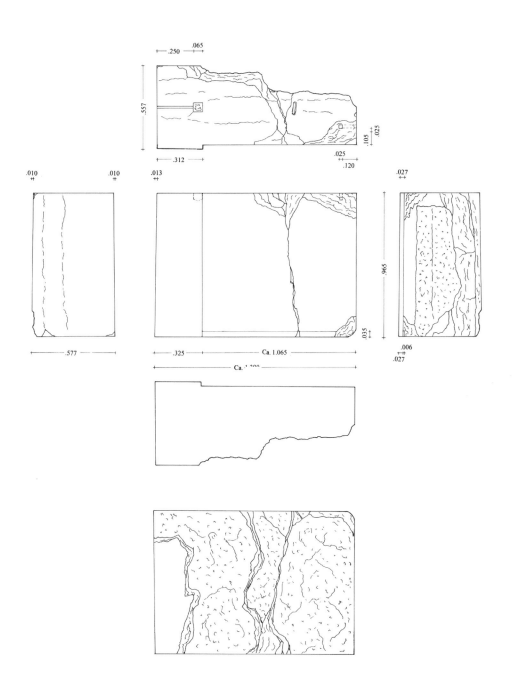

Orthostate block for anta, Δ40+Δ45.

PLATE 86

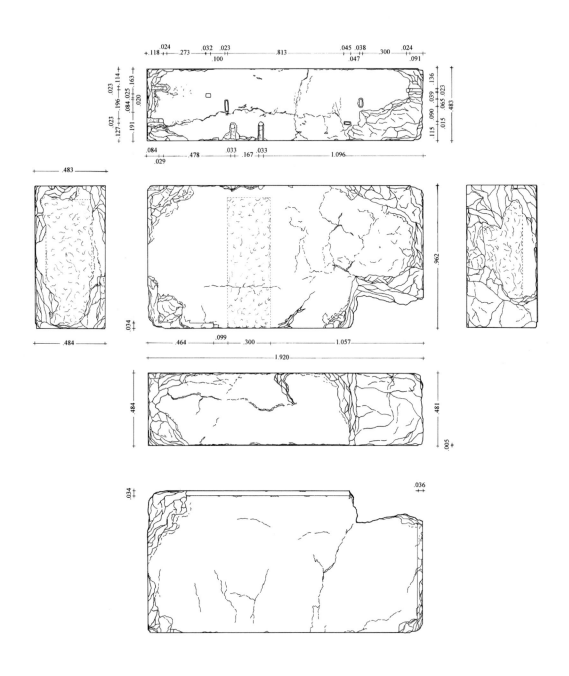

Orthostate block for intersection, Δ19.

Plates

PLATE 87

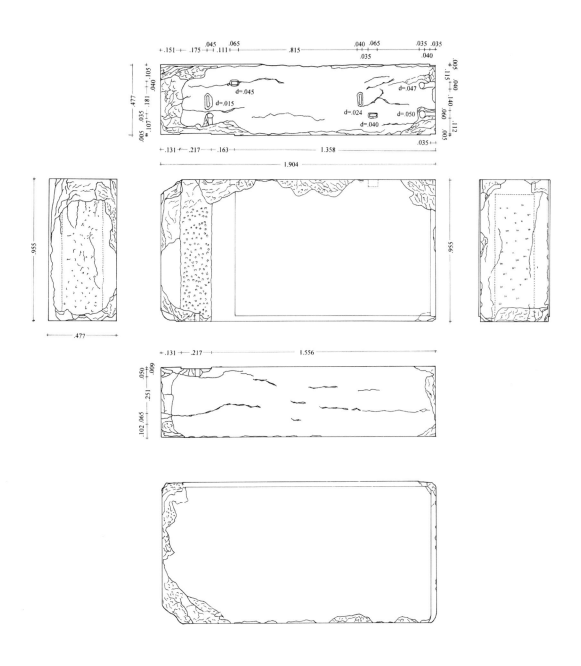

Orthostate block for intersection, Δ144.

PLATE 88

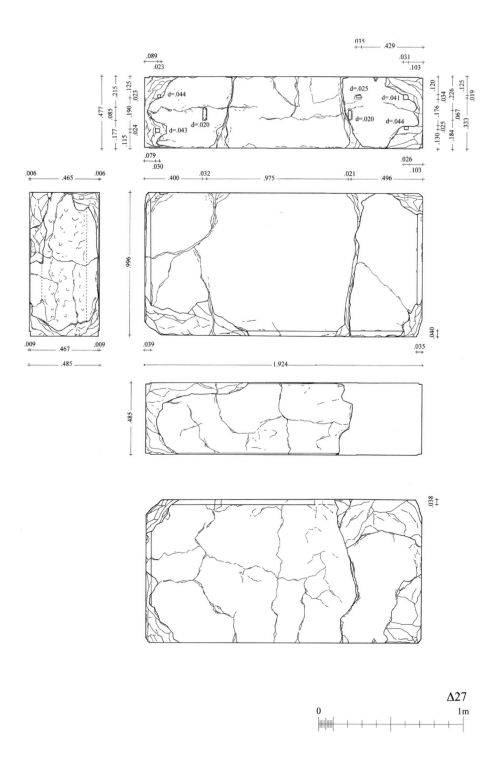

Orthostate block for pronaos side wall, Δ27.

Plates

PLATE 89

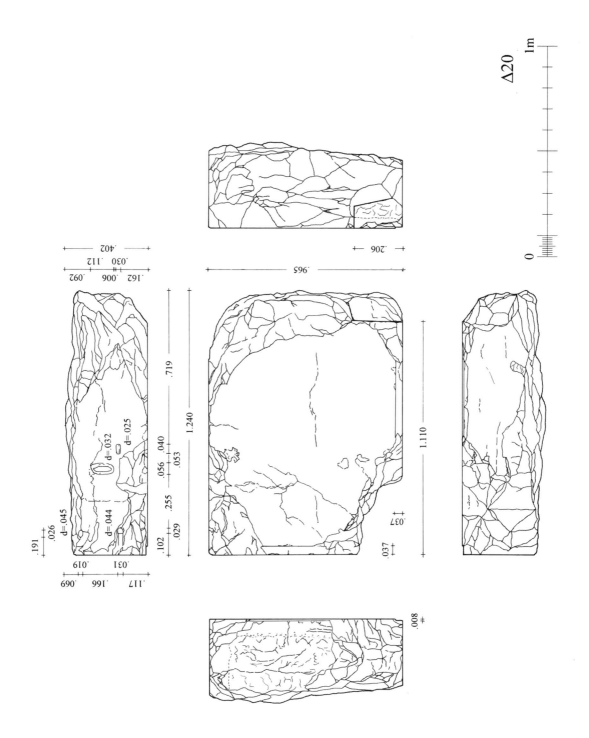

Orthostate block for pronaos separating wall, Δ20.

PLATE 90

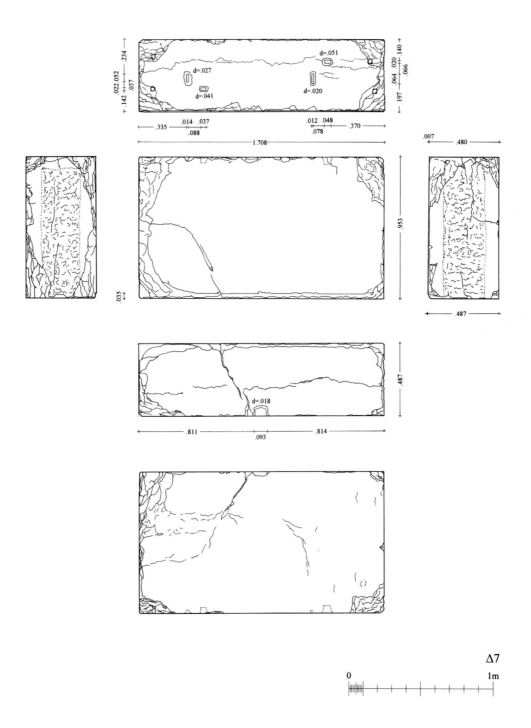

Orthostate block for opisthodomos separating wall, Δ7.

PLATE 91

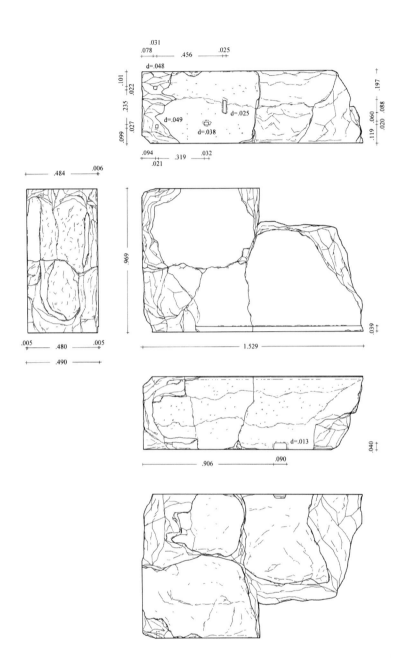

Orthostate block, Δ98+Δ98a.

PLATE 92

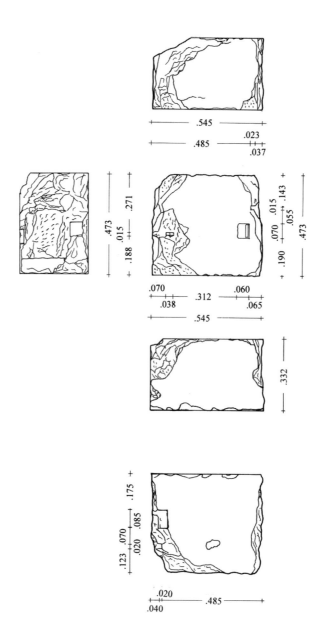

Δ68

Wall block, Δ68.

Plates

PLATE 93

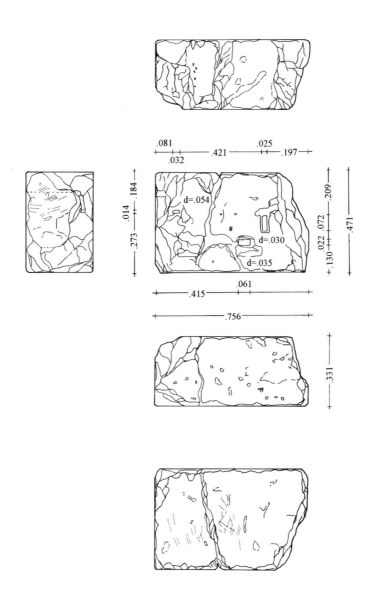

Δ105+Δ105α

Wall block, Δ105+Δ105α.

PLATE 94

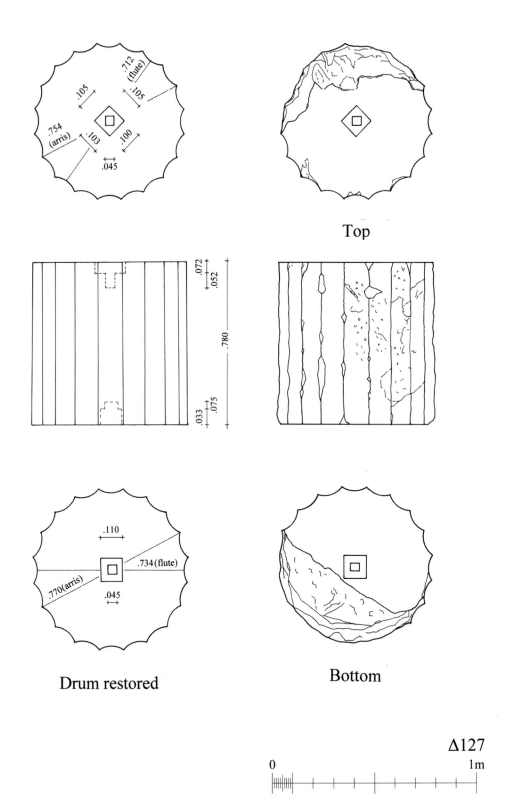

Column drrum, Δ127.

Plates

PLATE 95

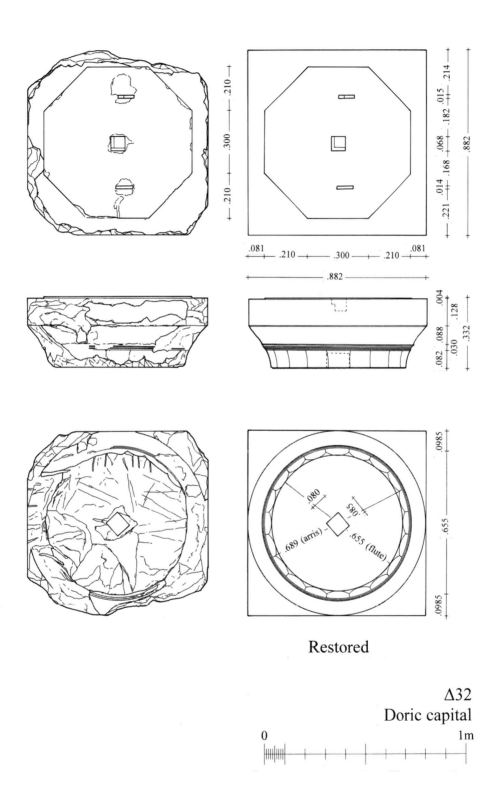

Restored

Δ32
Doric capital

Doric capital, Δ32.

PLATE 96

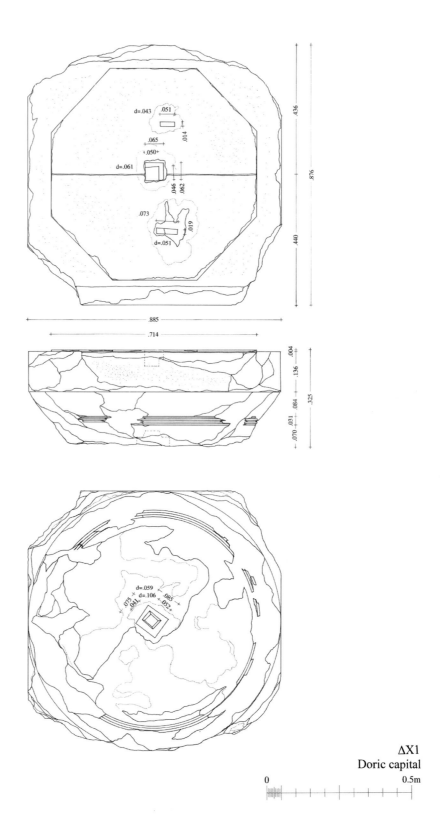

ΔX1
Doric capital

Doric capital, ΔX1.

Plates

PLATE 97

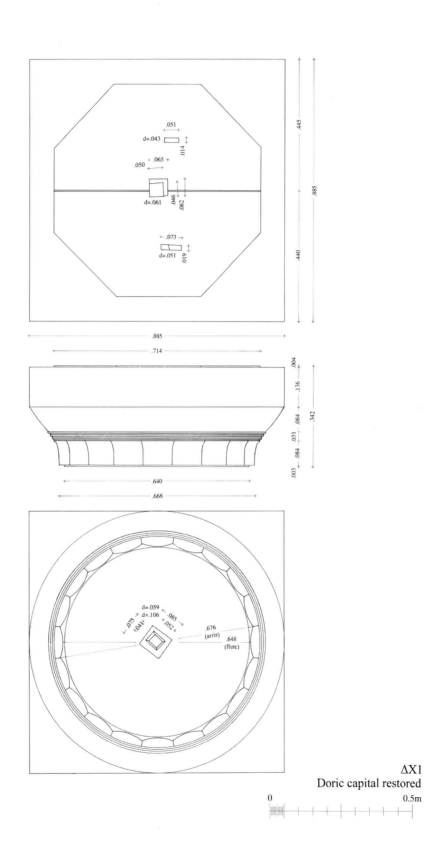

ΔX1
Doric capital restored

Doric capital, restored, ΔX1.

PLATE 98

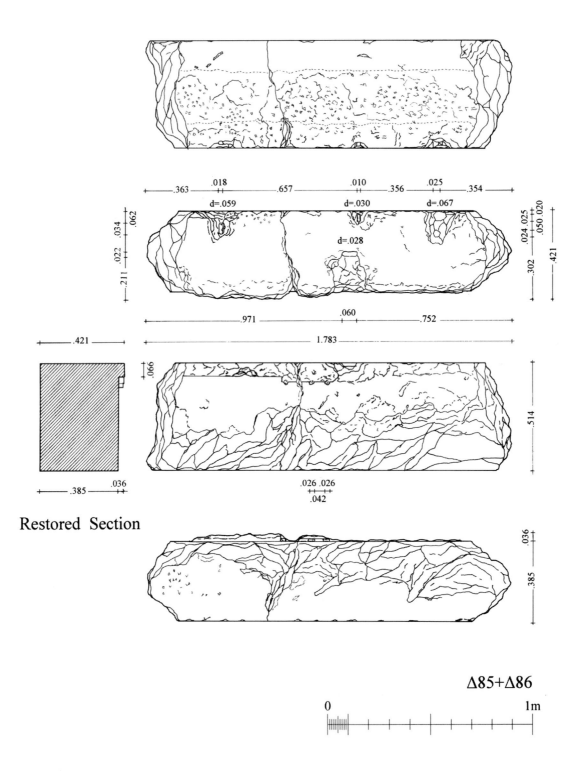

Architrave block, Δ85+Δ86.

Plates

PLATE 99

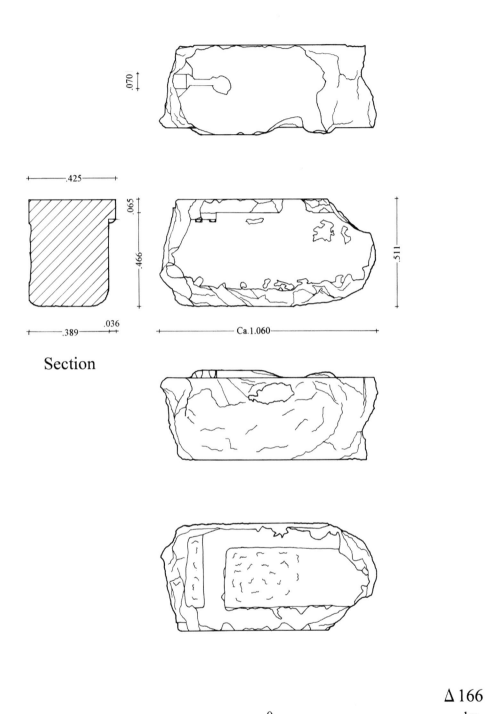

Architrave block, Δ166.

PLATE 100

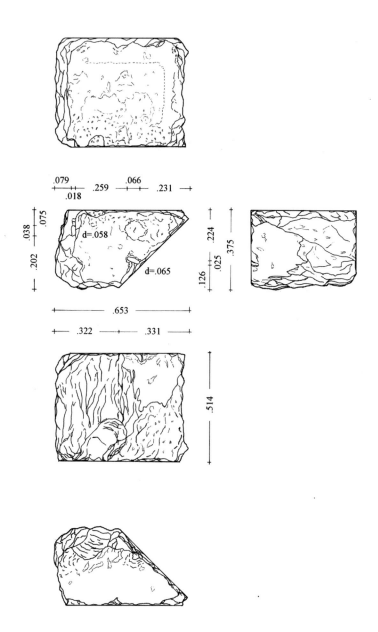

Architrave block, Δ294.

Plates

PLATE 101

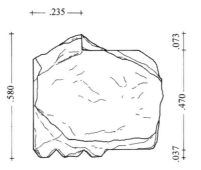

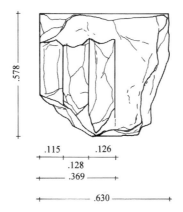

Δ159

Frieze block, Δ159.

PLATE 102

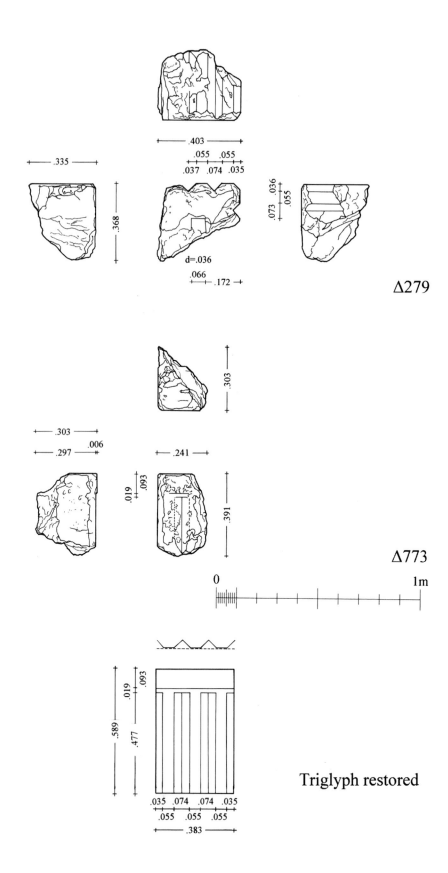

Frieze block, Δ279, Δ773.

PLATE 103

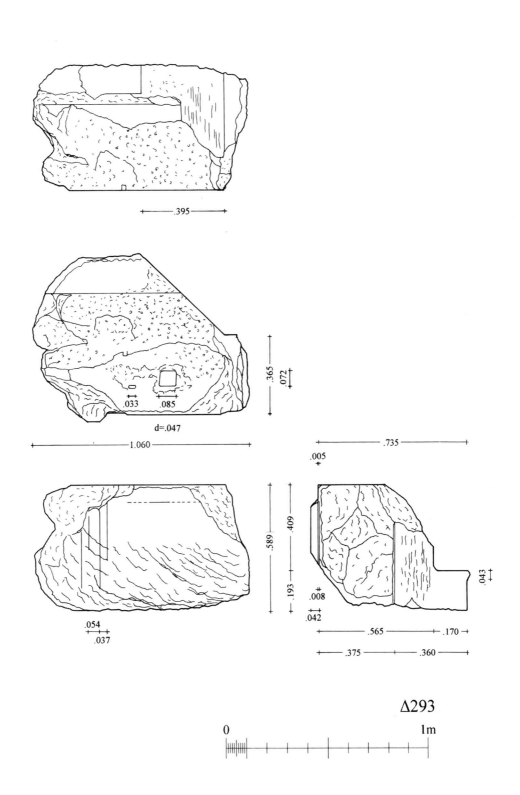

Frieze block, Δ293.

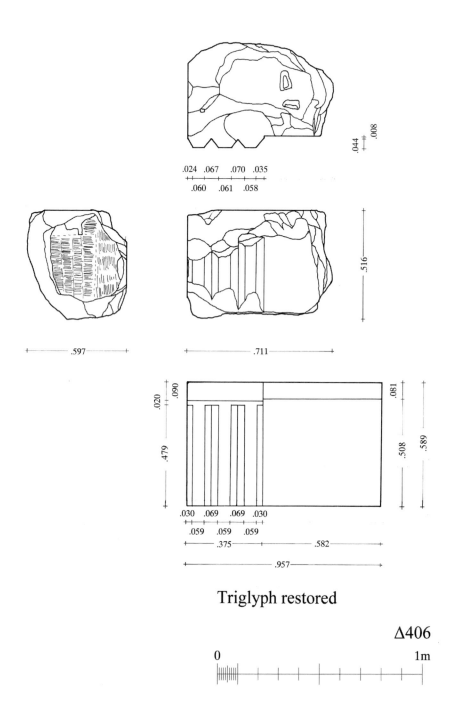

Frieze block, Δ406.

Plates

PLATE 105

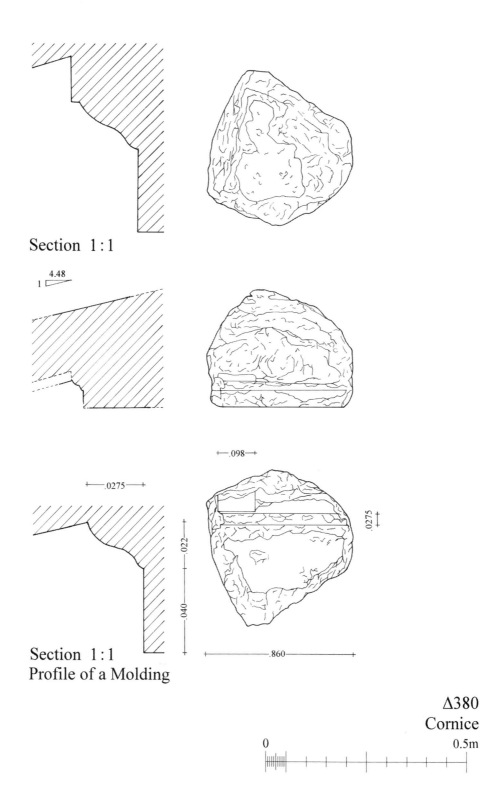

Cornice block, Δ380.

PLATE 106

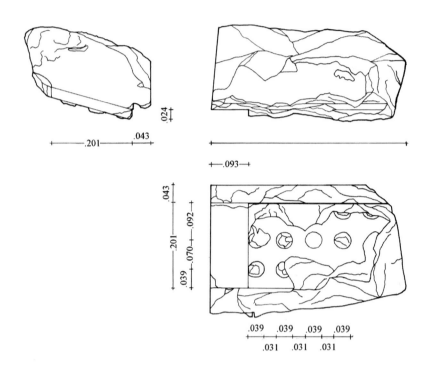

Cornice block, Δ717.

Plates

PLATE 107

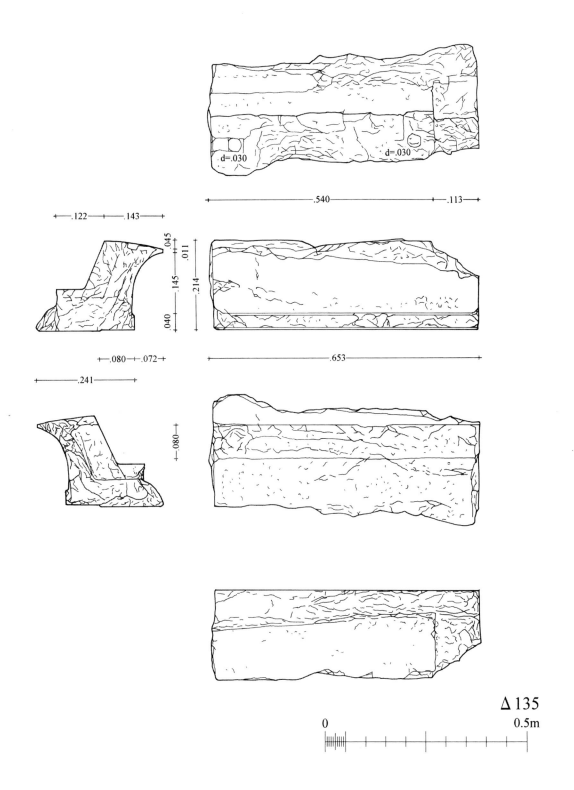

Sima block, Δ135.

PLATE 108

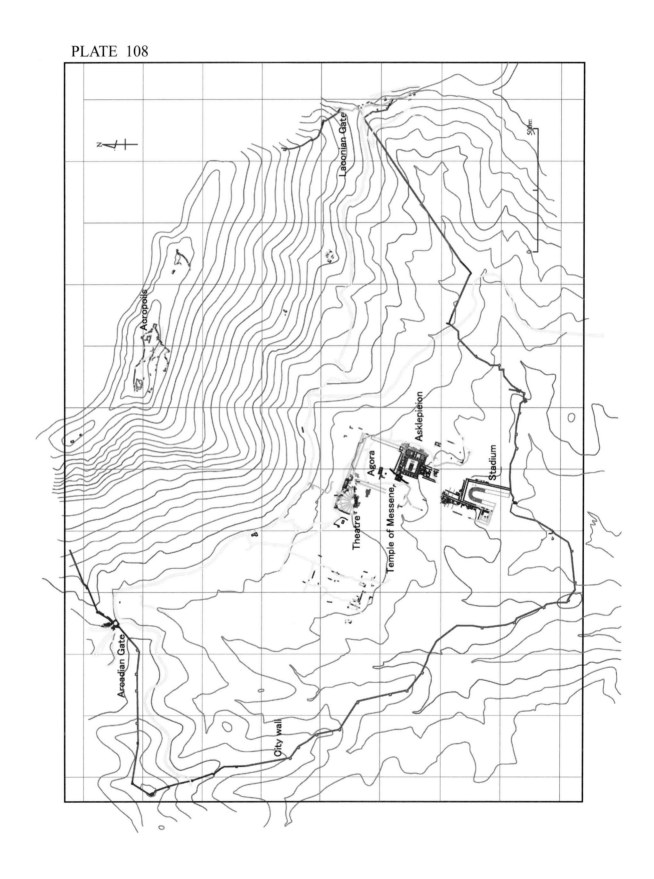

General plan of ancient Messene. (Courtesy of the Society of Messenian Archaeological Studies.)

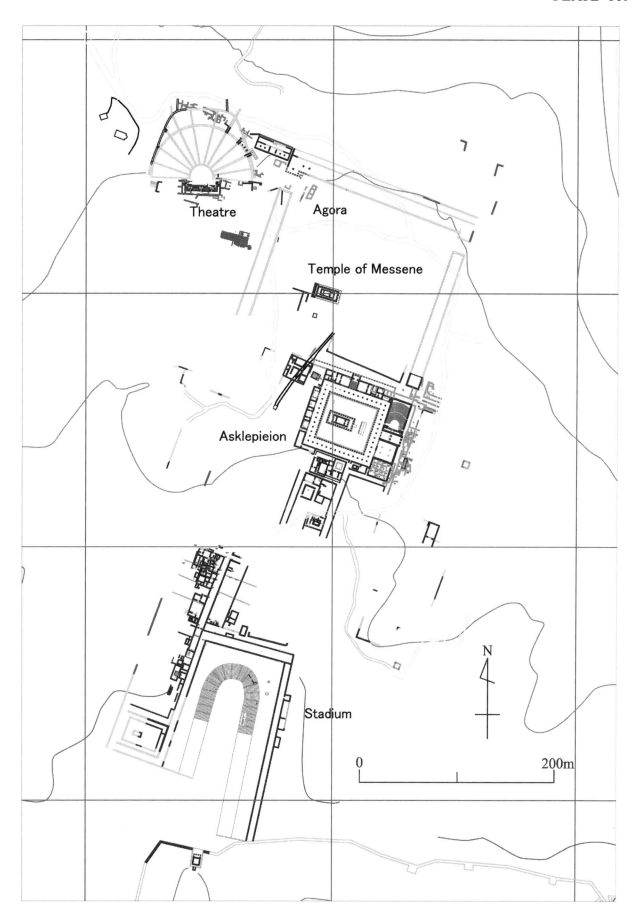

Central part of ancient Messene. (Courtecy of the Society of Messenian Archaeological Studies.)

PLATE 110

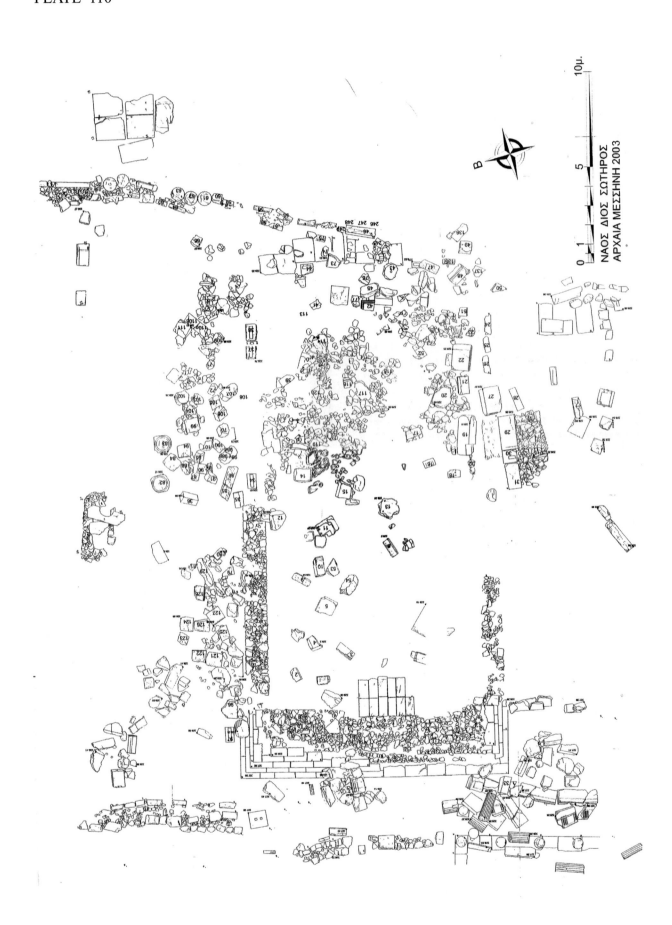

Plan of Temple of Messene, as excavated in 2003. (Courtesy of the Society of Messenian Archaeological Studies.)

PLATE 111

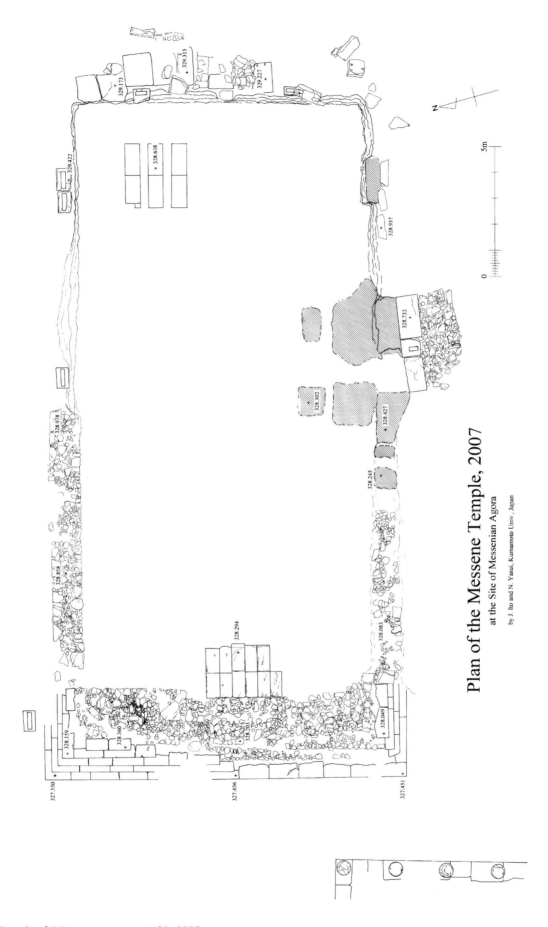

Plan of Temple of Messene, as excavated in 2007.

PLATE 112

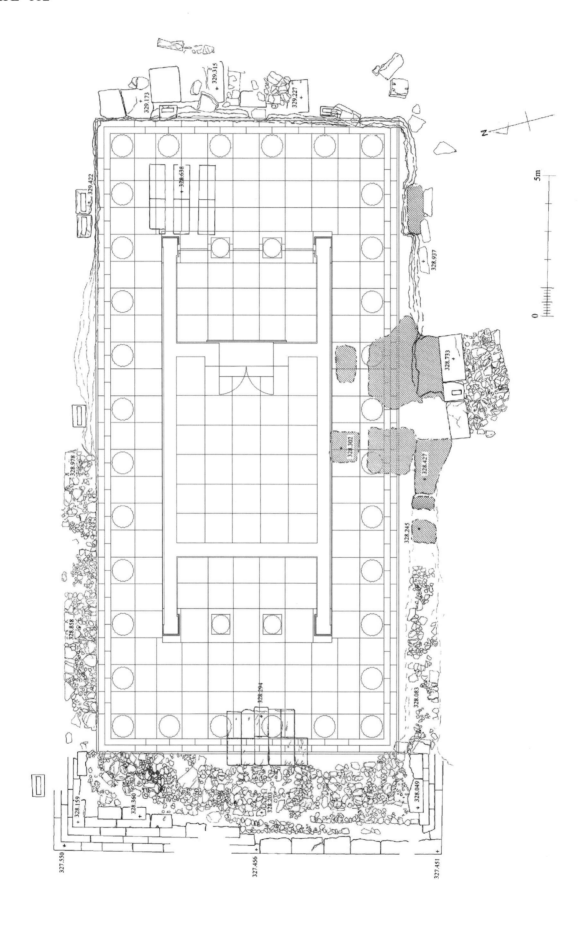

Reconstructed plan of Temple of Messene, superimposed on the plan as excavated.

PLATE 113

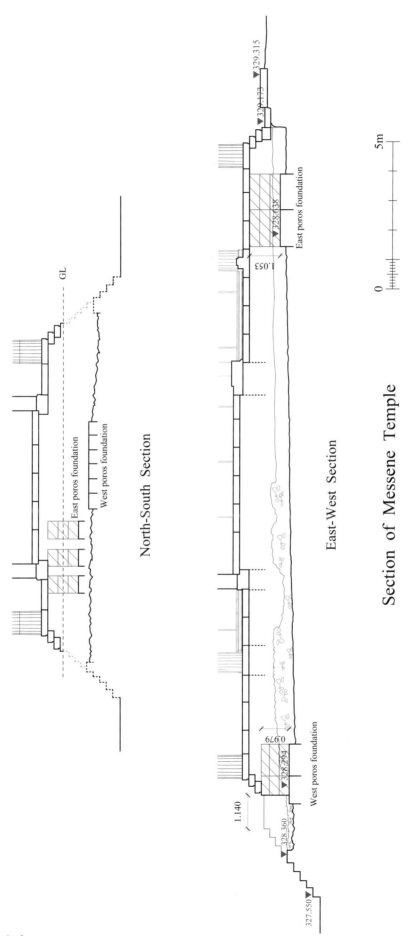

Sections of temple platform.

PLATE 114

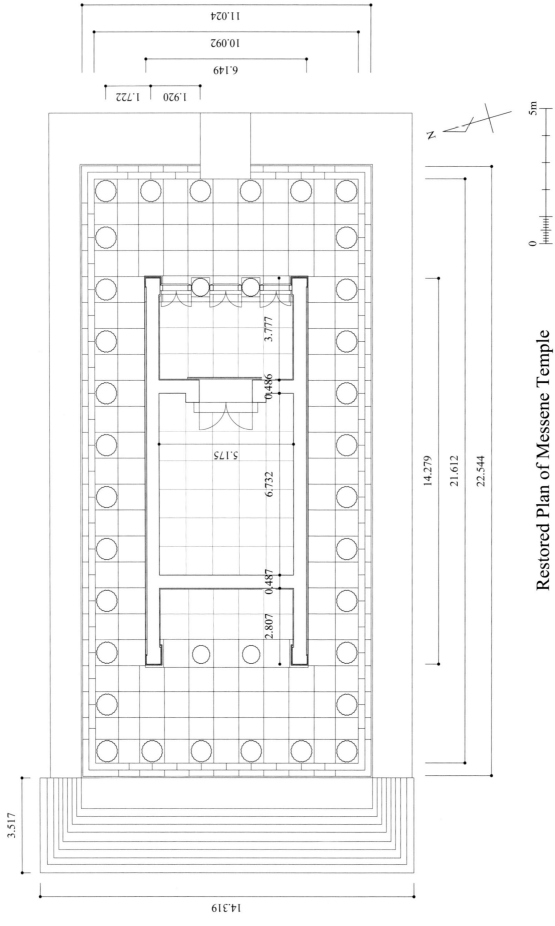

Reconstructed plan of the Temple of Messene.

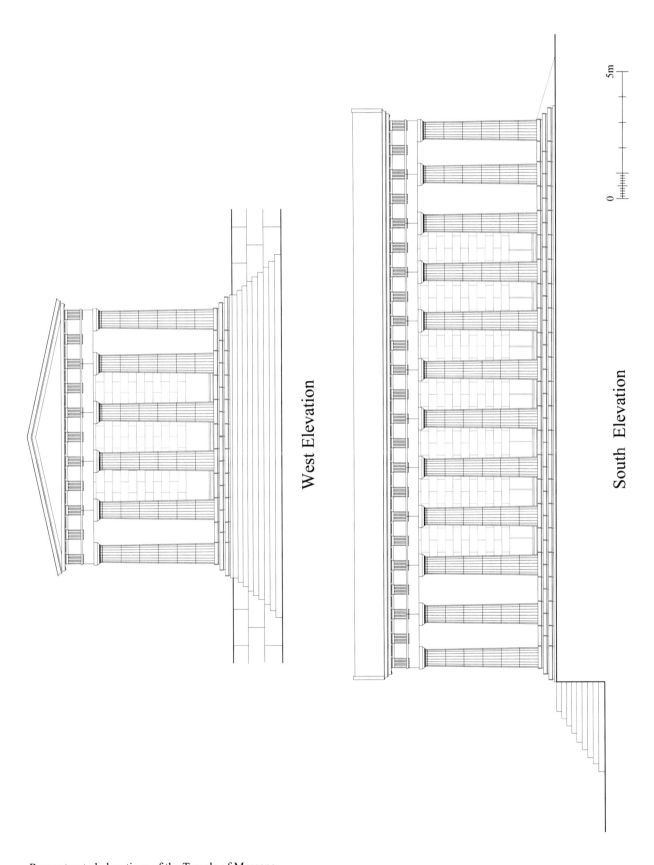

Reconstructed elevations of the Temple of Messene.

PLATE 116

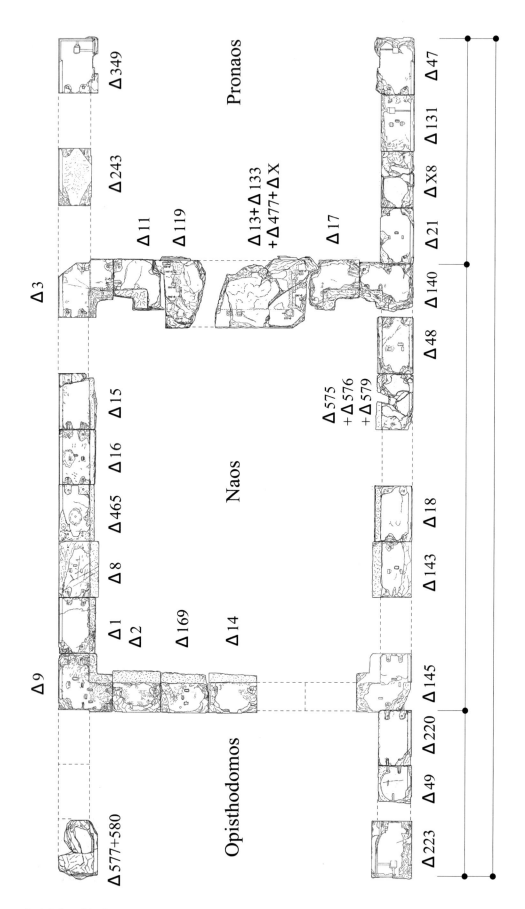

Placement of toichobate blocks.

PLATE 117

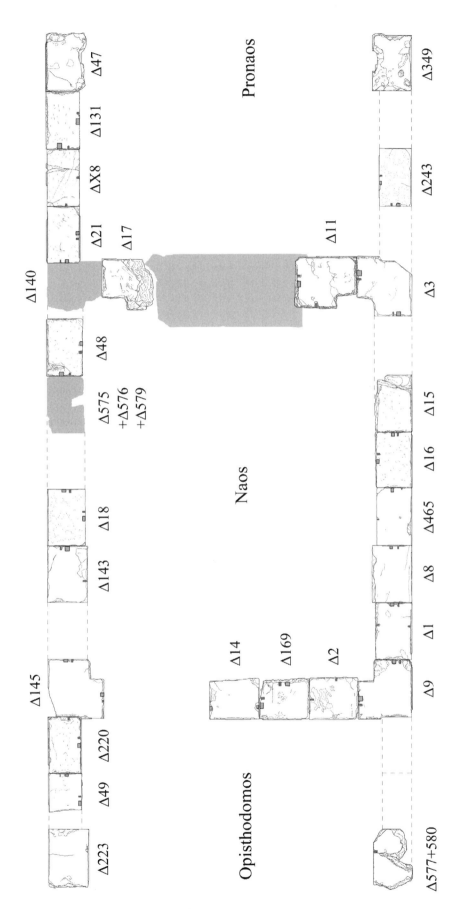

Placement of toichobate blocks, (from the bottom looking-up).

PLATE 118

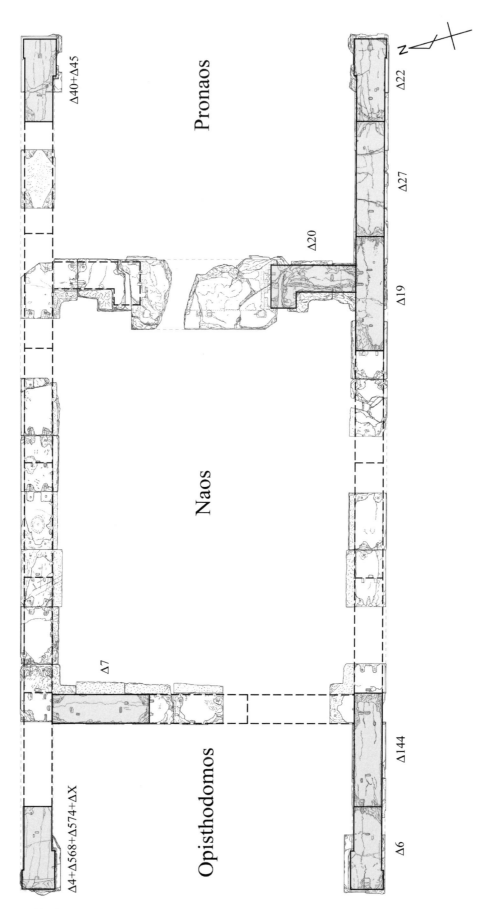

Placement of orthostate blocks.

PLATE 119

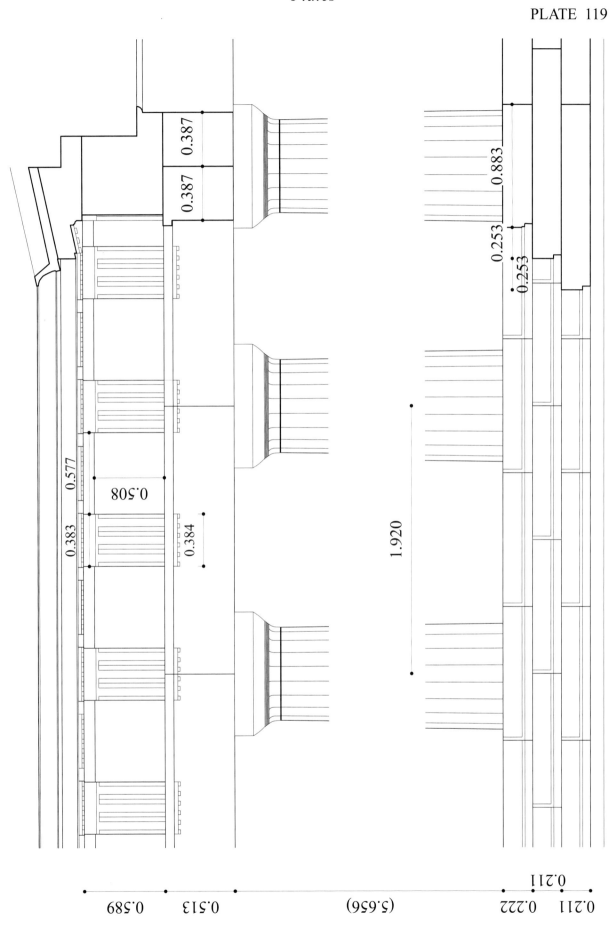

Details of Doric order.

PLATE 120

Table (1)-1 Doric temples from 4th to 1st century BC

	Place	Name of temples	Date	Country	Area Code	Columns	Reference
1	Aegae	Temple of Demeter	263-241	Turkey	D	distyle in antis	Born 1889
2	Aegae	NW Temple	2nd c. BC	Turkey	D	6x12	Born 1889
3	Aigeira	unknown	Hellenistic	Greece	A	6x11	Sioumpara 2006
4	Alabanda	Temple of Artemis/ Hekate	200	Turkey	D	6x11	Sioumpara 2006
5	Alexandreia Troas	unknown	300?	Turkey	D	6x11	Sioumpara 2006
6	Apollonia/ Kyrene	unknown	300	Libya	E	6x11	Knell 1983, Stucchi 1975, Sioumpara 2006
7	Assos	Heroon	3rd or 2nd c. BC	Turkey	D	prostyle	Clarke 1902
8	Athens	Temple of Kronos and Rhea	mid-2nd c. BC	Greece	B	6x9	Traulos 1971
9	Athens	Nikis Monument	320-319	Greece	B	6 prostyle	Dinsmoor 1910
10	Delos	Dodekatheon	early 3rd c. BC	Greece	C	6 amphi prostyle	Will 1955
11	Delos	Temple of Apollo (peripteral)	314-280	Greece	C	6x13	Dinsmooor 1975
12	Delos	Temple of Asklepios	early 3rd c. BC	Greece	C	4 prostyle	Robert 1952
13	Delphi	Temple of Apollo	373-320	Greece	B	6x15	Lacoste 1920, Dinsmoor 1975
14	Demetrias	Agora temple	294	Greece	B	6x10	Marzolff 1976
15	Emecik/Old Knidos	Temple of Apollo	end of 4th c. BC-early 3rd c. BC	Cyprus	C	6x11	Berges 2000
16	Ephesos	Temple on the Marketplace	kaiserzeitlich	Turkey	D	6x10	Sioumpara 2006
17	Epidauros	Temple of Asklepios	380	Greece	A	6x11	Knell 1971, Tomlinson 1983, Lechat 1895
18	Epidauros	Temple of Artemis	300	Greece	A	6 prostyle	Tomlinson 1983, Sioumpara 2006
19	Eretreia	Temple of Dionysos	Mid-4th c. BC	Greece	B	6x11	Knell 1983, Sioumpara 2006
20	Gortys	Temple of Asklepios	first half of 4th c. BC	Greece	C	6x11	Ginouvès 1956
21	Ilion	Temple of Athena	second half of 3rd c. BC	Turkey	D	6x12	Hoepfner 1969
22	Kallio	unknown	early Hellenism	Greece	B	5x10	Sioumpara 2006
23	Kallithea	Temple of Zeus	second half of 4th c. BC	Greece	B	6x11	Knell 1983, Sioumpara 2006
24	Kalydon	Temple of Artemis	360-350	Greece	A	6x13	Dyggve 1948
25	Kassope	Temple of Aphrodite	Mid-4th c. BC	Greece	B	6x10	Sioumpara 2006
26	Klaros	Temple of Apollo	3rd c. BC	Turkey	D	6x11	Knell 1983
27	Knidos	Temple of Apollo Karneios?	Hellenistic	Cyprus	C	6x11	Love 1970, Sioumpara 2006
28	Kos	Temple of Asklepios	200	Greece	C	6x12	Sioumpara 2006
29	Kourno	Small temple	second half of 4th c. BC	Greece	A	6x12	Schazmann 1932
30	Lebadeia	Temple of Zeus Basileus	150-100	Greece	B	6x13	Winter 1983, Sioumpara 2006
31	Lepreon	Temple of Demeter	175-171	Greece	A	6x12	Sioumpara 2006
32	Lindos	Temple of Athena Lindia	380-370	Greece	C	6x11	Knell 1983
33	Messene	Temple of Asklepios	early 3rd c. BC	Greece	C	prostyle	Dyggve 1960
34	Messene	Messene Temple	200	Greece	A	6x12	Sioumpara 2006
35	Molykreion	Temple of Poseidon	second half of 4th c. BC	Greece	B	6x13	Knell 1973
36	Nemea	Temple of Zeus	fist half of 4th c. BC	Greece	A	6x12	Hill 1966
37	Olympia	Metroon	330-320	Greece	A	6x11	Olympia II
38	Pergamon	Temple of Athena	400	Turkey	D	6x10	Born 1885
39	Pergamon	Shrine of the Royal Cult, peristyle	early 3rd c. BC	Turkey	D	unknown	Boehringer 1937
40	Pherai	Temple of Zeus Thaulios/ Ennodia-Hekate	230	Greece	B	6x12	Sioumpara 2006
41	Ptoioin	Temple of Apollo	300	Unknown	Unknown	6x13	Sioumpara 2006
42	Rhodos	Temple of Appollo Pythios	end 4th c. BC	Greece	C	6x11	Sioumpara 2006
43	Samothrace	Hieron	mid 2nd c. BC	Greece	C	prostyle	Lehmann 1969
44	Seleukeia/ Pieria	Temple of Isis-Aphorodite?	end 4th c. BC?	Turkey	D	6x12	Sioumpara 2006
45	Stratos	Temple of Zeus	321	Greece	B	6x11	Courby 1924
46	Sikyon	unknown	hellenistisch	Greece	A	6x18	Sioumpara 2006
47	Tegea	Temple of Athena Alea	345-335	Greece	A	6x14	Dugas 1924, Norman 1984
48	Thebe	Temple of Apollo	370	Greece	B	6x12	Sioumpara 2006
49	Troizen	Temple of Hippolytos or Asklepios?	4th c. BC	Greece	A	6x11	Knell 1978
50	Xanthos	Letoon Temple B	second half of 2th c. BC	Turkey	D	6x11	Metzger 1979, Sioumpara 2006

Doric temples from 4th to 1st century BC.

Table (I)-2 Other Doric buildings from 4th to 1st century BC

	City	Buildings	Date	Area	Area code	Reference
1	Assos	Stoa	3rd or 2nd c. BC	Turkey	D	Clarke 1902
2	Athens	Stoa of Attalos	159-138	Greece	B	Travlos 1971
3	Athens	Middle stoa (Gymnasium of Ptolemy)	second quarter of 2nd c. BC	Greece	B	Travlos 1971
4	Athens	Stoa in the Asclepieion	338-326	Greece	B	Allen 1911
5	Cyrene	portico B5	2nd c. BC	Libya	D	Stucchi 1965
6	Corinth	South stoa	end of 4th c. BC	Greece	A	Broneer 1954
7	Delphi	Tholos	365-335	Greece	B	Ito 2004
8	Epidauros	Tholos	380	Greece	A	Tomlinson 1983, Lechat 1895
9	Thasos	Paraskenia	330-320	Greece	C	Martin 1959, Coulton 1976
10	Thasos	North-west Stoa	300	Greece	C	Martin 1959, Coulton 1976
11	Pergamon	Athena Polias Stoa	197-159	Turkey	D	Bohn 1885
12	Pergamon	Stoa in the agora	175-150	Turkey	D	Doerpfeld 1902
13	Miletos	Bouleuterion	175-164	Turkey	D	Knackfuss 1908
14	Miletos	Delpinion Hall	340-320	Turkey	D	Knackfuss 1908
15	Olympia	Palaestra	3rd c. BC	Greece	A	Olympia II
16	Olympia	Gymnasion Hall	2nd c. BC	Greece	A	Olympia II
17	Olympia	Echo stoa	second half of 4th c. BC	Greece	A	Olympia II
18	Olympia	South stoa	Mid-4th c. BC	Greece	A	Olympia II
19	Olympia	Leonidaion	330	Greece	A	Olympia II
20	Oropus	Stoa st the Amphiaraion	360	Greece	A	Coulton 1968
21	Perachora	Stoa by the Harbour	last quarter of the 4th c. BC	Greece	B	Coulton 1964
22	Lindos	Propylaia	early 3rd c. BC	Greece	C	Dyggve 1960
23	Lindos	Stoa	second half of 3th c. BC	Greece	C	Dyggve 1960

Other Doric buildings except temples 4th to 1st Century BC.

PLATE 122

Table (2)-1 Column proportions of Doric temples

	Place	Name of temples	Date (graph)	Country	Area code	AbW	d	D	CH	AbH	EH	H	AbW/d	AbW/CH	AbH/CH	EH/AbH	AbW/D	d/D	H/D	H/CH	H/(AbH+EH)
1	Aegae	Temple of Demeter	-252	Turkey	D	559	455		242	78	110		1.229	2.310	0.322	1.410					
2	Assos	Heroon	-200	Turkey	D	554	422		259	94	82		1.313	2.139	0.363	0.872					
3	Athen	Nikis Monument	-320	Greece	B	903	672	844	338	133	125	5250	1.344	2.672	0.393	0.940	1.070	0.796	6.220	15.533	20.349
4	Delos	Dodekatheon	-275	Greece	C	712	564	690	247	92	87	4620	1.262	2.883	0.372	0.946	1.032	0.817	6.696	18.704	25.810
5	Delos	Temple of Apollo (peripteral)	-297	Greece	C			945				5200							5.503		
6	Delos	Temple of Asklepios	-275	Greece	C	640	500	600	243	82	103	4620	1.280	2.634	0.337	1.256	1.067	0.833	7.700	19.012	24.973
7	Delphi	Temple of Apollo	-347	Greece	B	1900	1298	1806	714	310	253	10590	1.464	2.661	0.434	0.816	1.052	0.719	5.864	14.832	18.810
8	Emecik/ Old Knidos	Temple of Apollo	-300	Cyprus	C	860	676		316	128	114		1.272	2.722	0.405	0.891					0.000
9	Epidauros	Temple of Asklepios	-380	Greece	A	1010	730	923	380	151	151	5700	1.384	2.658	0.397	1.000	1.094	0.791	6.176	15.000	18.874
10	Epidauros	Temple of Artemis	-330	Greece	A	704	510	590	272	100	106	4200	1.380	2.588	0.368	1.060	1.193	0.864	7.119	15.441	20.388
11	Ilion	Temple of Athena	-225	Turkey	D	1300	992	1240	459	191	141	8124	1.310	2.832	0.416	0.738	1.048	0.800	6.552	17.699	24.470
12	Kalydon	Temple of Artemis	-355	Greece	B	1110	850	1026	427	185	142	6300	1.306	2.600	0.433	0.768	1.082	0.828	6.140	14.754	19.266
13	Kos	Temple of Asklepios	-155	Greece	C	1515	1036	1270	484	212	186		1.462	3.130	0.438	0.877	1.193	0.816			0.000
14	Lepreon	Temple of Demeter	-375	Greece	A	837	640	830	375	140	136	4623	1.308	2.232	0.373	0.971	1.008	0.771	5.570	12.328	16.750
15	Lindos	Temple of Athena Lindia	-275	Greece	C	870	685	870	360	132	158	5600	1.270	2.417	0.367	1.197	1.000	0.787	6.437	15.556	19.310
16	Messene	Temple of Asklepios	-200	Greece	A		860	1000	500			7000						0.860	7.000	14.000	
17	Messene	Messene Temple		Greece	A	882	689	808	332	132	118		1.280	2.657	0.398	0.894	1.092	0.853			
18	Nemea	Temple of Zeus	-315	Greece	A	1760	1306.5	1628	630	250	227	10330	1.347	2.794	0.397	0.908	1.081	0.803	6.345	16.397	21.656
19	Olympia	Metroon	-400	Greece	A	890	655	850	343	139	139		1.359	2.595	0.405	1.000	1.047	0.771			
20	Pergamon	Temple of Athena	-275	Turkey	D	775	605	754	295	124	118	5260	1.281	2.627	0.420	0.952	1.028	0.802	6.976	17.831	21.736
21	Pergamon	Shine of the Royal Cult, peristyle	-230	Turkey	D	718	558	666	219	75	89	4660	1.287	3.279	0.342	1.187	1.078	0.838	6.997	21.279	28.415
22	Samothrace	Hieron	-150	Greece	C	1021	783	901	409.6	185	124	5660	1.304	2.493	0.452	0.670	1.133	0.869	6.282	13.818	18.317
23	Stratos	Temple of Zeus	-321	Greece	B	1360	1010	1290	505	202	180	7908	1.347	2.693	0.400	0.891	1.054	0.783	6.130	15.659	20.702
24	Tegea	Temple of Athena Alea	-340	Greece	A	1616	1209	1555	589	246	202	9474	1.337	2.744	0.418	0.821	1.039	0.777	6.093	16.085	21.147

Table (2)-2 Column proportions of other Doric buildings

	Place	Name of buildings	Date (graph)	Country	Area Code	AbW	d	D	CH	AbH	EH	H	AbW/d	AbW/CH	AbH/CH	EH/AbH	AbW/D	d/D	H/D	H/CH	H/(AbH+EH)
1	Assos	Stoa	-200	Turkey	D	819	649	776	255	90	120	5706	1.262	3.212	0.353	1.333	1.055	0.836	7.353	22.376	27.171
2	Athen	Stoa of Attalos	-149	Greece	B	771	656	742	272			5236	1.175	2.835			1.039	0.884	7.057	19.250	
3	Athens	Middle stoa (Gymnasium of Ptolemy)	-163	Greece	B	865	678	788	347	132	154	4970	1.276	2.493	0.380	1.167	1.098	0.860	6.307	14.323	17.378
4	Athens	Stoa in the Ascleteum	-332	Greece	B			750				4875							6.500		
5	Cyrene	portico B5	-150	Libya	D	1234	771.7	1029	441	191	164	6900	1.599	2.798	0.433	0.859	1.199	0.750	6.706	15.646	19.437
6	Corinth	South stoa	-325	Greece	A	1030	790	960	400	170	128	5700	1.304	2.575	0.425	0.753	1.073	0.823	5.938	14.250	19.128
7	Delphi	Tholos	-350	Greece	B	891	669	869	352	141	127	5927	1.332	2.531	0.401	0.901	1.025	0.770	6.820	16.838	22.116
8	Epidauros	Tholos	-380	Greece	A			992	380			6880						0.000	6.935	18.105	
9	Thasos	Paraskenia	-325	Greece	C	760	580	745	280	125	97	4950	1.310	2.714	0.446	0.776	1.020	0.779	6.644	17.679	22.297
10	Thasos	North-west Stoa	-300	Greece	C	743	595	742	245	66	67	5158	1.249	2.412	0.269	0.766	1.001	0.802	6.951	16.747	22.823
11	Pergamon	Athena Polias stoa	-178	Turkey	D	724	542	680	308	128	98	4995	1.336	3.175	0.424	0.977	1.065	0.797	7.346	21.908	29.382
12	Pergamon	Stoa in agora	-163	Turkey	D	561		542	228	86	84	4230		2.805	0.377		1.035		7.804	21.150	
13	Miletos	Buleuterion	-170	Turkey	D	850	615	750	200			5138	1.382	2.796	0.388		1.133	0.820	6.851	16.901	19.686
14	Miletos	Delphinion Hole	-330	Turkey	D			500	304	120	141	3530			0.395	1.175			7.060		
15	Olympia	Palaestra	-250	Greece	A	570	415	506	216	94	68	3410	1.373	2.639	0.435	0.723	1.126	0.820	6.739	15.787	21.049
16	Olympia	Gymnasion hole	-150	Greece	A	600	460	530	245	66	67		1.304	2.449	0.269	1.015	1.132	0.868			
17	Olympia	Echo stoa	-325	Greece	A	880	630	860	340	144	114		1.397	2.588	0.424	0.792	1.023	0.733			
18	Olympia	South stoa	-350	Greece	A	1115	850	1040	400	155	138		1.312	2.788	0.388	0.890	1.072	0.817			
19	Olympia	Leonidaion	-330	Greece	A	940	710	815	326	128	111	4990	1.324	2.883	0.393	0.867	1.153	0.871	6.123	15.307	20.879
20	Oropus	Stoa st the Amphiaraion	-360	Greece	A	671	505	656	254	102	87	4627	1.329	2.642	0.402	0.853	1.023	0.770	7.053	18.217	24.481
21	Perachora	Stoa by the Harbour	-313	Greece	B	650	460	625	235	100	90	4130	1.413	2.766	0.426	0.900	1.040	0.736	6.608	17.574	21.737
22	Lindos	Propylaia	-275	Greece	C	735	560		285	115	105		1.313	2.579	0.404	0.913					
23	Lindos	Stoa	-225	Greece	C	840	635	780	333	145	116	5000	1.323	2.523	0.435	0.800	1.077	0.814	6.410	15.015	19.157

Column proportions of Doric temples and buildings referenced.

226

Tables

PLATE 123

Table (3)-1 Entablature proportions of Doric temples

	Place	Name of temples	Date (graph)	Country	Area code	H	TW	MW	FH	AH	CorH	FH+AH	FH+AH+CorH	FH/TW	FH/MW	MW/TW	FH/AH	H/(FH+AH)	H/(FH+AH+CorH)
1	Aegae	Temple of Demeter	-252	Turkey	D				368	304	150	672	822				1.211		
2	Assos	Heroon	-200	Turkey	D		212	312	400	345	290	745	1035	1.736	1.179	1.472	1.159	4.217	3.581
3	Athens	Nikis Monument	-320	Greece	B	5250	420	624	681	564	221	1245	1466	1.621	1.091	1.486	1.207	4.667	4.035
4	Delos	Dodekatheon	-275	Greece	C	4620	360	479	580	410	155	990	1145	1.611	1.211	1.331	1.415	5.105	4.332
5	Delos	Temple of Asklepios	-275	Greece	C	4620	315	515	495	410	161.5	905	1067	1.571	0.961	1.635	1.207	4.117	
6	Delphi	Temple of Apollo	-347	Greece	B	10590	820	1220	1405	1167		2572		1.713	1.152	1.488	1.204		
7	Epidauros	Temple of Asklepios	-380	Greece	A	5700	441	688	688	610	210	1298	1508	1.560	1.000	1.560	1.128	4.391	3.780
8	Epidauros	Temple of Artemis	-330	Greece	A	4200	310	458	470	406	206	876	1082	1.516	1.026	1.477	1.158	4.795	3.882
9	Eretreia	Temple of Dionysos	-350	Greece	B		420-450		600	600		600		1.420					
10	Ilion	Temple of Athena	-225	Turkey	D	8124	580	863	858	736	282	1594	1876	1.479	0.994	1.488	1.166	5.097	4.330
11	Kallithea	Temple of Zeus	-325	Greece	B		420	672								1.600			
12	Kalydon	Temple of Artemis	-355	Greece	B	6300	498	752	820	768	290	1588	1878	1.647	1.090	1.510	1.068	3.967	3.355
13	Kos	Temple of Asklepios	-155	Greece	C		610	915	960	803	345	1763	2108	1.574	1.049	1.500	1.196		
14	Kourno	Small temple	-125	Greece	A				360	320		680	680				1.125		
15	Lebadeia	Temple of Zeus Basileus	-173	Greece	B		380	598	595	580		1175		1.566	0.995	1.574	1.026		
16	Lindos	Temple of Athena Lindia	-275	Greece	C	5600	475	729	740	620	240	1360	1600	1.558	1.117	1.194		4.118	3.500
17	Messene	Temple of Asklepios	-200	Greece	A	7000	478	716	800	639	199	1439	1638	1.674	1.252	1.498		4.864	4.274
18	Messene	Messene temple		Greece	A		383	577	589	513	175	1102	1277	1.538	1.021	1.507	1.148		
19	Molykreion	Temple of Poseidon	-375	Greece	B		455		645			645		1.418					
20	Nemea	Temple of Zeus	-315	Greece	A	10330	730	1142	1155	1030	317	2185	2502	1.582	1.011	1.564	1.121	4.728	4.129
21	Olympia	Metroon	-400	Greece	A		405	585	660	628	200	1288	1488	1.630	1.128	1.444	1.051		0.000
22	Pergamon	Temple of Athena	-275	Turkey	D	5260	312	478	538	508	208	1016	1224	1.724	1.126	1.532	1.126	5.177	4.297
23	Pergamon	Shine of the Royal Cult, peristyle	-230	Turkey	D	4660	311	520	478	387	260	865	1125	1.537	0.919	1.672	1.235	5.387	4.142
24	Pherai	Temple of Zeus Thaulios/ Ennodia-Hekate	-300	Greece	B		545	805			405			1.477					
25	Ptoioin	Temple of Apollo	-325	Unknown	Unknown		382	552	562	500	205	1062	1267	1.471	1.018	1.445	1.124		
26	Samothrace	Hieron	-150	Greece	B	5660	480	738	750	637	219	1387	1606	1.563	1.016	1.538	1.177	4.081	3.524
27	Stratos	Temple of Zeus	-321	Greece	B	7908	625	955	946	825	305	1771	2076	1.514	0.991	1.528	1.147	4.465	3.809
28	Tegea	Temple of Athena Alea	-340	Greece	A	9474	710	1081	1088	968	295	2056	2351	1.532	1.006	1.523	1.124	4.608	4.030
29	Thebe	Temple of Apollo	-370	Greece	B		770	1210		1118	290	1118	1408			1.571			

Table (3)-2 Entablature proportions of other Doric buildings

	Place	graph	Date (graph)	Country	Area code	H	TW	MW	FH	AH	CorH	FH+AH	FH+AH+CorH	FH/TW	FH/MW	MW/TW	FH/AH	H/(FH+AH)	H/(FH+AH+CorH)
1	Assos	Stoa	-200	Turkey	D	5706	355		529	420	175	949	1124	1.490			1.260	6.013	5.077
2	Athens	Stoa of Attalos	-149	Greece	B	5236	330	480		436	284	966	1250	1.606	1.104	1.455	1.216	5.420	4.189
3	Athens	Middle stoa (Gymnasium of Ptolemy)	-163	Greece	B	4970	409	600	718	563	264	1281	1545	1.756	1.197	1.467	1.275	3.880	3.217
4	Athens	Stoa in the Ascleteum	-332	Greece	B	4875	370	545	545	490	190	1035	1225	1.473	1.000	1.473	1.112	4.710	3.980
5	Cyrene	portico B5	-150	Libya	D	6900	646.8	827.5	955.5	808.5		1764		1.477	1.155	1.279	1.182	3.912	
6	Corinth	South stoa	-325	Greece	A	5700	455	715	745	634	230	1379	1609	1.637	1.042	1.571	1.175	4.133	3.543
7	Delphi	Tholos	-325	Greece	B	5927			634	586	186	1220	1406				1.082	4.858	4.216
8	Epidauros	Tholos	-350	Greece	A	6880			790	654	259	1444	1703				1.208	4.765	4.040
9	Thasos	Paraskenia	-325	Greece	C	4950	370	610	575	500	178	1075	1253	1.554	0.943	1.649	1.150	4.605	3.951
10	Thasos	North-west Stoa	-300	Greece	C	5158	366	538	604	520	237	1124	1361	1.650	1.123	1.470	1.162	4.589	3.790
11	Pergamon	Athena Polias stoa	-178	Turkey	D	4995	265	360	385	355	205	740	945	1.453	1.069	1.358	1.085	6.750	5.286
12	Pergamon	Stoa in agora	-163	Turkey	D	4230			380	260		640					1.462	6.609	
13	Miletos	Buleuterion	-170	Turkey	D	5138	356	523	527	490		1017		1.480	1.008	1.469	1.076	5.052	
14	Miletos	Delpinion Hole	-330	Turkey	D	3530				820		820						4.305	
15	Olympia	Echo stoa	-325	Greece	A				690	680	210	1370	1580				1.015		
16	Olympia	South stoa	-350	Greece	A	4990	485		770	680	230	1450	1680	1.588			1.132		
17	Olympia	Leonidaion	-330	Greece	A														
18	Oropos	Stoa at the Amphiaraion	-360	Greece	A	4627	312	450	479	432	186	911	1097	1.535	1.064	1.442	1.109	5.079	4.218
19	Perachora	Stoa by the Harbour	-313	Greece	B	4130	306		487	415	151	902	1053	1.592			1.173	4.579	3.922
20	Lindos	Propylaia	-275	Greece	C				424	470	185	894	1079				0.902		
21	Lindos	Stoa	-225	Greece	C	5000	350	530	535	450		985		1.529	1.009	1.514	1.189	5.076	

Entablature proportions of Doric temples and other buildings referenced.